Political Justice in a Republic

JAMES FENIMORE COOPER'S AMERICA

JOHN P. McWILLIAMS, JR.

Political Justice in a Republic

JAMES FENIMORE COOPER'S
AMERICA

University of California Press

Berkeley · Los Angeles · London

1972

University of California Press
Berkeley and Los Angeles, California
University of California Press, Ltd.
London, England
Copyright © 1972, by
The Regents of the University of California
ISBN: 0–520–02175–4
Library of Congress Catalog Card Number: 75–182283
Printed in the United States of America

The Belknap Press of Harvard University Press has granted permission to reprint quotations from *The Letters and Journals of James Fenimore Cooper*, ed. James Franklin Beard, Copyright 1960, 1964, 1968 by the President and Fellows of Harvard College.

American Quarterly has granted the author permission to revise and reprint his article "Cooper and the Conservative Democrat" from the Fall 1970 issue of *American Quarterly*, Copyright 1970 by the Trustees of the University of Pennsylvania.

Texas Studies in Literature and Language has granted the author permission to revise and reprint his article "*The Crater* and the Constitution" from the Winter 1971 issue of *Texas Studies in Literature and Language*, Copyright 1971 by the University of Texas Press.

FOR MY MOTHER
Brooks Barlow McWilliams
AND IN MEMORY OF MY FATHER
John P. McWilliams (1891-1972)

Acknowledgments

The Harvard University Press, *American Quarterly*, *Texas Studies in Literature and Language*, and the New York State Historical Association have been generous in granting copyright permissions. Raymond Ford and Susan Peters of the University of California Press have provided patient and needed editorial assistance. I am grateful to James D. Hart, Alan Heimert and Joel Porte, each of whom has read the manuscript in one of its stages, and offered valuable suggestions and advice. My deepest debts are to George Dekker and Norman Grabo, who have helped me redefine my subject and clarify my argument.

J.M.

Contents

A Chronology of
James Fenimore Cooper

1786   William Cooper establishes Cooperstown at the southern tip of Lake Otsego in New York.

1789   James Cooper born in Burlington, New Jersey. William Cooper moves his family to Cooperstown the following year.

1803   Cooper matriculates at Yale; dismissed for misconduct two years later.

1806–1808 Sails before the mast to England and the continent aboard the *Stirling*; serves as a midshipman in the United States Navy at Fort Oswego on Lake Ontario.

1811   Marries Susan Augusta De Lancey.

1811–1819 Lives as a gentleman farmer on family lands in Westchester County and Cooperstown.

1820   Writes *Precaution* and, in the following year, *The Spy* (1821).

1822–1826 Moves to New York City and writes *The Pioneers* (1823), *The Pilot* (1824), *Lionel Lincoln* (1825), and *The Last of the Mohicans* (1826).

1826–1833 Resides in Europe with his family. Lives most

frequently in Paris but takes long trips to England, the Low Countries, Switzerland, Germany, and Italy. Concern with and involvement in the European revolutionary movements of 1830. Writes *The Prairie* (1827), *The Red Rover* (1827), *Notions of the Americans* (1828), *The Wept of Wish-ton-Wish* (1829), and *The Water-Witch* (1830). After 1830, turns to novels that concern European politics: *The Bravo* (1831), *The Heidenmauer* (1832), and *The Headsman* (1833).

1833–1836   Returns to America and resides in New York City. Political correspondent for the *Evening Post*. *A Letter to His Countrymen* (1834), the A.B.C. Letters (1834–1836), and *The Monikins* (1835).

1836   Returns to Cooperstown and remodels Otsego Hall, William Cooper's home.

1836–1837   Publishes five volumes based upon his European travels.

1837–1838   The controversy over Three Mile Point causes Cooper to return to fiction with *Homeward Bound* and *Home As Found* (1838). Protracted libel suits against Whig editors begin. *The American Democrat* (1838), *Chronicles of Cooperstown* (1838), *History of the Navy of the United States* (1839).

1840   Resumes writing romances about the frontier and the sea: *The Pathfinder* (1840), *Mercedes of Castile* (1840), *The Deerslayer* (1841),

The Two Admirals (1842), *The Wing-and-Wing* (1842), *Wyandotté* (1843).

1844–1846　Defends the landlords' position in the Anti-Rent Wars by writing a trilogy titled The Littlepage Manuscripts: *Satanstoe* (1845), *The Chainbearer* (1845), and *The Redskins* (1846). Also writes *Afloat and Ashore* and *Miles Wallingford* (1844).

1847–1849　Writes the first American utopian novel, *The Crater* (1847). Last frontier and sea romances: *Jack Tier* (1848), *The Oak Openings* (1848), *The Sea Lions* (1849).

1850　　　Last social novel, *The Ways of the Hour* (1850).

1851　　　Dies in Cooperstown, leaving *The Towns of Manhattan* (also titled *New York*) unfinished.

Introduction:
Law and the Neutral Ground

> The law of Nature stands as an eternal
> rule to all men, legislators as well as
> others. The rules that they make for other
> men's actions must, as well as their own
> and other men's actions, be conformable
> to the law of Nature—i.e., to the will of
> God.
>
> JOHN LOCKE,
> *Second Treatise on Civil Government*

I

COOPER THOUGHT of himself, not as a writer of adventure romances, nor as a political analyst, but as a man of letters, a gentleman whose pen was in his nation's service. Convinced that self-disclosure was indiscreet, Cooper left few statements of general purpose. The few that remain, however, explicitly connect his fiction to his politics and indicate that his writings were to provide a defense for his nation—its lands, its history and, above all, its unique polity. In *Notions of the Americans* Cooper described himself as "a gentleman who is the reputed author of a series of tales, which were intended to elucidate the history, manner, usages, and scenery, of his native land."[1] After completing *The Bravo*, Cooper said

---

[1] *Notions of the Americans*, ed. R. E. Spiller, 2 vols. (New York, 1963), I, 254.

of America, "her mental independence is my object."[2]
And, most revealingly, when he laid down his pen in
1834, he declared himself an "American who wishes to
illustrate and enforce the peculiar principles of his own
country, by the agency of polite literature."[3]

Cooper fully expected that his nation's literature would
be distinguished by similar impulses toward political
and historical justification. Like the Young Americans of
a slightly later era, Cooper was convinced that it was
the primary duty of any American artist to proclaim the
political truths of his fledgling nation. The importance
of American literature was to be its advocacy of constitutional freedoms:

The literature of the United States is a subject of the highest
interest to the civilized world; for when it does begin to be
felt, it will be felt with a force, a directness, and a common
sense in its application, that has never yet been known. If
there were no other points of difference between this country
and other nations, those of its political and religious freedom,
alone, would give a colour of the highest importance to the
writings of a people so thoroughly imbued with their distinctive principles, and so keenly alive to their advantages.[4]

Because Cooper believed that "All fine writing must have
its roots in the ideas,"[5] he was willing to let the literary
quality of American literature wait upon its political instruction. For Cooper the uniqueness of American political ideas must constitute the uniqueness of its literature: "The only peculiarity that can, or ought to be

[2] *The Letters and Journals of James Fenimore Cooper*, ed. James
F. Beard, 6 vols. (Cambridge, Mass., 1960–1968), II, 84.
[3] *A Letter to His Countrymen* (New York, 1834), p. 98.
[4] *Notions of the Americans*, II, 122.
[5] *Letters and Journals*, IV, 350.

expected, in their [the Americans'] literature, is that which is connected with the promulgation of their distinctive political opinions."[6]

Astute contemporaries recognized that the main thrust of Cooper's writings had been his desire to serve as spokesman and guardian for the unformed republic. The *Memorial of James Fenimore Cooper* reveals that Cooper was valued chiefly as an historian of American culture and character, a graphic and passionate chronicler of the American frontier, not as a romancer nor as a social critic, but as a combination of the two. In the letters and speeches preserved in the *Memorial*, Bancroft, Prescott, R. H. Dana, Parkman, and Bryant all insist upon Cooper's importance as a national historian in fiction. Prescott's evaluation is representative: "surely no one has succeeded like Cooper in the portraiture of American character, taken in its broadest sense, of the civilized and of the uncivilized man, or has given such glowing and eminently faithful pictures of American scenery. His writings are instinct with the spirit of nationality, shown not less in those devoted to sober fact than in the sportive inventions of his inexhaustible fancy."[7]

"The spirit of nationality" led Cooper to explore the American experience in thirty-two volumes of fiction that encompass an impressive range of times, places, and cultures. Although seven of his novels are set in Europe, all of them save *Precaution* are concerned with questions of American identity. Written in no predetermined order, composed in haste, fitted into no overriding plan, Cooper's novels nonetheless leave his reader with a sense of

[6] *Notions of the Americans*, II, 101.
[7] *Memorial of James Fenimore Cooper* (New York, 1852), p. 31.

having acquired an extensive view of the development of American civilization. His fictional treatment of American history begins with Columbus in *Mercedes of Castille*, a book which Cooper hoped would become "a high wrought and standard fiction," "something that will take its place among the standard works of the language."[8] He wrote at least one novel dealing with every generation of Americans from 1675 to 1850, and devoted large sections of three works, *The Monikins*, *The Crater*, and *New York*, to prophecy on the national future. Despite his claim to have written only one true historical novel, *Lionel Lincoln*, he did extensive historical research when he felt it necessary—as in the writing of *Notions of the Americans* or *Mercedes of Castille*. Like Walt Whitman, Cooper was intensely of New York, yet wrote of many regions, classes, trades, and eras in an effort both to celebrate a conception of America and to defend it.

I shall study a selective number of Cooper's works, fiction and nonfiction, with regard for their author's declared purpose—as the writings of an "American who wishes to illustrate and enforce the peculiar principles of his country, by the agency of polite literature." I shall not consider Cooper as a mythopoetic romancer nor as a contributor to certain fictional traditions in America. These aspects of Cooper have been ably and thoroughly studied by D. H. Lawrence, Leslie Fiedler, R. W. B. Lewis, Yvor Winters, Richard Chase, Henry Nash Smith, and Joel Porte. Nor shall I consider biography or the post-1830 controversies, except where they have demonstrably influenced a given work. I cannot hope to supplement the

[8] *Letters and Journals*, III, 443.

biographical insights of Marcel Clavel, Dorothy Waples, and Ethel Outland, nor the painstaking and invaluable scholarship of James Beard.

Since the publication of James Grossman's critical biography, a number of critics have attempted to heal the breach between Cooper the romancer and Cooper the political and social critic. Marius Bewley, Donald Ringe, Kay Seymour House, and George Dekker have all explored ways in which the two Coopers can be seen as one, ways in which the political and social ideas of his nonfiction can be used to illuminate the novels. I hope to add to their findings by pursuing new methods which, like the sociological organization of House's *Cooper's Americans*, are not totally bound by chronology nor by the commitment to treat the entire Cooper canon. I attempt a more thorough treatment of fewer works than any critical study to date.

Because Cooper conceived of himself as a defender of American political values, the search for political justice became the dominant concern of his fiction. Cooper saw the problem of political justice in two separate ways. In fictions concerned with the frontier, or with preconstitutional America, Cooper and his Americans search for principles of political justice in their still unsettled land. In social fictions dealing with postconstitutional America, Cooper considers political justice to have been established by the Constitution of 1787 and is reluctant to believe that superior principles of government could be grafted upon it.

The controlling theme of political justice thus raises two related issues, one literary and one political. The first is the problem of determining the ways in which questions of national identity and political justice are treated within the seemingly apolitical settings of Cooper's tales. The second is the question of the consistency of Cooper's political views. Did Cooper adhere to a uniform set of political principles, or did Cooper's principles change significantly between 1833 and 1851? General discussion of both these problems must precede analysis of the individual works.

II

All readers of Cooper are confronted with the obvious but troubling fact that a Cooper tale is an uneasy melange of derring-do with abstract political and social commentary. Such topics as moral law, natural justice, or the American Constitution are debated by frontiersmen while in imminent peril of their lives. Questions of national identity are discussed in the untouched wilderness; mortgage laws are analyzed aboard ships in mid-Pacific. Civil laws, in effect on the eastern seaboard, can be curiously operative within the densest reaches of the American forest. These kinds of operatic conventions seem at times so forced as to render the world of Cooper's fiction absurd and unreal. Cooper, however, asks his reader to accept such stylization of experience as valid commentary upon pressing national issues. By what means can Cooper introduce complex political questions within the removed world of the frontier romance and yet avoid, in his best work, the danger of jarring discontinuity?

The most important of these techniques is Cooper's consistent use of a uniform kind of setting. All of Cooper's American fictions are laid in a time of social change.

Almost without exception, the social change assumes one of two forms: a revolution of government, or a shift in ownership of the land. Five novels occur during the American Revolution, three during the French and Indian Wars, one each during King Philip's War, the English conquest of New York, and the War of 1812. *The Pioneers, Home As Found*, and the Littlepage novels concern legal struggles for land ownership; the Louisiana Purchase is crucial to *The Prairie*. *The Monikins* and *The Crater* point toward national revolution of unspecified date, and *The Ways of the Hour* is concerned with changes wrought in mid-century life due to a new state constitution. All of Cooper's Americans, from Harvey Birch to Thomas Dunscomb, confront a time of shift or upheaval. The most honorable among them are placed in the difficult position of seeking permanent principles of moral and civil justice amid a world whose very definition is change.

We should not be surprised that, in Cooper's fiction, the American experience is one of continuing social and political flux. In *Notions of the Americans, Home As Found*, and *New York*, Cooper explicitly states, long before Henry Adams, that an accelerating rate of change is the only changeless quality of America. By seeking out times of violent upheaval for his tales, Cooper was not only imitating *Waverley* or *Rob Roy*, but insisting that his reader recognize that violent change within the fictional world is only typical of the essential quality of American life.

The spacial aspect of Cooper's settings is as consistent as the temporal. Cooper may place his characters in Connecticut, on the prairie, or on a Pacific island, but they all inhabit a single setting—constant in its fluidity. Characters are caught, not only in a time that gives them little fixity, but in a place that affords them less. Cooper's protagonists, most of them ordinary men, find themselves in environs where there is either no civil order or conflicting civil orders. In times of historical turmoil, his characters are fixed in precisely those places where disruptive social forces, be they troops, frontiersmen, Indians, or the rabble, become a serious menace to the harmonious life.

The time-honored division of Cooper's works into forest novels, sea novels, and social novels is thus a misleading oversimplification. The settings of nearly all the novels should properly be viewed as variations upon Cooper's own subtitle to *The Spy*, "A Tale of the Neutral Ground." In his fiction, the neutral ground assumes one of three forms. It may be a battlefield—an area fought over by conflicting forces but possessed by neither, as in *The Spy* and *Lionel Lincoln*. More commonly, it is either the sea or the forest, each of them conceived as a frontier, and unfolded before the reader at precisely the moment when man has invaded his environs but not possessed them, settled the land, but not yet brought it to a stable social order.

Cooper's settings are neutral ground in a second and more important sense. The sea, the forest, the prairie, or the border are themselves "neutral" in their effect upon character. Man may enter them and emerge with a heightened sense of natural piety, with that detachment from man's pursuits which often, in Cooper's works, indicates a higher morality and, paradoxically, renders one more humane. Or one may enter the neutral ground and use its lack of social order, its opportunities for unchecked liberty, in order to waste nature, kill men, and enforce injustice. Thus the neutral ground allows for both Deerslayer and Tom Hutter, Coejemans and Thousandacres, Long Tom Coffin and Christopher Dillon. Impassive and tolerant, the neutral ground reinforces the qualities a man brings to it.

Cooper uses the neutral ground for two distinctly separate purposes. Both Edwin Fussell and George Dekker have pointed out that for Cooper the neutral ground is a no-man's-land adapted from Scott's romances—both a testing ground for heroism and an exciting source of melodramatic action.[9] When Cooper is at his best, however, he endows the neutral ground with more significance than critics have yet acknowledged. R. W. B. Lewis made the interesting suggestion that "For Cooper the forest and the sea shared the quality of boundlessness; they were the *apeiron*—the area of possibility."[10] Lewis did not emphasize, however, that these two qualities, boundlessness and possibility, are the essence, not only of Cooper's frontier, but of his view of America. In many of Cooper's border tales, the immediate neutral ground, the setting of the action, is deliberately made to stand for the boundless promise of the entire land. Whereas Cooper's ocean is a place of boundless possibility that Cooper deliberately separates from America and its problems, Cooper's forest frontier is America itself.

Here arises a troubling if obvious problem. Cooper

[9] Edwin Fussell, *Frontier: American Literature and the American West* (Princeton, 1965), pp. 11–18, 48; George Dekker, *James Fenimore Cooper: The Novelist* (London, 1967), pp. 33–34.

[10] R. W. B. Lewis, *The American Adam* (Chicago, 1955), p. 99.

repeatedly defines American promise through the boundless landscape and the agrarian communities which were to be established upon its frontier. Communities like Templeton in *The Pioneers* were to combine the benefits of civilization and the State of Nature without the evils of either. Free of both commercialism to the east and savagery to the west, American frontier towns were to cultivate physiocratic virtues under the mild rule of republican law. Such towns would exemplify the ideal of the pastoral middle ground, whose importance for American literature has been convincingly demonstrated by Leo Marx's *The Machine in the Garden*. And yet, in novel after novel, Cooper shows us that the exigencies of the neutral ground prevent its ready transformation into his pastoral ideal. The land must first be settled and political justice established. Rather than leaping to utopian portrayals of agrarian communities, Cooper's novels concern the awkward transition between the State of Nature and the State of Civilization.

The heart of Cooper's novels is thus a struggle for power, a struggle for control of the neutral ground in a time of change and upheaval. In Cooper's fiction, what often seem to be endless patterns of escape, pursuit, and recapture, enlivened with glorious description and melodramatic death scenes, are in essence power struggles for possession of the American land. The larger, national meaning depends upon Cooper's ability to magnify the significance of a squabble over a local plot of earth. Admittedly Cooper only rarely makes conscious use of literary symbol, yet throughout his novels, the place of struggle attains far more importance than its intrinsic identity would seem to warrant. Westchester County,

Natty Bumppo's hut, the Valley of Wish-ton-Wish, Three Mile Point, the hutted knoll of *Wyandotté*, Tom Hutter's castle, Mooseridge and Ravensnest, and Mark Woolston's reef—all of these small, seemingly inconsequential bits of earth become representative of something far larger, the quality of a civilization or the American land itself. Cooper's novels search for answers to the greatest questions posed by the unrealized promise of his new nation: "Who shall inherit the American land?" "What form of society shall we establish?" and, above all, "What is the meaning of political justice in a republic?"

Cooper's penchant for enlarging the meaning of local and transient events influenced the form of his fiction. Searching for a technique with which to give national meaning to his tales, and groping toward the symbolism that was to serve later American romancers, Cooper happened upon what, for want of a better word, must be called synecdoche. His tales would deal with local struggles or historical events of lesser importance, yet through them Cooper would discuss the most grandly national of issues. Often, however, Cooper did not pause to clarify the exact relationship between the part and the whole. As a result, the reader sometimes feels a disparity between the small scale of Cooper's narrative and the ponderous uses to which he puts it. In successive sentences, one finds details of adventure and weighty statements of political theory. Cooper, however, often leaves the reader to draw whatever connection may exist between the two. Scalping Peter of *The Oak Openings*, for example, provides Cooper an opening for a discussion of the congressional demagogue. Podesta Vito Viti, an obscure Italian official in *The Wing-and-Wing*, is the occasion for a gratuitous attack on the bumbling officiousness of American bureaucrats.

Awkward as synecdoche may seem as a tool for fiction, it was exactly suited to Cooper's processes of thought. As a commentator upon national politics, Cooper repeatedly saw the largest of issues in the smallest of events. Cassio's review of *The Bravo*[11] was proof, to Cooper, of the essential quality of the American mind, deference to British aristocracy. Public misuse of Three Mile Point, a tip of land on a small lake in New York, signified sweeping changes in American attitudes toward property law. New York Anti-Rent Wars indicated a national catastrophe; the trial of Mary Monson illustrated faults, not only in the overhauled state judiciary, but in the republic itself.

Whenever Cooper enlarges the significance of a plot of earth in the neutral ground, he turns an exciting tale into a national statement, and, finally, into a study of the factors underlying the rise or fall of a civilization or a government. Those novels in which the action contains larger national dimensions are those I shall consider,

[11] This anonymous defamation, which appeared on June 7, 1832, was almost surely written by E. S. Gould, an American foreign correspondent who was avowedly antirepublican in his principles. S. F. B. Morse informed Cooper of Cassio's identity, and Cooper, at first indifferent to the review, began to assume, not without reason, that Cassio's attack was politically inspired. Cassio's review is one source of the misunderstanding that darkened the relations between Cooper and his country in the 1830s.

See Dorothy Waples, *The Whig Myth of James Fenimore Cooper* (New Haven, 1938), pp. 88–97.

Cooper's intemperate and disproportionate reaction to the hostile reviews of his European novels is the measure of the earnestness with which he defended American political values. Cooper was enraged, not by attacks on the literary merits of his books, but by attacks on their supposed antirepublicanism.

rather than those tales in which the neutral ground bears no wider significance. My emphasizing such novels as *Lionel Lincoln*, *The Redskins*, and *The Ways of the Hour*, and my ignoring of *The Last of the Mohicans*, *The Pathfinder*, and *The Sea Lions*, has, therefore, nothing to do with the intrinsic literary merit of the individual tale.

And yet I hope to demonstrate that Cooper developed markedly in his handling of the neutral ground. When he first uses his characteristic setting, in *The Spy* and *Lionel Lincoln*, the neutral ground is little more than a Scottlike no-man's-land;[12] questions of national identity can only be introduced by direct reference to historical aspects of the revolutionary war. *The Pioneers* shows a more skillful hand. Cooper discovers ways of making the tiny community of Templeton representative of American society at large. Six years later, when Cooper wrote *The Wept of Wish-ton-Wish*, he discovered a form of narrative that became a paradigm for a number of later novels including *The Deerslayer*, *Wyandotté*, and the Littlepage Manuscripts. He would describe how a representative group of settlers formed a self-enclosed community in the wilderness. By tracing the growth, maturity, and decline of the single settlement, he would describe the interworkings of larger social forces in America. It was not until writing *The Crater*, however, that Cooper combined the social novel with the adventure romance, and made both genres serve the theme of American identity in a satisfactorily symbolic form. By 1847 Cooper's gropings toward a more overtly national and symbolic form of fiction had led him far from the fault

[12] Dekker, *James Fenimore Cooper*, p. 33.

in handling of setting that Richard Chase condemned: "unless [Cooper] has been able to set some swift intrigue or combat in motion, the setting remains—even when thoroughly inventoried—scattered and inert, and fails to develop into that 'enveloping action' which in a coherent novel the setting should be."[13]

Cooper's characterization is admirably suited to fictions that describe symbolic struggles for control of the American land. Into the neutral ground come representatives of fixed social classes: Yankees, Dutchmen, gentry, blacks, squatters, Indians, and an occasional foreigner. As Kay Seymour House has shown, Cooper conceives these characters as types.[14] They bear remarkable resemblance to each other as they reappear throughout the novels, primarily because Cooper intends them to represent certain constant forces in American life. Individuals who exist outside of the fixed social types and classes also enter the neutral ground. Their names are memorable but few: Harvey Birch, John Paul Jones, Natty Bumppo, and Jacopo the bravo. All of them possess for Cooper an individual grandeur that not even the most admirable of his gentry can claim. The representatives of the fixed classes construct a form of rudimentary society by establishing settlements and agreeing upon laws. Upon the individuals, however, fall the burden of loneliness and the necessity of making the crucial decision—to acquiesce or to revolt, to remain or to flee.

As the social classes contend among themselves, and

[13] Richard Chase, *The American Novel and Its Tradition* (New York, 1957), p. 46.
[14] Kay Seymour House, *Cooper's Americans* (Columbus, Ohio, 1965), pp. 11–14.

as the individual contends against society, the establishment and continuance of political justice become issues as crucial to Cooper's frontiersmen as they are to the political theorist of the A.B.C. Letters or *The American Democrat*. Rights of land ownership in the neutral ground must be legally determined. Consequently, concepts of law, taken in their broadest sense, become the matrix for determining political justice. The laws instituted by the rudimentary society are an indication of its worth and strength. They form a standard of judgment both on those who construct them and those who uphold them. How, by whom, and for what purpose the law is formulated, how is it administered, and how it is upheld, determine the degree of political justice that the representative American settlement can claim. Cooper's plots thus rely upon legal conflicts. Trial scenes occur in twelve of his novels and impending trial alters the outcome of many more.

Cooper's continuing interest in the formulation of the law and its relation to justice is obviously attributable in great part to personal experience. His father had been both a congressman and a frontier judge, and James became expert by necessity in libel and New York property law. Susan Cooper noted that her father was so "partial to legal reading" that he eagerly studied legal questions that were quite independent of immediate controversies.[15] *The Letters and Journals of James Fenimore Cooper* attest to Cooper's continued fascination with the relation of law to political justice. The law of copyright, international law relating to naval impressment, Nullification, the issue

[15] Susan F. Cooper, *The Cooper Gallery* (New York, 1865), p. 367.

of French reparations, Jackson's removal of bank de-
posits, the congressional censure of Jackson, the Somers
Mutiny Affair—all of these issues absorb Cooper's interest and are evaluated through the framework of the law.

Only in the Littlepage Manuscripts and *The Ways of
the Hour* did specific contemporary problems of legal and
political justice provide the immediate raison d'être of a
novel. However, Cooper's acquaintance and experience
with legal questions, combined with his interest in the
facts of power and government on the frontier, consistently led him both to use the law as a source of
conflict in his novels, and, more importantly, to analyze
human behavior in terms of the law throughout his writings. By structuring novels around a legal conflict, Cooper
discovered a serviceable means of embodying republican
political values within the genre of the border romance.
As a metaphor through which to evaluate character, the
law provided Cooper both a fixity of absolute standards,
and an opportunity for debate among alternative ideas
of just behavior.

Personal experience is not the sole explanation for
Cooper's interest in the evolution of law and justice in
America. He was exploring a major issue of his day.
Perry Miller has shown that the period of Cooper's early
maturity was the era in which Hoffman, Story, and James
Kent (whom Cooper knew) were virtually creating
American law by adaptations from the British common
law.[16] Although Cooper's contemporaries were as hostile
to law as Natty Bumppo was, they were as willing to

[16] Perry Miller, *The Life of the Mind in America: From the
Revolution to the Civil War* (New York, 1965), pp. 99–121.

recognize the necessity of law as Judge Temple.[17] To create just laws for a nation without them was as imperative in higher judicial circles as it was at the foot of Lake Otsego. In his romances, his novels, and his social criticism, therefore, Cooper repeatedly explored the crucial issue of his times—the nature of political justice in the neutral ground that is America.

III

The most sensitive of Cooper's characters are aware that, in the effort to establish political justice, the great task is to choose one law among conflicting laws. There are, in fact, four distinct kinds of laws in Cooper's world—divine, moral, natural, and civil. When Cooper considers issues of government or political justice he shifts back and forth between these levels of law. None of the four kinds is explicitly defined, but each is used consistently, and all are essential to an understanding of the premises upon which Cooper's political thought rests.

Cooper's strong Deistic faith led him to the conviction that there exists in the mind of God a series of timelessly valid principles of absolute right called the divine law, and that God has given to each man an innate ability to discriminate between the Right and the Wrong in an earthly context. The following statement, wholly eigh-

[17] Miller argues that the popularity of Leatherstocking as a character, and *The Pioneers* as a novel, is attributable to the fact that Cooper "struck into the very center of what by 1823 had become a tormenting American dilemma" (*The Life of the Mind*, p. 100).

teenth century in style, diction, and thought, was written
by Cooper in the 1830s, but would not be out of place
either in *Precaution* (1820) or *The Sea Lions* (1849).

Those who think themselves set apart for the sole enjoyment
of the good things of this world, forget that this state of being
is merely a part of a great whole; that a superior Intelligence
directs all; that this divine Intelligence has established equit-
able laws, and implanted in every man a consciousness of
right and wrong, which enables the lowest of the scale to
appreciate innate justice, and which makes every man, in
some degree, critical in matters that touch his own welfare.[18]

The moral law, which Cooper repeatedly equates with the
Great and Ten Commandments, the Beatitudes, and biblical truth in general, is thus that portion of the divine law
that has been revealed to man.

For Cooper, as for Locke or Pope, natural law is the
will of God's providence operating in nature according to
observable principles. Such an easy coupling as "nothing
is easier than to offend against natural justice and the
laws of God"[19] recurs frequently in Cooper's writings.
In other contexts, natural law is synonymous with Cooper's libertarian politics, as in a reference to "the eternal
principles of natural justice which, in truth, contain the
essence of political liberty."[20] The primary function of
Cooper's appeal to natural law, however, is to emphasize
that natural law is a mirror of divine or moral law. For
Cooper, the God who created divine law, having created
natural law as well, has created them on identical principles, some of which can be discerned by men of natural

[18] *Sketches of Switzerland* (Philadelphia, 1836), part I, vol.
I, p. 177.

[19] *History of the Navy*, 2 vols. (Cooperstown, 1847), II, 32.

[20] *Sketches of Switzerland*, part I, vol. I, p. 208.

piety. An equally defensible conclusion is that moral law, being a part of divine law, must correspond to natural law. If both a beneficent Deity and man's submission are assumed, natural, moral and divine laws not only operate in eighteenth-century harmony; they become indistinguishable. Whenever Cooper theorizes about ideal political systems, natural, moral, and divine law become nearly interchangeable terms.

Cooper recognized no separation of morality from politics. There is an unswerving insistence throughout his fiction and social criticism that the moral or divine law must be the foundation of all civil law. In 1842 Cooper approved Dickens's proposal for an international copyright law with the following argument:

The holiness of the Deity is his justice. It is his unerring distinction, in all cases, between these eternal principles of right and wrong, which form good and evil. We should all endeavor—so far as an imperfect nature will allow us, and at a humble distance—to imitate this love of justice. Communities are, if possible, under greater obligations to do so, than individuals, on account of the greater results connected with their mistakes, of the influence of their example, and because less subject to be swerved by direct selfishness.[21]

For Cooper, then, the measure of political justice is the proximity of the civil to the divine law. This is the standard that Natty Bumppo applies to Templeton, that Fenimore Cooper applies to Venice or America, and that Mark Woolston applies to the creation of his utopia. The values that Cooper associates with divine law may shift slightly in his last years, but the standard of divine law itself is never relaxed.

[21] *Letters and Journals*, IV, 303.

As a political thinker, one of Cooper's assets is that he measures his ideals against reality without losing those ideals. The fourfold harmony between civil, moral, divine, and natural law is portrayed as a social reality only in *Notions of the Americans.* Elsewhere Cooper is forever detecting flaws in the scheme or in man's abilities to realize it. Most obviously, the divine laws to which Cooper appeals can never be comprehended by man. Far off, inscrutable, presumably absolute in truth, the principles of divine law form a credo to which Cooper and Natty Bumppo can only appeal with futile longing. Cooper's religious principles force him to make appeals to a divine law that can neither be realized nor described: "It is very true, that as we can understand only our relations to the Deity, without comprehending the relations which the Deity holds to us, it may be dangerous, or even impious, to pretend to deduce any reasoning from the great laws of God, which shall be strictly applicable to the obligations which man owes to his fellows."[22]

The moral sense that Cooper affirms—man's "consciousness of right and wrong" that has been implanted by the "divine Intelligence"—seems totally missing in many of Cooper's Indians and frontiersmen, to say nothing of more devious subversives such as Joel Strides or Jason Newcome. In work after work, Cooper shows how unrealizable is his own hope that man's moral sense is sufficient to govern him. The necessity of having the civil law, Cooper insists, arises from man's failure to live within the moral or divine law.

Cooper is all too aware of the ease with which man

[22] *Notions of the Americans,* II, 253.

misinterprets or perverts the terms "moral law" or "natural law." For Hurry Harry or Thousandacres, "moral law" signifies whatever he thinks is right and "natural law" whatever laws he cares to observe in nature. In Cooper's eyes, such misuses let down all barriers against personal relativism. Thus, Cooper's Yankees claim natural law as a sanction for squatter's rights, Natty refers to natural law to support his doctrine of use, but a Littlepage cites natural law in defense of property contracts.

The premises upon which Cooper's view of government rest are all dependent upon his recognition that, although natural justice must always be its standard, natural justice will always be perverted. The opening of *The American Democrat* reveals how ingrained the problem of civil and natural justice was to Cooper's mind:

Man is known to exist in no part of the world, without certain rules for the regulation of his intercourse with those around him. It is a first necessity of his weakness, that laws, founded on the immutable principles of natural justice, should be framed, in order to protect the feeble against the violence of the strong; the honest from the schemes of the dishonest; the temperate and industrious, from the waste and indolence of the dissolute and the idle. These laws, though varying with circumstances, possess a common character, being formed on that consciousness of right, which God has bestowed in order that men may judge between good and evil.[23]

Crucial assumptions of Cooper's political thought are evident in this passage. Like Jefferson or John Adams, Cooper's conception of law and government is entirely protective and preventative, a matter of guaranteeing

[23] *The American Democrat*, eds. G. Dekker and L. Johnston (Baltimore, 1969), p. 75.

individual or societal rights by proscription. Moreover, Cooper tends to equate "the immutable principles of natural justice" with "man's consciousness of right"; natural and moral law become synonymous. Finally, and most importantly, we note his Lockean insistence that the civil law can and must be based upon both the natural and the moral law.

If Cooper's primary standard of political justice is the proximity of the civil to the divine law, his secondary standard, even in the later years, is the extent to which political power is vested in the citizenry. In order to determine whether a given polity may be classified as a monarchy, an aristocracy, or a democracy,[24] Cooper always applies an unvarying set of criteria which seem to have become a habit of mind. Simply because a government possesses a monarch does not classify it as a monarchy, nor do the governmental machinery and the name of a republic qualify a nation to be truly republican. Cooper's yardstick is always the fact of power, the number of those who actually participate in the making of policy, whether they be one, a minority, or a majority.

Cooper's political analyses, starting from a determination of the identity and number of the rulers, in any of the three forms, then proceed to examine which social classes are in power and which are not, whether those classes in power are morally worthy of their charge, and whether those classes out of power could benefit their nation by

[24] Like Aristotle, Montesquieu, and Adams, Cooper envisions only three forms of government. He fits every government he analyzes into one of their subspecies. Both the *Letter to General Lafayette* and *The American Democrat* assess problems of government by formal comparison of monarchy, aristocracy, and democracy.

being included among the rulers. Inevitably, therefore, the extent of the franchise becomes an especially important touchstone of political evaluation for Cooper. Is the vote in a given political system dispensed so narrowly as to deprive a citizen of his natural rights and incite revolution, or is it so widely distributed as to put power into undesirable hands? In an attempt to determine the best available compromise to the franchise question, Cooper repeatedly considers the arguments for and against property and residence qualifications for voting.

Finally, Cooper focuses upon the balance between the powers of a government and the body of self-restricting laws it enacts. The constant standard that Cooper applies to America, England, France, Venice, and even the individual cantons of Switzerland is whether governmental authority is limited and defined by a written and stable code of law. Once the scope and power of the law are determined, Cooper examines whether individual civil laws, be they of Templeton, Berne, or Craterdom, are consonant with the divine law. In all of Cooper's American writings he assesses the degree to which civil laws encroach upon the natural rights and constitutional liberties of the individual.

IV

My approach to Cooper's American tales tries to combine his concerns with the neutral ground, the relation of civil to moral law, and the largest questions of national political justice. For these purposes, Cooper's handling of setting is of prime importance. The setting defines the political and national promise of the land; it also posits forces that classes and individuals struggle to overthrow. The ultimate test of a character's virtue is his ability to deduce a code of moral justice from his natural surroundings and then follow it. Cooper's characters, like Hardy's, are remembered against a landscape. Despite Cooper's frequent use of character contrast, his Americans are usually defined by their relation to their environment rather than their relation to others.

As a novel unfolds, any shift of power that occurs within the neutral frontier becomes of crucial importance —both intrinsically and as a symbolic rendering of historical forces in America. The following questions repeatedly arise: What class owns land at the novel's outset? What right have they to own it? And what kind of political justice are they attempting to institute? Are the codes of the settlement, whether written or unwritten, founded upon moral law? Which class rules at the conclusion of the tale? If there has been a shift in power, a change in statute or government, how and why has it come about? What sort of a future does Cooper envision for the new possessors of power and for the disestablished?

To examine the processes by which social order is established or overthrown restores the plot of Cooper's novels, the cause and effect relation of incident to incident, to primary importance as a tool of analysis. The credibility of a tale as fictional history of an American society depends directly upon the degree to which the linkage of events is plausible. If the incidents that lead to social change seem to arise from the actions of the characters themselves, the world Cooper portrays merits suspension of disbelief. If, however, a deus ex machina, unexplained changes in character, or timely revelations of long-buried information are employed to effect a desirable change of power, Cooper seems only to create puppets that play out preconceived ideas of republican integrity.

It seems inevitable that, on occasion, Cooper would refuse to allow his fictional America to work out its own future according to the very real historical forces operating within the neutral ground. Cooper wished to be both the spokesman for national ideals and the recorder of national fact:

The first object of a writer, should be the support of just and honorable sentiments. When an author of fiction has sufficiently respected this imperative obligation, it would seem that he has some right to felicitate himself that his pictures, whether of the passions, or of sensible objects, are so like the originals as to be recognized by those who are most familiar with the subjects.[25]

Cooper never abandoned the first of these obligations. His definition of "just and honorable sentiments" may have changed slightly in his last years, but his application of abstract standards of timeless moral truth to all he saw never varied. "Necessity is but a poor apology for any moral wrong" and "Expediency has no necessary connexion with the right,"[26] two phrases from an attack upon impressment, were so fundamental to his vision of the world that he rarely felt a need to state them.

The second "obligation," a plea for realism of character and physical detail, surprises the reader more accustomed to a Cooper whose "works aspire to the elevation

[25] *Letters and Journals*, II, 34–35.
[26] *History of the Navy*, II, 32, 34.

of romance" and who presents the *"beau-idéal"*[27] of character, but it is a plea characteristic of Cooper during the 1820s. More important is the fact that until the 1830s Cooper saw no problem in fulfilling the roles of both spokesman and factfinder; American facts confirmed American values. What would result, however, if Cooper's fictional assessment of the changing course of American life did not square with the promulgation of "just and honorable sentiments?"

Let us rephrase Cooper's dilemma in more general terms. Cooper was evidently searching for an unchanging code of political justice that would correspond to timeless divine laws. Yet his very definition of America was, as we have seen, an unformed land of endless change. When American change could no longer be called progress, one of Cooper's impulses was to attribute timeless political merit to the American Constitution, thus implying that divine laws had been permanently found. Another impulse was to continue to believe that absolute justice was unknowable and that the evils of American society would somehow work themselves out.

Given these impulses, what is the duty of a man of letters, like Cooper, who conceives of himself both as an advocate for American constitutional freedoms and as a realist? Cooper recognized that "the characters of institutions depend on the repositories of power, in the last resort,"[28] and yet became convinced that the power and the law had fallen into the wrong hands, and had

[27] "Preface to the Leatherstocking Tales" in volume 6 of the Darley Edition, *Cooper's Novels* (New York, 1861), p. x. All references to Cooper's novels are to the Darley Edition.

[28] *The American Democrat*, p. 89.

been misused. Should he forsake a realistic portrayal of America, manipulate the America portrayed in the neutral ground, and uphold "the just and honorable?" Cooper was to deceive himself with such manipulations in the resolutions of *Home As Found*, *The Redskins*, and, to a lesser degree, *The Pioneers*. A second alternative was to associate "the just and honorable" solely with the politics of the founding fathers and to denounce present reality. This tendency grew markedly in Cooper's thought after 1838. The third, and for Cooper the least attractive alternative, was to change his own political principles in order to adapt to the exigencies of a new age.

I shall argue throughout this study that it was not until the years that followed publication of *The Crater* in 1847 that Cooper changed his political convictions. Even in his last four years, Cooper's shift in political principles is so complicated by qualifications and by the problem of assigning auctorial authority to fictional characters that it will remain disputed. There is no evidence to conclude, however, that Cooper changed any of his political convictions before writing *The Ways of the Hour* and *New York*.

Criticism has rather consistently followed the older view of Cooper as a youthful liberal who adopted conservative or reactionary ideas upon returning from Europe in 1833. This picture, not markedly different from the Whig caricature, is simplistic because it is based on two separate confusions. We must distinguish, as Cooper did, between facts and principles. Cooper's conception of American political facts changed greatly after 1833, but his determination to retain his political principles remained constant. If we wish to ascertain the consistency of Cooper's political views, we must attend to the specific components of the polity that Cooper approves, and not to the vigor of his denunciations.

The second confusion arises from the continued misuse of the term "aristocracy." We are led to believe that Cooper wrote "democratic" novels about Europe in his early maturity and "aristocratic" novels about New York in later years. Cooper would have demanded a precise political definition of these words. For Cooper, the word "aristocracy" was a political not a social term, and one that could never be applied to the gentry of a democracy, who were vested with no political privileges.[29]

If we read Cooper's novels on his own terms, Cooper emerges neither as a youthful democrat nor as an aged aristocrat but, until 1850, as a consistent republican. Cooper frequently distinguished between a democracy, in which the citizens vote to determine policy, and a constitutional republic, in which citizens elect representatives to determine policy. He referred to America as a republic or as a confederated, representative democracy, but never as an unrestricted democracy. Although he was convinced that a true republic must derive political power from a widely based constituency, he never stated that

[29] Cooper insists rigorously upon these distinctions in *The American Democrat*: "We live in an age, when the words aristocrat and democrat are much used, without regard to real significations. An aristocrat is one of a few, who possess the political power of a country; a democrat, one of the many. . . . To call a man who has the habits and opinions of a gentleman, an aristocrat, from that fact alone, is an abuse of terms, and betrays ignorance of the true principles of government" (150–151). Cooper's counterattack against Whig editors was not solely motivated by self-justification. As a defender of republican values, Cooper wished to combat what he felt was dangerous political ignorance.

universal manhood suffrage was absolutely essential either to the federal or the state polity. Thus, for Cooper, the word "democrat" described no more than a man who believes in republican principles.

According to his conception of the needs of the historical moment, Cooper emphasized different aspects of his ideal republican polity, but he did not consider changing the polity itself until his last years. Those who characterize Cooper as a youthful democrat ignore his sensitive treatment of the Tory viewpoint in the revolutionary war novels. Cooper was most fervently "an American democrat" during his European years and not before them. Those who regret the so-called "aristocratic" tendencies in the later novels slight the possibility that America, not Cooper, was changing. More importantly, they ignore the troubling fact that not until 1847 did a presumably more "conservative" Cooper debate changes in his ideal polity. In dealing with Cooper, one must separate his aristocratic social convictions from his republican political convictions. Contemporary political labels do not apply. Cooper could rightly insist that he was both a democrat and a conservative because his unchanging political purpose was to conserve the individual liberties of the original republic. Believing that educated, propertied landowners should rule, Cooper nonetheless retained, in Marius Bewley's words, "a liberalism grounded in a sense of history that is rare."[30]

Bewley has also said of Cooper that he was "one of the most astute politico-social critics America has ever had."[31]

[30] Marius Bewley, *The Eccentric Design* (New York, 1963), p. 64.

[31] *The Eccentric Design*, p. 68.

This is a judgment which should be more widely shared. Admittedly, the repetitions and didacticism of Cooper's later works have contributed to the continuing disregard for his political and social writings in preference for the Leatherstocking Tales. An equally important cause of the neglect of Cooper's social fiction, however, has been an impatience with what seem to be triflingly local issues: Three Mile Point, Anti-Rent, trial by jury. Here the fault is ours if we fail to realize that the local squabbles are only individual manifestations of one vexing political dilemma for which Cooper could find no solution. How does a republican polity maintain desirable social and intellectual distinctions? How can the American system of government continue to place political power in the hands of those citizens best able to provide disinterested justice for the common weal? The writings of John Adams, Tocqueville, and Henry Adams, among others, testify how fundamental and persistent the problem has proven.[32] Cooper's willingness to grapple with it in all its complexity is another example of what is surely his greatest quality, moral courage.

In tracing questions of political justice in Cooper's American fiction, I have tried closely to respect both the chronology of Cooper's writings and the pertinence of Cooper's social criticism. By combining novels that are comparable in theme ("the revolutionary war") or setting

[32] Speaking of Cooper's portrayal of American life in the late novels, James Beard states that "For all its wealth of conscious insight, this fiction is so rich in unintended ambiguities that it persuades the modern reader chiefly of the existence of deep cultural dilemmas whose resolution was coming to seem, even to Cooper, beyond any power of human reason" ("Introduction" to *Letters and Journals*, I, xxx–xxxi).

("moral law in the wilderness"), I seek a concise way of studying the consistency of Cooper's political views. My ordering of Cooper's works is thus a compromise between chronology and theme that attempts to serve both.

By focusing on the problems of living the moral law and enforcing the civil law within the neutral ground, I have tried to select a theme large enough to contain Cooper's complexities and to illuminate the direction of his self-assumed role as fictional spokesman for the American republic. Simultaneously, however, I have restricted my scope to a study of specific social and political problems that are vital to Cooper's career and that must be understood in Cooper's own terms. James Beard rightly insists that "To be understood in the full context of his time and ours, [Cooper's] thought must be examined in terms of its own organic unity."[33] My intent is to show how Cooper works out questions of national destiny in fiction. I conceive of Cooper as a patriot who attempted the highly difficult task of exploring political justice in America by means of historical romances of the neutral ground.

[33] "Introduction" to *Letters and Journals*, I, xxv.

1. The American Revolution: Problems of Patriotism

> It can never be too often repeated, that the time for fixing every essential right on a legal basis is while our rulers are honest, and ourselves united. From the conclusion of this war we shall be going down hill. It will not then be necessary to resort every moment to the people for support. They will be forgotten, therefore, and their rights disregarded. They will forget themselves, but in the sole faculty of making money, and will never think of uniting to effect a due respect for their rights. The shackles, therefore, which shall not be knocked off at the conclusion of this war, will remain on us long, will be made heavier, and heavier, till our rights shall revive or expire in a convulsion.
>
> THOMAS JEFFERSON, *Notes on Virginia*

In Cooper's mind, the American Revolution formed the watershed of political history. If Cooper was to define American values for his country, he had to decide upon the essential significance of the revolutionary war. Five of Cooper's novels written before 1830 are concerned with the struggle for independence. *The Spy* and *Lionel Lincoln* deal with the revolutionary war directly. Three sea tales, *The Pilot*, *The Red Rover*, and *The Water Witch*, form a trilogy that describes the emergence of revolutionary fervor in America from the 1720s to the

outbreak of battle.[1] *Notions of the Americans*, the European travel volumes, and the *History of the Navy* assess
the war historically. Of the novels written after 1830,
only *Wyandotté* is primarily concerned with the revolutionary era, yet the American War for Independence is
frequently introduced as a reference point to establish
historical contrasts. Like Henry Adams in the *Education*,
Miles Wallingford and the Littlepages hearken back to
revolutionary times as a standard of political value
against which the present is measured. The frequency
with which Cooper returned to the revolutionary war
attests not only to the importance but to the difficulty of
his determining its significance.

In 1821 when Cooper decided to write his first tale of
the Revolution, he approached his subject with intense
but conflicting feelings. The son of a Federalist congressman, James Fenimore Cooper had been educated under
the staunchly antirepublican eyes of Thomas Ellison, rec-
tor of St. Peter's, Albany, a monarchist and a decided
Anglophile.[2] James's choice of spouse indicates no chaf-
ing against his heritage or education. His wife was a De
Lancey, a prominent family of patrician landholders who
were English in taste, Anglican in religion, and Federalist
in politics. More importantly for Cooper's fiction, the

[1] Thomas Philbrick, *James Fenimore Cooper and the Development of American Sea Fiction* (Cambridge, Mass., 1961), p. 58.

[2] Cooper's often quoted characterization of Ellison pictures him
as the very type of the comic Tory in America (*Gleanings in Europe: England* [New York, 1930], pp. 196–197). It is likely, however, that the youthful Cooper had accepted his teacher's prejudices, among which Cooper mentions a "most profound reverence
for the king and nobility," a "contempt for all classes of dis-
senters," and a detestation of democrats.

De Lanceys had remained loyal to the crown during the revolutionary war; John Peter De Lancey, James's father-in-law, had been a captain of the Pennsylvania Loyalists.[3]

Whenever as a mature man Cooper mentioned Federalism, he associated it with monarchism, never failing to observe that, though most Federalists had been republican, some of them, most notably Hamilton, had been monarchists at heart.[4] Yet Cooper also acknowledged the "deep reverence and admiration" toward England that he had "imbibed" as a child, and noted that, for him as for other presumably republican youths, England had been the "idol of their political, moral, and literary adoration."[5] Cooper never denied his pride in his marital connections nor his interest in the De Lancey genealogy, which had included, along with a number of Loyalists, a Lord of the Manor of Scarsdale.[6] Susan Cooper recalled her father's fondness for studying English heraldry, a fondness that extended to the reading of entire books on

[3] The fullest account of Cooper's connection with the De Lancey family, aside from the relevant letters and journals, is to be found in R. E. Spiller's biography, *Fenimore Cooper: Critic of His Times* (New York, 1931), pp. 59–68.

[4] *Letters and Journals*, II, 30–32, 180; *Sketches of Switzerland*, part I, volume II, p. 158.

[5] *Gleanings in Europe: England*, pp. 9–10.

[6] See, for example, *Letters and Journals*, IV, 492–495; V, 274–277: V, 306–310. The *Letters and Journals* force us to correct Spiller's conclusion: "With the Tory strain in his wife's family, Cooper never admitted any sympathy" (*Fenimore Cooper*, p. 62). Perhaps Leslie Fiedler was only following Spiller in judging that "Cooper's Toryism . . . is rather like Scott's Jacobite sympathies, a literary affectation" (*Love and Death in the American Novel* [Cleveland, 1960], p. 177). The unfortunate consequence of both judgments has been to disregard the complexities of Cooper's treatment of the revolution.

the British nobility.[7] At no point in his life did Cooper see any contradiction between a respectful interest in titled aristocrats as individuals and a thorough condemnation of aristocracy as a polity. During his European years, Cooper's pen flowed with diatribes against aristocratic oligarchy, while his letters to Mrs. Peter Augustus Jay were carefully noting the name and mannerisms of continental nobility.

By causes which have not and perhaps cannot be fully traced, Cooper added to his Federalist birthright a firm belief in the simple dignity of democratic man and a deep conviction that the natural rights of every human being entitle him to a maximum of liberty. Because of the American Revolution, a government had been founded upon these principles. If left free from the corrupting polity of European, specifically English aristocracies, the future of the new American world could know no limit. *Notions of the Americans* is Cooper's glowing tribute to precisely these familiar ideals, these unrealizable longings that have continued to appeal to Americans at least since the times of Jefferson.

From Cooper's writings, one can recover a scattered few of the factors that seem to have influenced the growth of his libertarian faith. Cooper speaks of the day in 1806 when, entering a royal English park and being informed that, mercifully, he was indeed permitted to enter, he suddenly understood the distinction between political franchise and political liberty.[8] Judging from the long sequence of sea dogs and democratic old salts in Cooper's sea tales, together with the autobiographical impli-

[7] *The Cooper Gallery*, p. 122.
[8] *Gleanings in Europe: England*, pp. 248–249.

cations of *Ned Myers* and *Afloat and Ashore*, Cooper's years in the navy, both on the ocean and at Oswego, surely bolstered his nationalism and toned down social pretension. The Castle Garden Ball for Lafayette and Sully's portrait of Jefferson also seem to have affected him deeply. Until more direct influences are recovered, however, we must continue to regard these factors not as causes but as manifestations of Cooper's growing commitment to Republican rather than Federalist ideology. It is unlikely that the sources of Cooper's mature political faith will ever be fully known.

Out of this uneasy combination of a Federalist heritage, libertarian political principles, and a strong nationalism, Cooper began to write of the revolutionary war. Inevitably he adopted a many-sided view of its significance. Like Jefferson, he was sure that the American Revolution had been a crisis in which men, acting beyond themselves in accord with principles and not self-interest, had succeeded in envisioning and creating a polity that ushered in a new era of political virtue.[9] Yet Cooper was never to be sure, no matter how long he struggled for one definitive interpretation, exactly what those principles had been. His acquaintance with Tory and Federalist viewpoints had led him to understand the wide varieties of opinion that had existed in America between 1760 and 1787. In writing of the war he would not gloss over those differences.

[9] "There are periods in the histories of all countries, in which entire nations may be said to be on their good behavior. These are the times of struggles and changes, when attention is drawn to the acts of public men, and principles have unusual influence. Such was the case at the commencement of the American revolution" (*The American Democrat*, p. 195).

One can trace three sharply distinct views of the American Revolution in Cooper's writings. Whenever he feels called upon to give an historical justification for the war, he becomes "an enthusiastic admirer of the conduct of the Americans throughout those trying scenes" and declares that the era as a whole should be placed "in comparison with any thing that history may boast."[10] In *Notions of the Americans* and the historical sections of *Lionel Lincoln*, he glorifies the war as a true revolution in which bands of sturdy yeomen democrats, oppressed by English tyranny, fought for the natural rights of man. He insists that the American militia were "men battling for the known rights of human nature"[11] and flatly declares that "The War of 1776 was purely a war of principle."[12]

One of the climactic moments in *Notions of the Americans* is Lafayette's triumphant reception by the House of Representatives in 1824. Cooper approvingly records the speech in which Lafayette attributes American prosperity to revolutionary ideals that closely resemble Thomas Paine's:

What better pledge can be given of a persevering national love of liberty, when those blessings are evidently the result of a virtuous resistance to oppression, and of institutions founded on the rights of man and the republican principle of self-government.[13]

Whenever Cooper justifies the revolution on the basis of such phrases as "natural rights" or "the rights of man,"

[10] *Notions of the Americans,* I, 75.
[11] *Notions of the Americans,* I, 217.
[12] *Notions of the Americans,* II, 195.
[13] *Notions of the Americans,* II, 143.

he is appealing beyond civil governments to principles of natural and divine law, much as Jefferson had done in "A Summary of the Rights of British North America." From *Notions of the Americans* and *Lionel Lincoln*, as from many of Jefferson's writings, the reader pictures a united nation of simple republicans who claimed that Parliament had no natural right to tax the colonies. Even in later years, Cooper asserted that "the revolution proceeded from a denial of the right in parliament to tax the colonies at all, and not from any particular imposition."[14]

In other passages, however, Cooper's view of the war is far more moderate. The struggle is considered to be an unwilling recourse to arms by dignified men and not a national revolution fought for natural rights. Cooper emphasizes that the Americans sought no separation from the crown, but were simply trying to regain civil rights guaranteed them under the British constitution:

The thirteen United Colonies . . . now commenced a struggle with the mother country, not to obtain a political independence, for few thought of so great a change when blood was first shed, but to regain rights that were inherent in the governing principles of the institutions under which they had long lived, and which were assured to them formally in a variety of ways.[15]

Whereas Cooper's first view of the Revolution implies the primacy of natural over civil law, the second implies

14 *Sketches of Switzerland*, part II, vol. I, p. 66.
15 *History of the Navy*, I, 42. Like George Bancroft, Cooper accepted the notion that the first generation of Puritans were America's Ur-democrats. In 1831, he insisted that "democracy is not an experiment in America; it has endured, in fact, two centuries" (*Letter to General Lafayette* [New York, 1931], p. 41).

that natural laws can only be guaranteed by civil constitutions that must, in turn, be respected. This view, not
unlike that of John Adams in *A Defence of the Constitutions*, is more characteristic of later than earlier
Cooper. However, one can find its origin in *Notions of
the Americans*. Cooper there assures his reader that the
grandeur of the American Revolution was precisely that
it was a dignified reform movement and not a rebellion.
Cadwallader tells Cooper's bachelor that "The Americans
had no revolution, strictly speaking; they have only preceded the rest of Christendom in their reforms, because
circumstances permitted it."[16] Later on, Cooper repeats
his point, insisting that "We have ever been reformers
rather than revolutionists. Our own struggle for independence was not in its aspect a revolution."[17]

When adopting either of these viewpoints, Cooper
thinks of the Revolution as a struggle of the colonies to
vindicate either their natural or their civil rights. In *The
Spy* and *Wyandotté*, however, the reader is not experi-
encing a great struggle for popular rights but a brutal
civil war. When Cooper was freed from the pressures of
making an historical statement, family loyalties and the
facts of local history came more readily to his mind.[18]
Cooper then imagines the colonists, not as future Americans, democrats or Tories, but as English citizens deeply
divided among themselves. In the *History of the Navy*,
Cooper acknowledged that "The war, in one sense, was a

[16] *Notions of the Americans*, II, 339.

[17] *Notions of the Americans*, I, 269.

[18] New York City remained heavily loyalist throughout the war.
New York State provided more troops for the king than for Con-
gress (Samuel Eliot Morison, *The Oxford History of the American
People* [New York, 1965], p. 237).

civil war,"[19] an admission he had previously made only in fiction. Once Cooper conceives the Revolution as a civil war, the standard by which he judges his characters shifts. Political principle becomes less important than gentlemanly fidelity to whichever principle one chooses.

Like Cooper's view of the revolutionary war, his view of individual civic virtue is a delicate combination of heritage and political conviction. In all of Cooper's writings, he accords unqualified praise to only three men: Washington, Lafayette, and John Jay.[20] He speaks of them in constant, sometimes embarrassing, and sometimes humorous superlatives.[21] In considering the importance these three men held for Cooper, image is more important than fact. Despite the many differences among

[19] *History of the Navy*, I, 90.

[20] See Cooper's five-page tribute to Washington in *Notions of the Americans*, II, 190–195, or his passages on Lafayette in *Sketches of Switzerland*, part II, vol. I, pp. 8–152, and *Gleanings in Europe: France* (New York, 1928), pp. 331–345. Dekker's *James Fenimore Cooper* concentrates almost exclusively on the importance of John Jay, yet in all of Cooper's writings, John Jay figures importantly only in *Notions of the Americans*. Washington and Lafayette, however, are introduced into such unlikely places as *The Chronicles of Cooperstown* or the second part of *Sketches of Switzerland*, and are repeatedly mentioned in the *Letters and Journals*.

[21] Cooper tells of hiring a French governess for his children: "We engaged a governess for the girls, not long after our arrival, and she proved to be a bigoted catholic, a furious royalist, and as ignorant as a calf. She had been but a few weeks in the house, when I detected her teaching her *élèves* to think Washington an unpardonable rebel, Lafayette a monster, Louis XVI a martyr, and all heretics in the high road to damnation. There remained no alternative but to give her a quarter's salary, and to get rid of her" (*Gleanings in Europe: France*, p. 128). The comedy of the passage is at Cooper's expense.

their lives and opinions, Cooper molds all three into a single composite ideal made up of many discrete values, both social and political.

In dwelling upon the social values of the three men, we are apt to forget that Cooper has selected these particular figures because they had turned his political ideals into an historical reality. Either as diplomats or military commanders, all three were heroes of the American revolutionary war. Cooper eulogizes Lafayette as a man who "dedicated youth, person, and fortune, to the principles of liberty."[22] Washington, "a leader worthy of a cause so righteous," acted throughout the war, Cooper says, upon certain "immutable principles of justice and truth":[23] a dignified distaste for oppression and a belief in the individual's unassailable right to liberty.

Because Cooper never idealized a Tom Paine or a John Paul Jones, we must recognize that, for Cooper, the truly model American must exemplify certain social values in addition to republican political views. The similarities between the tributes to Washington or Jay in *Notions of the Americans*, and the passages on Lafayette in the European travel books, reveal that all three men came to typify a social class and a way of life. All are pictured as principled gentlemen living as an acknowledged patrician class on a landed estate. Yet all three pride themselves on their simple, forthright republican ways. Lafayette is the marquis who, contemptuous of feudal distinctions, has deliberately altered the medieval character of La Grange.[24] Washington's republican simplicity is

[22] *Notions of the Americans*, II, 215.
[23] *Notions of the Americans*, II, 195, 190.
[24] *Gleanings in Europe: France*, pp. 331–345.

evident in the bareness of his tomb. Cooper's descriptions
of La Grange, Bedford, and Mount Vernon repeat phrases
and create nearly identical pictures. To concentrate on a
lesser known example, Cooper portrays La Grange both
as Bléneau-farm and an ancient family chateau. Rural,
productive, and comfortable, La Grange has the permanence of the self-contained estate. The house, neither
large nor ostentatious, is made of stone. "The habits of
the family are very regular and simple, but the intercourse
has the freedom and independence of a country-house."[25]
La Grange, Bedford, and Mount Vernon combine simple
tastes with gentlemanly farming, patrician associations
and an assurance of belonging. In the Wallingford and
Littlepage novels, Cooper was again and again to picture
landed estates that embody these social values.

Through Jay, Lafayette, and Washington, Cooper associates republican virtue with the patrician gentleman
who is a disinterested upholder of liberty. Cooper's ideal
revolutionary is a man, like John Jay, of "moderation,
dignity, and firmness,"[26] so principled that he can seem,
at times, stiffly dispassionate. Such men exemplify for
Cooper the great values of individual disinterest and
social privacy. Cooper's inveterate suspicion of parties,
organizations, and associations is reflected in his rev-
erencing the detachment of his principled gentlemen.
Nonetheless, their lonely independence of spirit, a quality
they share with Natty Bumppo, raises a vexing problem.
Lafayette, Jay, and Washington are all pictured as principled gentlemen in retirement, not in action. Although their

[25] *Gleanings in Europe: France*, p. 344.
[26] *Notions of the Americans*, I, 75.

retirement endows them with the virtue of disinterested integrity, it also associates them with a past age and deprives them of present power. It is, therefore, not accidental that Cooper chose Lafayette's triumphal tour of 1824 for the organizing narrative of *Notions of the Americans*. In order to complete his paean to America, Cooper had to provide dramatic proof that the American citizenry still recognized the leadership of men of the highest quality.

Washington and Jay were Federalists, Lafayette a Frenchman. It would seem that Cooper's education and upbringing led him to praise only those heroes of the American Revolution who became Federalists, and to maintain a discreet silence concerning the more radical of American revolutionaries. It is to Cooper's great credit that, as the years distanced him from the prejudices of his heritage, he became increasingly willing to admit Jefferson to his pantheon of revolutionary heroes. If it was not sympathetic exposure to Jeffersonian thought that led Cooper to forsake his Federalist training, Cooper's changing evaluation of Jefferson is at least the truest measure of his newer loyalties.[27]

As we have seen, Thomas Ellison, Cooper's pedagogue, was an Anglophile who "detested a democrat as he did the devil" and "cracked his jokes daily about Mr. Jefferson and Black Sal, never failing to place his libertinism in strong relief against the approved morals of George III."[28] This prejudice against Jefferson evidently remained in

[27] Only George Dekker has explored in any detail the importance of Jefferson to Cooper's thought (*James Fenimore Cooper*, pp. 110–112, 145–147).

[28] *Gleanings in Europe: England*, p. 197.

Cooper's mind in 1823, when Cooper visited West Point and saw Thomas Sully's portrait.

The fine letter in which Cooper describes his reaction to Sully's painting seems intentionally structured to be the record of a political conversion. Cooper begins by detailing youthful misconceptions:

You know my antipathies, as you please to call them, to Mr. Jefferson. I was brought up in that school where his image seldom appeared, unless it was clad in red breeches, and where it was always associated with the idea of infidelity and political heresy. Consequently I would have gone twice as far to see the picture of almost any other man. The moment I entered the library and cast my eyes on the picture, I desired the gentleman with me to wait.[29]

Under the excitement of Sully's artistry, Cooper recalls that he quickly left the room in order to bring a mysterious connoisseur named M—— (Charles Matthews) to judge the quality of the portrait. Assured by M—— that the painting is "one of the finest portraits he had ever beheld," Cooper affirms that Sully's work has "a dignity, a repose, I will go further and say a loveliness . . . that I never have seen in any other portrait."

After so consciously elaborate an opening, Cooper's letter ends with fittingly simple sentences that reveal how the image of Jefferson the Jacobin turned into the image of Jefferson the dignified libertarian:

In short, I saw nothing but Jefferson, standing before me, not in red breeches and slovenly attire, but a gentleman, appearing in all republican simplicity, with a grace and ease on the canvas, that to me seemed unrivalled. It has really shaken my opinion of Jefferson as a man, if not as a politician; and when

[29] *Letters and Journals*, I, 95.

his image occurs to me now, it is in the simple robes of Sully, sans red breeches, or even without any of the repulsive accompaniments of a political "sans culotte."

In a letter of 1835 to the sculptor Pierre Jean David, Cooper broadened even further the significance he found in Sully's painting. By claiming that, in the figure of Jefferson, Sully had portrayed the essential qualities of any American, Cooper tried to claim a hope as a fact: "On y voit le beau ideal de l'homme et, en même temps l'homme lui même. . . . L'attitude est non seulement celle de l'individu, c'est l'attitude d'un Americain."[30] Because of the importance Cooper attributes to Sully's portrait, it may not be an exaggeration to say that, for Cooper, the experience of seeing it was the catalyst that fused in his mind the figures of the American democrat, the agrarian gentleman and the patrician revolutionary, thereby creating the sole unit of transcendent social value Cooper was never to abandon.

While in Rome in 1830, Cooper purchased Randolph's four-volume edition of Jefferson's writings and read it with interest and care.[31] Cooper did not hide his enthusi-

[30] *Letters and Journals*, III, 175–176. In this passage, Cooper applies the phrase "beau ideal" to Jefferson, as he was later to apply it to Natty Bumppo. This odd linking of Leatherstocking with the libertarian gentry surfaces again in the commodore's familiar statement, "I set down Washington and Natty Bumppo as the two only really great men of my time" (*Home As Found*, p. 229).

It is equally characteristic of Cooper that he desires to see, in Jefferson, the prototype of the American. When Cooper had written to Horatio Greenough about a proposal for a statue of Washington, he had urged Greenough to consider that Washington was representative of the national character because of his simple natural dignity (*Letters and Journals*, I, 390).

[31] *Letters and Journals*, I, 412.

asm: "What do you think of Jefferson's letters? Have we not had a false idea of that man? I own he begins to appear to me, to be the greatest man, we ever had."[32]

In September of 1830 Cooper wrote a journal entry declaring his admiration for Jefferson as a man of "equanimity of temper" and "philosophical tone of mind."[33] By 1830 Cooper mentions only two lingering objections to Jefferson's ideas. Qualifying Jefferson's fears that Federalism had been a monarchical conspiracy, Cooper argues that Jefferson's attacks on noble title and political privilege, however right in purpose, were precipitant in manner:

One of the chief merits of all our political innovations is, that they have been gradual, and that they have rather followed, than preceded opinion, while he appears to have expected that men were to abandon all their ancient ideas, to satisfy a theory that many deemed a little doubtful.[34]

The second criticism is only an acknowledgment of Cooer's own political forebodings. Cooper declares that Jefferson's fear of executive powers was misplaced. The true danger to a constitutional republic, Cooper declares as early as 1830, is legislative usurpation, the possibility of unchecked congressional demagoguery.[35]

By the 1830s Cooper had found in Jefferson a democrat who believed in an agrarian society and a landed patrician who insisted upon a maximum of individual freedom. Most importantly, Jefferson substantiated Cooper's conviction that, in a republic, a social aristocracy

[32] *Letters and Journals*, I, 411.
[33] *Letters and Journals*, II, 31.
[34] *Letters and Journals*, II, 33.
[35] *Letters and Journals*, II, 32.

is entitled to no privileges beyond the natural rights guaranteed in the Constitution:

Jefferson was the man to whom we owe the high lesson that the *natural* privileges of a social aristocracy are in truth no more than their *natural* privileges. With us, all questions of political rights, except in the case of the poor slaves, are effectually settled, and yet every visible interest is as secure as it is anywhere else.[36]

Thus, Jefferson's distinction between a "natural aristocracy" of virtue and talent and an "artificial aristocracy" of wealth and birth became Cooper's distinction as well.[37] Although Cooper was later to argue that men of wealth and birth should be voted into political power, he never argued that they be voted into power solely because of wealth and birth. Until Cooper's very last years, he remained vehemently critical of special political privilege for any class. If Cooper has an aristocratic bias, it is a bias toward Jeffersonian natural aristocracy and not toward Adams's longings for distinctions of title. Cooper's fondness for the American Constitution is not to be equated with John Adams's fondness for the British. Whereas Cooper came to detest England, John Adams accepted England as a model of political and social virtue.

In the persons and residences of Lafayette, Jay, Washington and—finally—Jefferson, Cooper found a precarious union between a patrician way of life and strongly

[36] *Letters and Journals*, II, 180.

[37] Cooper could be referring to many passages in which Jefferson drew this distinction. Among the most memorable are Jefferson's letter to John Adams, October 28, 1813, and the sections of the *Autobiography* in which Jefferson discusses the bills he submitted to the Virginia Legislature in 1777 for abolishing entail and primogeniture.

republican political principles. Through these historical
figures of the American Revolution, Cooper continually
affirmed a single pattern of civic, political, and social
virtue. But his conception of the war itself remained
vacillating and unsure. Because he could see the war as
a libertarian revolution, a necessary reform, or a civil
war, Cooper's novels of the revolutionary era avoid the
patriotic hectoring and naive melodrama of such novels
as John Neal's *Seventy-Six*. The vogue of American historical novels that followed publication of *The Spy*
reveals that the readers of the new nation had a considerable appetite for tales of revolutionary glory. Cooper,
however, projected into the revolutionary romance contradictory feelings of pride and regret, of faith in the new
polity and distrust of its consequences.[38] The warfare of
1776 brought forth conflicting feelings within Cooper
and pointed up the precarious balance Cooper had struck
between his political and social ideals.

"THE SPY"

In all five of the prefaces to *The Spy*, Cooper insisted that
his theme was patriotism. The second preface, written
during the flush of the novel's success, states: "The Author believes that most of the good will, with which "The
Spy" has been received, is owing to 'love of country.' If
he has in any degree contributed to this feeling, his prin-

[38] Marius Bewley made the fresh and still largely unexplored
suggestion that Cooper's novels of the American Revolution "are
not only an outward record of the Revolutionary struggle; they
are also a dialectic between opposing sides, with the answer held
in suspension" (*The Eccentric Design*, p. 81).

cipal object is attained."[39] In the fourth preface of 1831, writing with Harvey Birch, the Skinners, and perhaps the Polish rebellion in mind, Cooper revealed the immense moral value he placed in patriotic enthusiasm:

Of all the generous sentiments, that of love of country is the most universal. We uniformly admire the man who sacrifices himself for the good of the community to which he belongs; and we unsparingly condemn him who, under whatever plea of sophism or necessity, raises his arm or directs his talent against the land to which he owes a natural allegiance.[40]

If, by patriotism, Cooper meant an honorable and disinterested adherence to one's political principles, whether loyalist or American, *The Spy* admirably suits his didactic purpose. If, however, Cooper intended his "patriotic" novel to justify the American Revolution, as his prefaces imply he did, *The Spy* can only be considered a fascinating contradiction.

Cooper's attempt to inculcate "love of country" raises perplexing questions. In an historical romance that might have pitted oppressive redcoats against simple, decent republicans, nearly every act of violence is committed by Skinners, who are native forces. Sir Henry Clinton commands British troops in the area, but they are hardly ever seen and never villainized. The Cow-boys, who by all canons of patriotism and revolutionary fervor, should be the villains, appear but once, not as marauders but as agents of retributive justice upon the Skinners. The Cow-

---

[39] *The Spy*, 2nd ed. (New York, 1822), p. xii.

[40] *The Spy* (Leipzig: Bernhard Tauchnitz, 1842), p. v. The fourth preface was written in Paris, April 4, 1831, and was first included in Bentley's English edition of *The Spy* published in the same year.

boys, Cooper notes, are led by a De Lancey (236). The word "Tory" is used only by the Skinners, not by the regular American army. Cooper's last preface discloses that Harvey Birch was modeled upon a spy who was employed to thwart the Cow-boys. In the action of his tale, however, Cooper never pictures Birch acting against any English irregulars. Rather than telling Mr. Harper secrets concerning English troop movements, Harvey Birch seeks out and aids a British officer, Captain Wharton, who is falsely accused of being a British spy.

The events of Cooper's novel clothe the American Revolution with little patriotic glory. Rather than uplifting his reader with clear-cut and stirring victories, Cooper has pictured the war as a series of aimless and inconclusive skirmishes, purposeless but deadly. The English, not the Americans, emerge the victors. Harvey Birch, Cooper's embodiment of patriotism, is appallingly mistreated by American forces, but not by the British. Sarah Wharton is driven mad, Dunwoodie is wounded and the Locusts is burned. Captain Lawton, the only heroic American commoner besides Harvey Birch, is killed at the end of the action. The events of the novel confirm Sarah Wharton's account of the effects of revolution:

You now have the fruits of rebellion brought home to you; a brother wounded and a prisoner, and perhaps a victim; your father distressed, his privacy interrupted, and not improbably his estates torn from him, on account of his loyalty to the King. (172–173)

Even Peyton Dunwoodie, American officer and convinced libertarian, has grave doubts: "his reflections on the victory brought with them no satisfaction that compensated for the sacrifices by which it had been purchased" (125).

At the end of the novel, the living inhabitants of the Locusts wearily remove to an unravaged estate in Virginia, at the same time that Birch retreats westward. Nowhere in the novel does Cooper explicitly glorify the Revolution.

The chief problem posed by regarding *The Spy* as a patriotic eulogy is embedded deep within the book's structure. Harvey Birch devotes nearly all of his energies to the freeing of a British infantry captain from seizure and captivity by the Americans. George Washington travels miles into the mountains in order to liberate the same British captain from Washington's own troops. The great leaders of the cause of American liberty, the one highborn and the other low, are thus portrayed serving British interests. In a novel that supposedly teaches love of country, Cooper defines heroism through two characters who value abstract principles of justice over patriotic ardor. While the reader's admiration for Washington and Birch increases, his opinion of the sacredness of the American Revolution suffers in proportion.

Cooper is not concerned with praising Americans or vilifying Tories. Wharton the English officer and Dunwoodie the American are equally admirable. Cooper's scorn falls not on the honestly erring Tory but on the hypocrites and temporizers who follow no principle save self-interest. When Mr. Wharton attempts to remain neutral by moving to the neutral ground, he is motivated more by a desire to maintain the propertied, gentlemanly life than he is by an honest division of personal scruples. Caught between his Tory daughter and his American daughter, between tepid American principles and Tory friendships, Wharton is psychically immobilized. Cooper punishes Wharton unmercifully, not because Wharton is neutral, but because Wharton, although little concerned with political principle, is very concerned to use neutrality in order to maintain comfort. Cooper never asks his English citizens to take the American side in the civil war; he asks only a hard decision based on political and moral principles.

Into all the novels dealing with the Revolution, Cooper inserts short, set debates between loyalists and rebels on the worthiness of the revolutionary cause. Cooper does not resolve these debates; he weights them in favor of the Americans, but allows Tory spokesmen to voice strong arguments. The pompous and cowardly Wellmere, who Cooper vehemently insisted was not a portrait of all Englishmen,[41] utters sharp retorts concerning the hypocrisy of those who fight for liberty and slavery simultaneously. Wellmere even foresees another form of slavery that may haunt the republic:

Slavery, sir; yes, even slavery; you are putting the tyranny of a mob on the throne of a kind and lenient prince; where is the consistency of your boasted liberty? (191)

Cooper refutes Wellmere, not by logical argument, but by turning him into a bigamist. In this early novel, Cooper is already raising the insoluble issue of his later work. Here, however, Cooper assigns an opinion that was later to be his to the novel's English villain.

Cooper's setting serves as another means of tempering any naive revolutionary enthusiasm. The neutral ground between the British and American lines is described in

[41] The revised "To James Aitchison," dedicatory foreword to *The Spy*, 4th ed. (New York, 1824), unnumbered.

such a way as to make heroic deeds difficult to achieve and impossible to memorialize. The neutral ground has no border and no definition. Its roads are often impassable and its contours seem actively to resist being known. The Episcopal minister, spokesman for the moral law, skulks along the road in woman's garments. The neutral ground is conquered alternately by both armies, but controlled by neither. Any acts of heroism that transpire within it thus become historically meaningless, however crucial to the individual characters. Because the neutral ground forces those who brave it to assume a mask, and then to shift the mask at a moment's notice, neither individuals nor troops can be clearly identified.[42] In a world where all is fluid and changing, where Harvey Birch says "all places are now alike, and all faces equally strange" (202), it is impossible to argue the simple rectitude of the American cause.

In the first chapter Cooper defines the political nature of the neutral ground: "In short, the law was momentarily extinct in that particular district, and justice was administered subject to the bias of personal interests, and the passions of the strongest" (13). The total absence of civil law in the neutral ground thus provides Cooper a standard for judging the comparative merits of loyalists and Americans. The moral laws that govern Tory or Rebel conduct in the neutral setting reflect upon the merit of larger political causes.

[42] Donald Ringe shows how effectively Cooper defines the neutral ground in the opening scene. Cooper's three leading characters, all masked behind false identities, meet during a thunderstorm, but remain dangerously unknown to one another (*James Fenimore Cooper* [New York, 1962], p. 30).

Cooper compares three separate means of establishing moral justice in the neutral ground. Some characters are governed by the restraint of individual morality. To deal with the unrestrained, the opposing armies have created military tribunals. If these fail, there is always a recourse to pure force. *The Spy* convincingly demonstrates that individual restraint is rare, military tribunal a travesty, and that sheer force is just only on occasion. The action of the novel moves continually toward greater brutalities. When the leader of the Skinners crows that "The law of the neutral ground is the law of the strongest" (204), the reader is forced to accept this appeal to sheer force as a condition of existence. Because so many act upon the Skinner's creed, it becomes a truth.

Cooper contrasts two kinds of war that arise in such a setting. The official war, between the Regulars and the Continentals, Howe's army and Washington's, is fought by the military in accord with so many scruples of honor that it hardly seems to exist. The actual war, between the Cow-boys and Skinners, or more accurately, between the Skinners and all of society, is ruthless beyond any expectation. Cooper implies, without seeming to recognize it, that the true significance of the Revolution is not the historical battles between British and Americans, but an interclass conflict in America.

In contrasting the two wars, Cooper draws an obvious connection between social class and individual morality, between the elegant Whartons and Dunwoodies, who combat politely for abstract principles, and the lowborn Skinners, who butcher for plunder. Cooper is too honest, however, wholly to believe that virtue is dependent upon birth or military rank. Mr. Wharton and Wellmere are obviously upper class. More importantly, the conditions of the neutral ground have driven the American army to use the Skinners: "The convenience, and perhaps the necessities, of the leaders of the American arms, in the neighborhood of New York, had induced them to employ certain subordinate agents, of extremely irregular habits, in executing their lesser plans of annoying the enemy" (24). More repellent than any of the killings is the fact that the American army "was to be seen giving the sanction of something like legality to acts of the most unlicensed robbery, and, not unfrequently, of bloodshed" (24). *The Spy* is a novel in which Cooper can, on the one hand, praise Washington as "the acknowledged hero of an age of reason and truth" (456), and then admit that Washington's fellow officers could only win independence by underhandedly employing the Skinners.

The Skinners are Cooper's first embodiment of lawless, rootless forces threatening America from underneath. Because they operate with the approval of the controlling military, the Skinners are more openly violent than Bragg or Newcome can afford to be. Nonetheless Cooper attributes to the Skinners the tactics which make their descendants so insidious. Lawton calls the Skinners "Fellows whose mouths are filled with liberty and equality, and whose hearts are overflowing with cupidity and gall" (329). He even suspects that the Skinners may prove the force of the future. When the leader of the Skinners tells him, "we shall have a free government, and we, who fight for it, will get our reward" (238), Lawton ruefully agrees. Like Cooper, Lawton recognizes that the people may become prey to demagogues: "The time must arrive when America will learn to distinguish between a patriot and a robber" (316).

When individual moral restraint fails in Westchester, vigilante justice or military tribunal are the only barriers against anarchy. Cooper compares the merits of the two forms of justice by relating them to his controlling image of the gallows and to the crucial problem of defining the spy. The plot of the novel is built upon analogous action. Both Harvey Birch and Henry Wharton are wrongly accused of being English spies. Both are unjustly condemned to execution by the American army, both escape, and both are haunted by the gallows, symbol of sham military justice. Although Harvey Birch fled because he knew that justice was unobtainable, Wharton, principled gentleman that he was, rigidly stood trial.

Cooper intended his novel to argue the superiority of civil law to military tribunal. In the opening chapter, he flatly declared that "oppression and injustice were the natural consequences of the possession of a military power that was uncurbed by the restraints of civil authority" (24).[43] Cooper fashioned the military trial of Henry Wharton to illustrate this thesis. The Skinners, who should be brought to formal justice, rove free. Henry Wharton, who visited his father, is sentenced to execution as a spy.

In Cooper's trial scenes, he is always interested in ex-

[43] Like Melville, Cooper frequently criticized the justice of military courts. He underscored the falsities of military tribunals in *The Wing-and-Wing*, condemned the expediencies of the naval court in the Somers Mutiny case, and grimly forewarned of bayonet justice in *New York*.

posing the contradictions by which injustice works. The judges profess that "although we are a court of martial law, yet, in this respect we own the principles of all free governments" (344). However, when Wharton cogently points out that, in the neutral ground, the boundary lines by which spying can legally be determined do not exist, his judges are forced to drop their rationalizations about picket lines and admit the true source of their power:

Its name, as a neutral ground, is unauthorized by law; it is an appellation that originates with the condition of the country. But wherever an army goes, it carries its rights along, and the first is, the ability to protect itself. (345)

By this appeal to raw power and self-interest, the court reveals that its military justice is not different in kind from the Skinners' "law of the strongest," however different it may be in practice. The court's claim to follow "the principles of all free governments" is shown to be expedient pretense.

Cooper repeatedly emphasizes that Wharton is being executed, not because he truly was a spy, but because of pressures for severity stemming from the recent André affair.[44] An additional irony is that the American military judges suspect the guiltless English captain simply because he has consorted with Harvey Birch, the greatest of American patriots. Cooper calls the judgment passed

[44] See pp. 101, 341, 348. In *Notions of the Americans*, Cooper dwelt on the André affair at length (I, 217–222). Cooper criticized André, not for his Tory principles, but his weakness. To Cooper André's willingness to serve as a spy was a violation of the codes of a gentleman and an officer, whereas the lowness of Birch's origin and his lack of military rank absolve his spying from any taint of dishonor.

upon Captain Wharton an example of "those construc-
tions and interpretations of law that inflicted punishment
without the actual existence of crime" (356). Frances
Wharton, an avid republican and American sympathizer,
shows how the miscarriage of American justice reflects
on the merits of the American position: "Is this the cause
I have so ardently loved? Are these the men that I have
been taught to reverence?" (352).

The court's injustice creates the prototype of a situation to which Cooper will often return in later fiction.
The forces of disorder, whether they be social, legal, or
military, disrupt a static, social framework and produce
grave injustices threatening social disintegration. These
forces can only be curbed by the actions of a landed
gentleman who remains at the head of society, yet detached from it. The gentleman becomes the only dispen-
ser of justice and upholder of liberty. In this instance,
Washington, who possesses the necessary powers, intervenes to save Henry Wharton and restore a measure of
justice. By allowing Birch to act as Washington's agent,
Cooper keeps Washington above the action[45] and builds
an effective contrast between Birch's ability to save himself and Wharton's comparative helplessness.

In such a place as the neutral ground, the gibbet should
figure as the sole agent of justice, yet Birch lives in mental terror of it. As Frances and Henry Wharton brush
by the gibbet in flight, they recoil as from a living crea-
ture. In one magnificent scene, however, Cooper reverses

[45] George Lukács demonstrated that Scott heightened his reader's interest by permitting the historical hero to appear only at
climactic moments (*The Historical Novel* [New York, 1965], p. 38).
Cooper presumably followed Scott's example.

all of its connotations. The gallows, symbol of a false military justice, suddenly becomes the symbol of a truer form of justice, extralegal vengeance. Harvey Birch watches the Cow-boys calmly build a gallows and hang the Skinner chieftain—the American who had robbed Harvey, burned his house, and ransomed him to the military. Prior to this hanging, the only other act of true justice in the novel had been the extralegal whipping of the Skinners by Lawton's men, a whipping administered, says Lawton, by "the law of Moses—forty, save one" (240). Thus, although the very existence of the Skinners pleads the need for the firm rule of statute law, retaliatory justice carried out by the individual is preferable to statutes misused by military tribunals.[46]

Despite the evident satisfaction of author and reader with the punishments meted out to the Skinners, Cooper does not condone retaliatory justice as a principle. As the Cow-boys coolly ride away from the gallows, Cooper shows us that, for Harvey Birch, vengeance is as horrid as it is pleasurable:

Birch continued gazing on this scene with a kind of infatuation. At its close he placed his hands to his ears, and rushed toward the highway. Still the cries for mercy rang through his brain, and it was many weeks before his memory ceased to dwell on the horrible event. (437)

Sadistic retribution, even when justly applied, is not a moral law to which either Harvey Birch or his creator could subscribe. When next we see Harvey, he refuses all reward but a tribute from "the noble, upright, impartial

[46] James Grossman, *James Fenimore Cooper* (Stanford, 1967), p. 28.

Washington" (351) and departs westward to newer settlements.

The resolution of this scene provides the surest index to Birch's character. Recognizing that neither military tribunal nor vindictive force provides political justice, Birch flees from Westchester. He is thus forced to be "a pilgrim through life" (147) in search of truer principles of justice than he has found in the American neutral ground. Suspected to be the devil, hunted by Americans and Skinners, Birch raises a question he knows is rhetorical, "who is there to do me justice?" (203). What he most desires, "I would wish all good men to judge me with lenity" (247), is the very thing he can never have. Significantly, it is Birch who, at a climactic moment in the novel, delivers Cooper's sharpest criticism of the laws that operate in the neutral ground. Telling Henry Wharton that only he, Birch, can save Wharton from the American gibbet, he says:

Yes, such are their laws; the man who fights, and kills, and plunders, is honoured; but he who serves his country as a spy, no matter how faithfully, no matter how honestly, lives to be reviled, or dies like the vilest criminal! (376)

In Harvey's world one may rely only on oneself, Washington and one's Bible. Harvey Birch is the one man who is integral with the surrounding environment. Yet, simultaneously, he is the only man for whom everyone in the neutral ground is a danger, and who therefore can truly belong only in his mountain hideaway.

Harvey Birch and his disillusioned withdrawal provided Cooper with a paradigm for one of his two definitions of heroism. Harvey Birch is the fictional father of Long Tom Coffin, Natty Bumppo, the Rover, Jacopo the bravo and, in lesser degrees, Raoul Yvard and Moses Marble. These heroes are all, at bottom, simple democratic men, eminently capable in and at one with their environment. All, however, are lonely isolates, stoics who defect from a civilization they cannot endure. Convinced that political justice cannot be instituted by men, they prefer the moral laws that are visible in nature. In many cases, the heroes share the highest principles which their society professes but does not practice. Retreating to maintain their own values, or simply to be alone, such men become stoics laced with self-pity, activists with a wide streak of fatalism.

Given the many reservations in Cooper's praise of American revolutionary conduct, it is not surprising that Cooper conceived *The Spy* as a glorification of love of country, but dedicated his book to an "educated, liberal, and intelligent"[47] Englishman, James Aitchison. Two dedicatory letters to Aitchison, dropped from later editions, were doubtless designed to prepare a potential market by conciliating any English readers. They do an admirable job, referring to "the many valuable qualities which form the ground-work of an Englishman's virtues," protesting against all objections that *The Spy* is prejudicial against the English character, and apologizing for "any weakness in the exhibition of national partiality."[48]

Despite all the inglorious aspects of the Revolution,

[47] The revised "To James Aitchison," dedicatory foreword to *The Spy*, 4th ed. (New York, 1824), unnumbered.

[48] The first quotation is from the revised "To James Aitchison." The second is from the original "To James Aitchison," dedicatory foreword to *The Spy*, 2nd ed. with first and second prefaces (New York, 1822), unnumbered.

however, *The Spy* fully celebrates "love of country" in one very special sense. In his fourth preface to the novel, Cooper distinguishes between real and false patriotism:

There is a purity in real patriotism which elevates its subject above all the grosser motives of selfishness, and which, in the nature of things, can never distinguish services to mere kindred and family. It has the beauty of self-elevation, without the alloy of personal interest.[49]

Harvey Birch perfectly exemplifies a definition of patriotism, not as praise of country, but as a love of country so disinterested that no amount of mistreatment or disillusion can quell it.

Because Harvey must illustrate "real patriotism," Cooper cannot allow Washington to acknowledge Birch's services at the war's end.[50] To reward Birch with money or recognition would be to sully the purity of his devotion to liberty. Reward can only be a tribute from Washington, a climactic speech in which Cooper specifies the origin of the true revolutionary hero: "That Providence destines this country to some great and glorious fate I must believe, while I witness the patriotism that pervades the bosoms of her lowest citizens" (454).[51] Such patriotic statements dull our memory of the events of the novel. Because the speech is Harvey's reward, it carries

[49] Fourth preface to *The Spy* (Leipzig, 1842), p. v.

[50] Although Cooper wrote his last chapter before the tale itself was complete, he never implied that the resolution was unsatisfactory for any other reason than its haste (Cooper's "Introduction" to *The Spy*, Darley Edition, p. xi).

[51] Kay Seymour House remarks that Washington speaks to Birch "with a mouthful of eagle feathers" (*Cooper's Americans*, p. 214).

the stamp of truth. Whenever Cooper's plot, handling
of setting, or exploration of justice lead the reader to
doubt Cooper's faith in American achievement, Harvey's
faith always remains, a reproach to any reader who
might suspect that Cooper's values are in conflict.

Cooper has also upheld patriotism by simple association of character. The convincing and lovable among the
subsidiary characters—Lawton, Sitgreaves, and Betty
Flanagan—are all dedicated democrats accompanying
the American army. And, then there is *The Spy's* concluding scene, for which Cooper has characteristically
reserved his most improbable stagings of patriotic
melodrama. Cooper pulls out all stops in order to convince us that the sickening brutalities of 1780 had a
glorious issue. American victories in the War of 1812
and the sublimity of Niagara Falls are both invoked in
order to justify the principles for which Birch and Lawton fought. In a last effort to emphasize that national
glory has followed reconciliation, Cooper introduces a
symbolic figure of pure fantasy, Wharton Dunwoodie,
whose name is a composite of the Tory and the American, and whose "hair shown in the setting sun like ring-
lets of gold" (457). When Harvey Birch sees Wharton
Dunwoodie, he draws the inevitable association: "'tis like
our native land . . . improving with time;—God has
blessed both" (458).

The figure of Wharton Dunwoodie, the belated recognition of Birch's services, and Birch's death on the field
of victory have served to excuse, but not condone, the
events of 1780. Thus the reader is led to forget that,
earlier in the tale, Cooper had invoked an unrealized
American ideal:

Who would be ruled when he can rule? The only rational ground to take, is that every community has a right to govern itself, so that in no manner it violates the laws of God. (192)

Cooper may have described these words as "good sense" (192), but assigned them to his comic surgeon Sitgreaves, because he realized how inappropriate they seemed in context. The neutral ground of Westchester was not a community, nor did the men within it seem to regard the laws of God. To what extent the neutral ground represented his nation, Cooper was unwilling to speculate. Nonetheless, within *The Spy* itself, the neutral ground comprised the entire revolutionary world, and the possibilities for rational self-government, if such figures as Harper or Birch were absent, seemed small indeed.

JOHN PAUL JONES

By showing that Cooper's three early sea tales describe the gradual emergence of revolutionary feeling in three separate generations of Americans, Thomas Philbrick clearly demonstrates Cooper's urge to celebrate maritime nationalism.[52] Given this urge, one would expect that Cooper's praise of American achievements on the sea frontier would extend to a glorification of the American Revolution. Everywhere there is evidence of this intent. *The Water-Witch* roundly condemns English colonial governments for not "referring all to the rule of right" and not laying "their foundations in natural justice" (122). The fall of Yorktown and the emergence of the American

[52] *James Fenimore Cooper and the Development of American Sea Fiction*, pp. 42–83.

navy are hymned at the end of *The Red Rover*. John Paul Jones's naval exploits are invoked in the original preface to *The Pilot*. Tom Tiller, the Rover and John Paul Jones, the heroes of the three tales, are all conceived as prerevolution revolutionaries, mysteriously wronged by the English government. Each is described as a physically heroic Ur-American, an unknowing devotee of man's natural right to liberty.

These are the ingredients of thoroughly chauvinistic novels. In final form, however, none of these novels leaves an unqualified sense of the glory of establishing American independence. The chief problem lies in the conception of the hero. The closer Cooper looks at the prerevolution revolutionary, the more he fears that these American heroes are not wronged libertarians but excessive individualists. Within all three men Cooper uncovers streaks of selfishness and violence. In *The Water-Witch*, the American hero is cast as a smuggler, and in *The Red Rover* as a pirate. The Byronic conventions Cooper is following clothe the renegade with sinister glamor. Try though Cooper may to explain away these renegade qualities in his heroic Americans, the taint of violent outlawry remains. Disinterested patriotism cannot easily be attributed to characters that resemble Manfred or Conrad of *The Corsair*.

If the three tales are considered in historical sequence, the American heroes become progressively more suspect. Tom Tiller is revealed to be an honorable smuggler, who only seeks to restore a daughter to her father. Because Cooper apotheosizes Tiller into a sea god, Tiller's former identity is nearly forgotten. The Rover does not emerge so unsullied. He may be a victim of British injustice, but he has murdered a man who insulted the colonies. The Rover's ship, unlike Tiller's graceful brigantine, bristles with armament. He tyrannizes over his crew. Although Cooper eventually reveals that the Rover, far from being a pirate, is a man so honorable as to disband his crew rather than do injustice to an English naval lieutenant, the sinister qualities of the Rover are not easily erased. The strongest impression we have of his character remains his entrance into Newport. Masked as a lawyer, dressed in green, red of skin and snapping his whip, the Rover is, in truth, the very devil of a disciplinarian.

The dangerous and lonely individuality of Tom Tiller or the Rover could largely be excused by the fact that they lived before their time. John Paul Jones, however, lives during the proper historical moment. Whatever undesirable traits he might have must be laid to his account. In *The Pilot*, Jones complains of youthful mistreatment under the British and the closed purse of Congress. Cooper, however, shows no evidence to confirm either charge; Jones is allowed to stand or fall on his own merits.

Criticism has yet to account for Cooper's fascination with John Paul Jones.[53] Three times during his career he wrote extensively of him—in *The Pilot*, the *History of the Navy*, and *Lives of Distinguished American Naval Officers*. The last of these is even unbalanced by Cooper's

[53] Yvor Winters and George Dekker have analyzed *The Water Witch* and Thomas Philbrick has thoroughly studied *The Red Rover*, but little attention has yet been paid to *The Pilot*. Donald Ringe explores the themes of self-discipline and obedience in the novel (*James Fenimore Cooper*, pp. 37–41). The only discussion of the heroism of John Paul Jones is the brief, uniformly negative judgment by Kay Seymour House (*Cooper's Americans*, pp. 190–191).

interest in Jones; over one hundred pages in a five-hundred-page volume treating nine naval officers are devoted to him alone. In the two later accounts, Cooper's task, to write accounts of American naval heroism, results in rather labored and idealized portraits of Jones. The comparative license of an historical romance, however, freed Cooper to express more complex feelings. *The Pilot* is Cooper's only extended study of an historical figure of the revolutionary war. Whether Cooper's portrait of Jones is an act of deliberate debunking or uneasy praise is difficult to assess.

At the outset, we must recognize that a determination to better the sea scenes of *The Pirate* was not the sole purpose for which *The Pilot* was written. The original preface declares an intent to revivify the fading memory of John Paul Jones and thereby to immortalize the deeds of the heroes of the Revolution. Cooper complains that "Every one has heard of the victory of the *Bon-Homme Richard*, but how little is known of the rest of [Jones's] life, and of the important services of the remarkable man who commanded, in our behalf, in that memorable combat."[54] Regretting that the heroes of the great era are dying, Cooper concludes: "If his book has the least tendency to excite some attention to this interesting portion of our history, one of the objects of the writer will be accomplished."[55] The original preface, in short, prepares the reader for an historical romance recording the "important services" of a great and representative hero of the American Revolution; competition with Scott is not mentioned.

[54] First preface to *The Pilot*, first ed. (New York, 1823), p. vii.
[55] First preface to *The Pilot*, p. viii.

In ways especially important to a naval historian, the pilot fulfills his preannounced role. Oblique references to Jones's great naval triumphs are scattered through the novel. Cooper never fails to mention, in each of his three accounts of Jones, that it was he who first raised the pine tree and rattlesnake flag on board the *Alfred*. Within the narrative, Jones functions as Cooper's ideal seaman. Only he possesses the absolute skills necessary for the piloting of the frigate through storm and over shoal. Jones' abilities, self-possession, and courage earn him unquestioned mastery over everything and everyone he encounters.

Moreover, Jones possesses many of the traits of the Cooper hero. A man of humble birth and total competence, his defenses of American principles and his outcries on behalf of liberty often ring true. He characterizes himself as "a man with a soul not to be limited by the arbitrary boundaries of tyrants and hirelings, but one who has the right as well as the inclination to grapple with oppression, in whose name soever it is exercised" (169). Jones may boast that "I have lived to bear the banners of the new republic proudly in sight of the three kingdoms, when practised skill and equal arms have in vain struggled to pluck it down" (167), but his rhetoric conforms to fact. Alone, embittered, and self-sufficient, like so many of Cooper's heroes, Jones's final disappearance in a solitary sailboat leaves a void of power and ability in the American navy.

At other times, Jones is described as a hypocrite or, even worse, a careerist of revolutions. His seeming devotion to libertarian principles may only mask his hunger for glory. Cooper repeatedly exposes the falsity of Jones's

pride in honors bestowed upon him by French royalty
for services in a republican cause. On the last page of the
novel Cooper questions a love of liberty that ends, as
Jones's did, "in the service of a despot!" (486). Cooper
later described these last years of service to Catherine
the Great as "a revolting account of intrigues, bad management, and disappointment."[56]

Many of Jones's most ringing declarations are unconscious revelations of the contradiction of his motives: "I
left the country, because I found nothing in it but oppression and injustice, and I could not invite you to become
the bride of a wanderer, without either name or fortune"
(165). Speaking to Griffith of "the great purposes of our
struggle," Jones characteristically reduces revolution to
self-interest:

There is glory in it, young man; if it be purchased with danger, it shall be rewarded by fame! It is true, I wear your republican livery, and call the Americans my brothers; but it is
because you combat in behalf of human nature. Were your
cause less holy, I would not shed the meanest drop that flows
in English veins to serve it; but now, it hallows every exploit
that is undertaken in its favour, and the names of all who contend for it shall belong to posterity. (241–242)

As such instances of self-contradiction accumulate, Jones
appears more and more to be a man who cloaks his ambition under an antimonarchical tirade. His image of
himself as "a Quixote in the behalf of liberal principles"
(413) is too self-consciously paraded to be entirely convincing. What troubles Cooper is that his own conception of virture is so like Jones's posture.

[56] *Lives of Distinguished American Naval Officers* (Philadelphia,
1846), II, 104.

If Harvey Birch's patriotism is proven by his anonymity and silence, Jones's patriotism is discredited by
rhetoric and desire for notoriety. Having no trust in
God or man, Jones alternates between bitter resignation
and scornful outburst. The judgments passed upon him
by characters unconcerned with his seamanship are uniformly critical. Alice Dunscombe believes him "a man,
who has been goaded by fancied wrongs to forget his
country and home, and who is suddenly clothed with
power to show his resentments" (172). Griffith finally
concludes that Jones's devotion to America "proceeded
from desire of distinction, his ruling passion" (486). The
saddest moment of the book is the pilot's fleeting admission, "I am not, Alice, the man I would be, or even the
man I had deemed myself" (412).

Although Cooper exalts Jones's historical achievements, he simultaneously creates a plot that seems designed only to reveal Jones's failures. The motivation of
the pilot's action is both petty and absurd; the reader is
amazed that so great a hero as Jones has little better to
do than kidnap the maiden lovers of American naval
officers. As soon as Jones forms his scheme for taking
English hostages to Congress, Griffith asks "would it
effect the great purposes of our struggle? or is it an exploit, when achieved, worth the hazard you incur?"
(241). Even Jones himself, asked directly about the failure
of the expedition, admits " 'tis lost . . . 'tis sacrificed to
more private feelings" (394). As in *The Spy*, the narrative of *The Pilot* is historically inconsequential.

The total characterization of Jones is thus contradictory and perhaps intentionally enigmatic. Cooper himself
offers no summary judgment beyond occasional refer-

ences to "restless ambition and the pride of success" (413) or to "visionary expectations of a wild ambition" (421). In the main, however, Jones emerges not as an admirable hero but as a study of misguided individuality. Cooper does not determine for his reader whether Jones is a man for whom liberty is a rationale for selfishness, or whether an extreme but sincere devotion to liberty has warped his character. The distinction, however, is important. If the former, Jones is a hypocrite mouthing democratic principles; if the latter, the principles themselves come under question. In either case, however, Jones's self-concern reduces him to the role of the pilot, a knowledgeable guide through moments of danger, who lacks the disinterestedness necessary for abiding loyalties.

The Byronic framework that surrounds Jones thus has contradictory effects. During nautical and visual scenes, the Byronic conventions raise Jones to a lonely and heroic grandeur. When, however, his words are closely examined, the facade collapses. Given the contrast between Cooper's declared intent and his actual characterization, the portrait of Jones must represent either deliberate debunking or Cooper's indecision. Because the first seems so inconsistent with Cooper's temperament during the 1820s, it is more likely that Cooper is unwittingly expressing his own divided feelings concerning the integrity of the revolutionary hero.

The contradictions in Cooper's assessment of Jones continue long after completion of *The Pilot*. The two historical accounts largely absolve Jones from the charge of political hypocrisy. Cooper later stated, "There is reason to think Jones had a real attachment to the colonies, as well as to the principles for which they contended; and it is certain that, having fairly cast his fortunes in them, he had just as good a moral right to maintain both as any native of the country."[57] Privately, however, Cooper became increasingly suspicious of any suggestion of cant, and these suspicions resulted in a surprising criticism of his own novel:

> With the character of Paul Jones, as given in "The Pilot," Mr. Cooper, at a later day, was himself dissatisfied. It was not sufficiently true to reality. The pilot of the frigate was represented as a man of higher views and aims, in a moral sense, than the facts of the life of Paul Jones would justify. The commander of the Ranger was in truth a bold and daring adventurer, a skilled seaman, a brave partisan, an ambitious man—but he was scarcely the enthusiast in private feeling, in political views, described in the pilot of the frigate.[58]

It is impossible to square Cooper's retrospective view of the pilot as an "enthusiast . . . in political views" with the book itself. Nonetheless, Cooper's change of feeling explains his deletion from the final preface of earlier statements of patriotic intent. Even in his summary statement in the *History of the Navy*, Cooper was reduced to describing Jones with such a contradiction as "in motives, much disposed to disinterestedness, though ambitious of renown and covetous of distinction."[59]

Cooper implied, but nowhere declared, that John Paul Jones exemplified qualities of the American revolutionary mind. Herman Melville had little doubt of it: "intrepid, unprincipled, reckless, predatory, with boundless ambition, civilized in externals but a savage at heart, America

[57] *Lives of Distinguished American Naval Officers*, II, 15.
[58] *The Cooper Gallery*, p. 77.
[59] *History of the Navy*, I, 118.

is, or may yet be, the Paul Jones of nations."[60] Whether Melville, who had reviewed *The Red Rover* and *The Sea Lions*, was developing a suggestion from Cooper, cannot be proven or disproven. It is interesting that one of the "Extracts" supplied by the "Sub-Sub-Librarian" of *Moby Dick* is a quotation from *The Pilot*. Cooper's view of John Paul Jones, though it subsumes Melville's, is far more equivocal and less savage. In later years, however, Cooper's view of Jones, like his view of America, was to resemble Melville's warning.

"LIONEL LINCOLN"

The problem of patriotism is most evident in *Lionel Lincoln*. No reader to my knowledge has ever been satisfied with the book, and all have been dissatisfied for similar reasons. Cooper does not clearly link his gothic tale of the sins of the Lincolns with his historical account of revolutionary Boston. Ralph and Job Pray, the heroic revolutionary patriots, are characterized, respectively, as a maniac and an idiot, thus associating revolutionary ardor with insanity. The technical hero, Lionel Lincoln, remains a colorless, totally unindividualized officer who gains neither new awareness nor new loyalties from his experiences. Cooper's inconsistent ending thus robs the tale of whatever potential meaning it might have had.[61]

These criticisms are incontestable and need be bela-

[60] *Israel Potter* (New York, 1957), p. 170.
[61] Grossman, *James Fenimore Cooper*, pp. 40–43; Ringe, *James Fenimore Cooper*, pp. 41–42; Dekker, *James Fenimore Cooper*, pp. 37–42.

bored no further. We need now to seek the reasons underlying Cooper's failure. The excuse of hasty writing is not sufficient for a novel whose historical sections were so meticulously researched. To say that Cooper did not know what issues he had constructed is contradicted by the book itself, which raises its issues very clearly. There remains the possibility that the failures of Lionel Lincoln the character and *Lionel Lincoln* the novel, like the portrait of John Paul Jones, reflect conflicting feelings within Cooper himself.

In a preface of 1832 Cooper admitted that *"Lionel Lincoln* is not what its author hoped it would have been."[62] Discussing in opaque generalities "the difficulties he encountered in writing this his only historical tale," Cooper attributes his failure to a particularly American demand for consistency of characterization. What author and reader were unwilling fully to recognize, Cooper reasons, was the fact that "the most opposite qualities are frequently the inhabitants of the same breast." It is odd that the statement, though it has obvious significance for the protagonist of the novel, seems in context to refer primarily to Cooper himself.

Applying the suggestion of inner inconsistency to the tale yields a possible interpretation of Cooper's failures. In marked contrast to *The Spy* and *The Pilot*, the historical portions of *Lionel Lincoln* provide an unqualified justification of the revolutionary war. In selecting a fictional narrative to suit the purpose of glorifying the Revolution, Cooper decided to write a tale describing the

[62] Third preface to *Lionel Lincoln* (London, 1832), quoted entire in Arvid Schulenberger, *Cooper's Theory of Fiction* (Lawrence, Kansas, 1955), p. 26.

political conversion of a noble British officer of divided sympathies. For Cooper to write so aggressively patriotic a tale, however, meant that he must dismiss the complicating notion of civil war and exclude all his doubts about the purity of American conduct. As Cooper progressed through his novel, his unwillingness to oversimplify his own views grew ever stronger. Because he did not intend to rewrite the fine but wholly patriotic accounts of Concord and Breed's Hill, and because he would not oversimplify his own feelings, Cooper decided—consciously or unconsciously—to scotch his ending. Lionel Lincoln would not be converted to American loyalties.

This phantasy demands substantiation. Cooper's desire to glorify the Revolution is most obvious in his selection of historical setting. Superficially, Boston of 1775 is portrayed as a neutral ground like Westchester. A dangerous, uneasy stalemate exists between the British garrison in Boston and the American forces in the surrounding countryside. Concord, Charlestown, and Dorchester constitute the neutral ground where battles are fought. In *Lionel Lincoln*, however, the stalemate is resolved as it had not been in *The Spy*. History furnished Cooper with clear justification for his patriotism in the historical sequence from the American flight on Lexington Green to Howe's ignominious retreat from Boston. Cooper turned the progression to full patriotic advantage.

In *The Spy* and *The Pilot* Cooper had drawn no clear distinctions of merit between the British and American forces operating in the neutral ground. *Lionel Lincoln* reveals a persistent desire to eulogize the Americans by downgrading both British character and British power.

The British troops are repeatedly characterized as arrogant, often brutal invaders, fending off their inevitable downfall by wine and derision. The Americans, by contrast, are uniformly pictured as simple, decent, resolute yeoman who have imprisoned the British in their seaport garrison. Even within Boston itself the British troops retain the power, but have no control, over the plucky Americans who have remained.

In *Lionel Lincoln* there are no American forces like the Skinners to cloud simple moral distinctions. Conversely, there is not one mention of civilians loyal to the crown in the entire tale. Cooper's descriptions of the retreat from Concord, the battle of Breed's Hill, and the fortification of Dorchester Heights portray the uprising of an entire people, a folk, against redcoats and mercenaries. The political nature of the neutral ground has decidedly changed:

In this manner, both parties stood at bay; the people living in perfect order and quiet, without the administration of the law, sullen, vigilant, and, through their leaders, secretly alert; and the army, gay, haughty, and careless of the consequences, though far from being oppressive or insolent, until after the defeat of one or two abortive excursions into the country in quest of arms. (78)

It seems that the yeomen of Massachusetts, unlike those of Westchester, are capable of living the moral law without civilian or military control.

In this novel Cooper does not qualify his summary judgments of the history of the Revolution. He is writing of "those important results which have established a new era in political liberty, as well as a mighty empire" (72–73). In speaking of colonial resistance to taxation without representation, he states that "the direct and plain argument was clearly on the side of the colonies" (73). Blame is quite specifically placed, neither on George III nor on Parliament, but on "the besotted servants of the king" (74) and "the unconstitutional attempts of the ministry" (75) who denied to the colonies their British constitutional rights when they imposed the Stamp and Townshend Acts. Cooper's care to blame Lord Bute, not king nor Parliament, shows an underlying respect for British political institutions.

Cooper repeatedly praises the self-restraint of the oppressed colonists. Throughout the controversies the Americans are said to have exhibited "a guarded care not to exceed the limits which the laws had affixed to the rights of the subject" (76). Cooper insists that the colonists would assent to all British civil laws that are founded on moral laws. Rebellion was an unwilling and last resort. The last barrier to total justification of the colonial position is the question of the legality of provincial legislatures and the Continental Congress during 1774 and 1775. Cooper's position is admirably frank. Admitting that such bodies were not "legally constituted," he simply appeals beyond civil to natural justice by adding that "their recommendations possessed all the validity of laws, without incurring their odium" (76). In later works, Cooper was again to deny the civil legality of ad hoc popular bodies, but his feelings toward the natural justice of their decrees were to decisively darken.

Cooper's determination fully to justify the principles of the Revolution is evident in all of the battle scenes. The description of the fortification of Breed's Hill, for example, points toward a particular political statement:

Ignorant of the glare of military show; in the simple and rude
investments of their calling; armed with such weapons as they
had seized from the hooks above their mantels; and without
even a banner to wave its cheering folds above their heads,
they stood, sustained only by the righteousness of their cause,
and those deep moral principles which they had received from
their fathers, and which they intended this day should show
were to be transmitted untarnished to their children. (222–223)

Such a statement would be totally out of place in *The
Spy*. The American of *Lionel Lincoln* is a sensible yeoman who, having recognized that constitutional liberty
is a moral law, steadfastly fights for natural rights formerly granted him under the British constitution.

The suspension of civil law in Boston forces recourse
to the same codes of political justice that had devastated
Westchester: military tribunal and the law of might.
Here, however, both principles operate to the discredit
of the British rather than the Americans. Two trials are
contrasted in *Lionel Lincoln*. The trial of Seth Sage, by a
self-appointed military court, condemns the American
for shooting at an Englishman during the retreat from
Concord, although Seth's judges, as he maintains, were
the ones violating British law. Further irony is added
when Cooper reveals that this injustice is only a form of
judicial bribery; the court releases Seth providing he becomes an illicit provisioner for the British troops.

Cooper contrasts this comic miscarriage of justice with
a serious one. In the most powerful scene of the novel,
Job Pray, the American revolutionary who is starving,
diseased, and feeble-minded,[63] is beaten by a howling

---

[63] Like Hetty Hutter, Job Pray is mentally enfeebled because,
although he can distinguish good from evil, he cannot understand
the ease with which Christian law is betrayed in the neutral

mob of Irish soldiers. The "crime" he has committed, the one of which Seth was accused, affords him no legal self-defense. The greatness of the scene, however, comes not only from its stark portrayal of sheer vindictive brutality, but from the irony of the refrains with which Cooper has prepared it. Job, the prophet of American triumph and British downfall, has six times exclaimed "The People will teach them the law." Although Job cannot explain his meaning, he surely refers to the moral law that decrees the individual's right to liberty. As the Irish soldiers prepare to kill Job, they shriek out six times the only moral law they have learned in Boston, "Blood for blood." Unlike the Americans in *The Spy*, the Americans in *Lionel Lincoln* act within the moral law, while the British increasingly act without it.

Into this world, at once so treacherous and yet so conducive of American patriotism, Cooper places a wavering hero derived, in all probability, from Scott's first novel.[64] Disembarking in Boston in April of 1775, Lionel Lincoln is Boston born but English by habit and education. A British major and a member of Parliament, heir of the noble Lincolns, Lionel's instinctual belief is that rebellion "would be both a mad and an unlawful act" (48), and that "the utmost required is . . . a redress of grievances" (88). At the same time, however, Cooper informs us that Lionel had "a natural interest for all that involved the safety and happiness of the place of his birth" (90). The young noble himself insists, on a number of occasions, that "I am not one of those who affect

ground. His name combines two of the qualities, persecution and piety, characteristic of Cooper's revolutionary hero.

[64] Dekker, *James Fenimore Cooper*, pp. 21–23, 37–42.

to undervalue my own countrymen; for you will remember that I too am an American" (48). Polite, intelligent, and a man of principle, Lionel knows little of the Revolution and far less of his American family. Even before the battle of Lexington he is asking a leader of the Revolution, "Is sympathy with the oppressed incompatible with loyalty to my prince?" (95).

Cooper confronts Lionel Lincoln with every conceivable justification for conversion to the revolutionary cause. Lionel constantly meets or employs Ralph and Job Pray, who are not only convinced patriots and victims of British mistreatment, but, unknown to Lionel, his own father and half-brother. Job and Ralph take Lionel on a patriot's tour of Boston, showing him proof after proof of British tyranny and American rectitude. Ralph constantly appeals to Lionel to change his allegiance.

To summarize Lionel's experiences is to reveal how clearly Cooper has planned a novel of patriotic conversion. Lionel first glimpses Boston as the British flags are being lowered (17). His next sight is of Job Pray being beaten by the British grenadiers (21). Having saved Job from his own soldiers, Lionel is confronted by the contrast between the warehouse hovel of the Prays and the cold, wealthy splendor of his great-aunt's mansion. Later in the novel, Lionel moves away from Mrs. Leechmere's house because of suspicions of her aristocratic selfishness. Cooper allows Lionel a choice between the Tory and the American maiden, whereupon Agnes Danforth, the sprightly American, tells him to resign his British commission (48). Ralph and Job take Lionel to the Liberty Tree and to a Sons of Liberty meeting, where Lionel with surprised approval comments upon the moderation, rationality, and respect for law of all of its members (97). Horrified by the senseless slaughter of American soldiers at Lexington, Lionel learns the reality of British conduct in the neutral ground: "Great God! . . . what is it ye do? Ye fire at unoffending men! Is there no law but force?" (131). He reacts strongly against the English plundering of Concord and later attacks Parliament with uncharacteristic savagery. Significantly, Lionel long remains an observer both at Lexington and Breed's Hill, half-reluctantly joining the British troops only after blood has been shed. Reflecting upon his march to Lexington and Concord, Lionel nearly rejoices in the outcome: "a people are never certain of their rights until they are respected" (155).

The soldier for whom Lionel expresses the greatest admiration is neither Gage, Burgoyne, nor Clinton, but Israel Putnam, whom Lionel regards as a modern Cincinnatus (186). Lionel is deeply interested to learn that many "gentlemen" have sided with the American forces (186). When Job Pray shows Lionel the Old South Church, used by the British as a stable, Lionel denounces the military he is serving as fools who have forgotten the laws of God (299). Suddenly, after his marriage to Cecil, Lionel is unaccountably missing. The reader learns only that Lionel has left Boston with Ralph and is in American territory. After arousing expectations that Lionel will be converted, Cooper tells us nothing further of Lionel until the conclusion.

When Lionel reappears, Cooper inflicts upon him the crushing weight of his family's past crimes and simultaneously forces the issue of conversion. Ralph exacts a promise from Lionel that, upon hearing the truth con-

cerning his English ancestry, Lionel will "swear eternal
hatred to that country and those laws, by which an innocent and unoffending man can be levelled with the beasts
of the field, and be made to rave even at his Maker, in the
bitterness of his sufferings" (433). Lionel consents,
swearing "I will league with this rebellion" (433), provided only that Ralph will give proof of his assertions.

Lionel hears a history of evil that constitutes an overwhelming attack on the avarice and brutality that stem
from English aristocratic privileges. The dwelling and
person of Mrs. Leechmere become symbols of the evil
that forms an inseparable part of Lionel's English heritage. Cooper's clumsy handling of these absurd gothic
details may render his attack on English aristocracy
totally unconvincing, but the tale of family horror is integral to his purposes. The sins of the Lincolns become
the evidence of English colonial misrule. Gothic tale and
historical narrative serve the same end. At the point
when Lionel reenters the novel, the cumulative forces of
both his political and familial experiences are simultaneously brought to bear upon him, demanding his conversion to the principles of the Revolution and the land of
his birth.

In the last chapter, Lionel directly violates the promise
he has made his father by remaining wholly indifferent
to any change of conviction or allegiance. Lionel and
Cecil calmly retire to their new life as landed British
aristocrats, remaining only long enough to commit a
culminating act of insensitivity, the burying of Ralph and
Job beside the body of Mrs. Leechmere in the armorial
Lincoln tomb. Such a conclusion would be consistent
with the body of the novel only if Cooper had been criti-

cal of Lionel's failure to live up to his experience. By sending Lionel Lincoln off to England without any comment whatever, Cooper reverses the direction of his narrative and the book's structure collapses.

Surely Cooper recognized that his ending violated the political conversion he had so carefully prepared. Up until this point, there had been no need to explore the inner divisions in Lionel's mind. His conflicting loyalties were evident in the situation. To concentrate upon them would have been to raise a real question of political merit that Cooper, in this novel, was anxious to avoid. If Cooper could not bring himself to oversimplify his complex feelings by converting his honorable loyalist officer, neither could he commend Lionel for Toryish indecision when his fictional purpose was so blatantly patriotic. Auctorial silence was the disastrous, inevitable result.

There is an obvious, important objection to this explanation for Cooper's inconsistent ending. Ralph and Job Pray are clearly intended to be heroic, patriotic figures, not unlike Harvey Birch, whose qualities and actions argue the American cause. If Cooper was intending a thoroughly patriotic novel, why from the outset does Cooper emphasize Job's idiocy and Ralph's growing insanity?[65] There are two possible answers. In the process of clarifying the obscurities of his plot, Cooper intended to account for these mental illnesses by tracing their cause to the inhumanity of the ambitious Mrs. Leechmere. The awkward unraveling of these familial tangles at the end of the novel reveals that Cooper intended

[65] When Cooper introduces Ralph, he describes him as bowed, aged, wrinkled, with wildly fluttering hair and eyes that shoot forth "glowing rapid glances" (15).

Ralph's insanity to reflect discredit, not upon Ralph's revolutionary feelings, but upon aristocratic vanity. A second explanation would be that, subconsciously, Cooper intended to counter the patriotic surface of his novel by associating madness with revolution. To anyone but a narrow Freudian, the first seems far more likely.

The failure of *Lionel Lincoln* is vital to the development of Cooper's fiction. The book was to be the first in a series of thirteen novels to be collectively entitled "The Legends of the Thirteen Republics." From this title and from the contents of *Lionel Lincoln* itself, it is not difficult to reconstruct the purpose of the entire work. The Legends were doubtless conceived as a series of historical romances cast during the revolutionary war, one devoted to each state, all of them to be nationalistic and republican in tone. Probably Cooper hoped to achieve a comprehensive survey of American history and a ringing affirmation of American political values. William Gilmore Simms' seven historical romances of the American Revolution, though confined in setting to South Carolina, were to realize the patriotic purposes of Cooper's "Legends" with impressive success.

Many reasons for Cooper's abandoning the project can be surmised. In 1826, one year after publication of *Lionel Lincoln*, Cooper left America for seven years in Europe, where both the time and the facilities for the necessary historical research were lacking. Cooper had already written both *The Pioneers* and *The Pilot*, books that afforded him his three most congenial subjects: Natty Bumppo, the frontier, and the sea. The important first volume of the series, rightly devoted to Massachusetts, had been a failure. Finally, Cooper may have felt unable or unwilling completely to restrict himself within a preplanned program of historical fiction that would affirm the unalloyed glories of the American past. Certainly his three historical romances, taken together, disclose the difficulty Cooper found in deciding upon the essence of the American Revolution. The ideals of the Revolution, however noble, were difficult to define precisely and rarely conformed to historical fact. Idealizing the historical fact, however—as Cooper had done in *Lionel Lincoln*—had proven even less satisfactory. It is probable that Cooper resolved never again to write an "historical tale" in the manner of Scott. When, in 1843, Cooper completed his last novel of the Revolution, he had developed fictional techniques that allowed him to treat questions of national identity while avoiding the strictures of historical fact. Whatever deficiencies *Wyandotté* may display, an inconsistent view of the meaning of the American Revolution is not one of them.

"WYANDOTTÉ"

During the eighteen years between *Lionel Lincoln* (1825) and *Wyandotté* (1843), Cooper's patriotism had in no way abated, but the visible and present justifications for patriotism had nearly disappeared. The American Revolution and the ideals for which its heroes had fought, seemed now forgotten. In chapter XXI of *Home As Found* the Effinghams view Templeton's celebration of Independence Day. The fourth of July has degenerated into a willful display of American vulgarity. Citizens are only interested in fireworks, squeaking bands and pretentious dress. The oration, delivered, significantly, by a lawyer, Mr. Writ, is a composite of demagoguery and cant. Writ's speech flatters the people but makes no mention of the principles for which the revolutionary war was fought or the institutions it created. The great era is ignored.

Cooper's justifications of the Revolution in his social criticism shifted to accord with changes of political feeling. In *Notions of the Americans* and *Lionel Lincoln*, the cause of the Revolution had been righteous resistance of English ministerial oppression by the heroic American yeoman. By 1839, however, Cooper had become increasingly fearful of legislative powers. In the *History of the Navy*, he projects his fear into an account of the causes of the Revolution: "Immediately after the peace of 1763, commenced that legislative usurpation on the part of the mother country, which twenty years later terminated in the independence of the colonies."[66] The British Parliament, exonerated in *Lionel Lincoln*, is now held to be solely responsible for the revolutionary war. The heroism of oppressed farmers is hardly mentioned.

A corollary of Cooper's distrust of Parliament is an increased sympathy for the executive powers of a monarchy; "this portion of the empire [Parliament], by extending its legislation unduly over the others, was substituting a new and dangerous master, for a prince who might be supposed to know no difference in his affection for his subjects."[67] This surprisingly complimentary reference to the British king is then confirmed:

[66] *History of the Navy*, I, 37.
[67] *History of the Navy*, I, 38.

While, however, this was probably the principle that lay at the root of the difficulties with America, few saw it in theory; facts invariably preceding opinion in a country as purely practical as this. Legislative usurpation, in the abstract, was resisted; while few perceived the difference between a legislation that was effectually checked by the veto of an independent monarch, bearing an equal relation to all the parts of a vast empire, and a legislation that not only held this, but all the other material powers of the crown, directly or indirectly, in subjection.

Cooper's statement, which may have been intended as a support of Jackson's use of the veto, is startling in its implication. If England had in fact had the benefit of an independent monarch with a veto, and if the few Americans who perceived it, had thought and acted rightly, they would not have resisted. In short, monarchy—or a strong executive power—is acquiring qualities of benevolence and disinterestedness.

The wronged, lowborn, democratic revolutionary had been the major vehicle for Cooper's declared object of patriotism. In the later novels however, this figure becomes suspect. Ithuel Bolt of *The Wing-and-Wing*, the novel that, in Cooper's canon, immediately precedes *Wyandotté*, is a fine example of the transition. Like Harvey Birch, Bolt is a lowborn Yankee, a man of disguises, completely competent within his environment. Like Birch, Ithuel has been deeply wronged by both English and Americans, and, like Birch, he is proud of his republicanism. He boasts of the "Granite" participation in the battle of Bunker Hill, and repeatedly contrasts American liberty both to English monarchy and to the tyranny of the British navy, with which he is all too well acquainted.

The resemblance between the two characters goes no farther. Upon the outline of the old revolutionary hero Cooper has superimposed one of the types which haunt his later novels—the Yankee sharpster. Six feet of New Hampshire bone, angular, shifty-eyed, and self-possessed, Ithuel has had his eye on the main chance through an unending series of trades. Bolt talks of the great fight against England, but neglects ever to specify whether he played any part in it. When Bolt does speak of America, his intention is not to further truth, but to foment revenge against the British. The shifty and calculating nature of the man makes his devotion to American liberty seem hypocritical. A perversion of the heroic revolutionary isolate, Bolt has all of Harvey Birch's acuity and abilities, but none of his capacity for disinterested patriotism.

When, therefore, Cooper wrote a belated last fiction upon the revolutionary war, he approached his theme from these changed presuppositions: a distrust of his old conception of the revolutionary hero, an unadmitted yearning for the executive dispatch of a monarchy, and a belief that his contemporaries were indifferent to revolutionary truths. Distrust of contemporary tendencies in American life led Cooper to distrust the past. Accordingly, the origin of contemporary cultural problems is traced back to the once heroic era of the Revolution. The object of a fiction on the revolutionary war is no longer to instill love of country, but to write a parable about the power of demagoguery:

One of the misfortunes of a nation, is to hear little besides its own praises. Although the American revolution was probably as just an effort as was ever made by a people to resist the first inroads of oppression, the cause had its evil aspects, as well as all other human struggles. We have been so much accustomed to hear everything extolled, of late years, that could be dragged into the remotest connexion with that great event, and the principles which led to it, that there is danger of overlooking truth, in a pseudo-patriotism. . . . That there were demagogues in 1776, is as certain as that there are demagogues now, and will probably continue to be demagogues as long as means for misleading the common mind shall exist.[68]

This introductory reference to the probable justice of the American Revolution proves to be unique. Cooper was not unaware that his overwhelming emphasis on the "evil aspects" of the Revolution was something new to his historical fiction. Before *Wyandotté* went to press, Cooper quietly described it as "a border story, treated differently from its predecessors, time, commencement of the American Revolution."[69]

In *Wyandotté* fictional narrative and historical significance are neatly conjoined as they had not been in any of the three previous revolutionary tales. Escape and pursuit sequences are discarded in favor of the cleanest and simplest of plots. The Willoughby family purchase, settle, and build their home, "The Hutted Knoll," in the neutral wilderness. Their community is later besieged by a combination of whites and Indian mercenaries, and the Willoughbys withdraw. This narrative, so similar to *The Wept of Wish-ton-Wish*, *The Deerslayer*, and *The Crater*, forms a timeless tale of the rise and fall of a rudimentary civilization. At the same time, however, Cooper applies a very specific chronology to the narrative. The first section of the novel, laid in 1765, describes the build-

[68] Preface to *Wyandotté*, pp. v–vi.
[69] *Letters and Journals*, IV, 382.

ing and the promise of the knoll. The middle section, comprising nearly all of the novel, deals with the fulfillment and downfall of the community during 1775 and 1776. The concluding chapter tells of the return visit of the survivors in 1795.[70] While the archetypal plot generalizes the significance of the sacking of the knoll, the chronological framework forces the reader to think of the tale in historical terms. The experiences of the Willoughbys thus become representative, not only of American civilization, but of American civilization throughout the revolutionary era.

The shift in Cooper's thinking about the Revolution is most evident in his handling of his leading character. Captain Willoughby is a thorough reworking of Mr. Wharton of *The Spy*. The aged landowner of divided loyalties has become a representative central figure rather than a peripheral caricature. In the person of Willoughby, Cooper endows Mr. Wharton with influence, dignity, and a mind. Willoughby's neutrality is seriously and thoroughly treated. In contrast to both Wharton and Lionel Lincoln, Willoughby's vacillations are neither condemned nor glossed over.

All imaginable worthy but conflicting political pressures are placed upon Willoughby. An English veteran of the French and Indian Wars, born in England, Willoughby has married an American wife. He, the Englishman, is sympathetic to the Americans; she, the American, is sympathetic to the British. Willoughby's son Robert is a British major in the forces defending Boston. Twice Robert journeys through dangerous territory to the knoll

[70] Cooper had effectively used the same tripartite structure in *The Red Rover*.

to beg his father to join the English army. Willoughby's future son-in-law, Evert Beekman, is a colonel in the American army; he also journeys to the knoll to ask Willoughby to accept a commission. The captain has a daughter sympathetic to the Americans and an adopted daughter who is Tory. Having inherited an English baronetcy that his son deeply desires, Willoughby half-heartedly refuses it in order to be an American frontier gentleman.

Willoughby's political convictions are as reasonable, as scrupulously balanced, as his personal loyalties. A strong believer that the colonies should "render unto Caesar the things which are Caesar's" (95), Willoughby nevertheless feels that the parliamentary taxes are most unjust. Although he thoroughly understands the advantages of monarchy, stating that "a good king is a good thing, and a prodigious blessing to a country," Willoughby can also say, with the same breath, "a people needs look to its political privileges if it wish to preserve them" (114). The captain expresses strong fears of a republican government, but calls the Declaration of Independence "a creditable document, and . . . eloquently reasoned" (250). Desiring America to remain a colony, he is truly sympathetic to all colonial grievances. An English soldier and a member of the New York Colonial Assembly, Willoughby sends General Gage a letter which is so sympathetic to the Americans that he does not sign it (162–163).

With the sole exception of Willoughby's admitted hope that America will remain a colony, all of these convictions are expressed in Cooper's own pronouncements upon the American Revolution. Cooper and Willoughby draw different conclusions that are based on identical antitheses of principle. Although Cooper would surely deny any parallel between himself and his central character, the increasing respect that he has afforded the loyalist leanings of the divided old neutral is in itself a silent admission. We may wonder, however, whether Cooper's feelings have truly changed or only surfaced. The figure of Willoughby openly raises questions of contradictory political merit that had to remain implicit in the earlier historical tales that were designed to praise the Revolution.

Willoughby's style of living bears an equally interesting comparison to Cooper's social tenets. Somewhat of a martinet in discipline, the captain is the undisputed governor of an idyllic social hierarchy composed of faithful Irish and Scotch retainers, household blocks, Dutch tenants, and Yankee tenants, in that order of preference. The captain owns all the land and has established the Anglican church. At the outset of the novel, Cooper describes with great care the beauty and fecundity of the knoll, built before the Revolution by continued and honest effort, and rendered seemingly secure by its remoteness from civilization and the strength of its fortifications.

Both the captain's politics and his knoll represent a very positive good. They constitute the best and most honorable retreat from a world in which absolute allegiance to king or Congress necessitates oversimplification and moral wrong. Robert Willoughby, the Tory son who believes he is fighting for an unjust cause, is asked by his beloved to change his loyalties:

I would in a minute, if I knew where to find a better. Rely on it, dearest Maud, all causes are alike, in this particular; though

one side may employ instruments, as in the case of the savages, that the other side finds it its interest to decry. Men, as
individuals, may be, and sometimes are, reasonably upright—
but bodies of men, I much fear, never. The latter escape responsibility by dividing it. (273)

In none of the previous novels of the Revolution would
Cooper's technical hero ever have claimed that "all
causes are alike." Nor would the hero have denied that
virtue could reside in the American people as a whole.
Nonetheless, Robert Willoughby here declares what the
plot of *The Spy* had only implied; political integrity is
more important than political allegiance.

Robert's speech is true to the world of the novel. For
Captain Willoughby to declare any political allegiance
would be to forsake important convictions and responsibilities. Unlike Wharton's neutrality, Willoughby's is
evidence of principle. Although Cooper is openly critical
of Willoughby's brutality, of his imprudence, and of his
exaggerated sense of security, he is not critical of Willoughby's politics. There is little movement through four
hundred pages of *Wyandotté*, because Cooper is concerned to build his reader's fear of impending disaster
by portraying a man of principle, drifting in an excru-
ciating but necessary indecision, while a summer passes,
independence is declared, and his community remains
unprotected.

Near the end of the novel, Willoughby summarizes his
feelings about the Revolution to an old Indian acquaintance and sometime employee, Saucy Nick:

"I am neutral, Tuscarora, in the present quarrel. I only defend
myself, and the rights which the laws assure to me, let whichever party govern, that may."

"Dat bad. Nebber neutral in hot war. Get rob from bot' side. Always be one or t'oder, cap'in."

"You may be right, Nicholas, but a conscientious man may think neither wholly right nor wholly wrong. I wish never to lift the hatchet unless my quarrel be just." (432–433)

Willoughby knowingly acts against his interest rather than violate moral justice. Such a position is as admirable as it is naive. Within an hour Nick coldbloodedly murders Willoughby in revenge for past floggings. Shortly thereafter Willoughby's honorable maintenance of a conscientious neutrality earns its reward. His knoll is sacked; his servants, his wife, and his only daughter are murdered. To make a decision entails loss of integrity. Not to make a decision is suicide.

Willoughby's faith in "the rights which the laws assure to me" is only pathetic. In *Wyandotté* there is no civil law, not even the military tribunals of *The Spy* or *Lionel Lincoln*. Only Willoughby himself is governed by self-imposed moral laws. Cooper has, however, found a new law operating in the revolutionary world, "people's law." Joel Strides introduces the concept while telling the captain of the "Indians" who threaten him:

There's two laws in operation at this time; the king's law, and the people's law. I take it, this party comes in virtue of the people's law, whereas it is likely the law the captain means is the king's law. The difference is so great, that one or t'other carries the day, just as the king's friends or the people's friends happen to be the strongest. These men don't like to trust to their law, when the captain may think it safest to trust a little to his'n. (324)

Joel's distinction is absolutely correct. He knows that the king's law, suspended in 1776, can be enforced only by the might of Willoughby, and that "people's law" is anything he and his cohorts can devise.

At the Hutted Knoll in 1776, the king's law falls, not to American constitutional law, nor to any settled government, but to "people's law." The problem of demagoguery is thus traced back to the very root of the American nation. Claiming a sham legal authority, using the unsettled conditions of 1776, pseudo-patriots effect the only revolution in the novel by pulling down Willoughby and his way of life. This unexpected revolution depends upon the all-important irony that a gang of Yankee scum and their Mohawk mercenaries are demanding "the surrender of the Hut and all it contained, to the authorities of the Continental Congress" (326). This supreme example of "people's law" is itself only a cloak for the people's thirst for land, plunder and revenge upon the gentleman. Having conveniently damned Willoughby, a colonial sympathizer, as a Tory, they ravage his knoll in the name of the Congress to which he is sympathetic. The ironies are further compounded when the Continental army arrives to stop the destruction being wrought in the name of the Continental Congress.

Cooper combines into one figure, Joel Strides, all the different social ills responsible for the knoll's overthrow. Like many of his fellows in Cooper's late fiction, Joel is, at once, the Yankee invading New York, the demagogue, the land overseer of a gentleman's estate, and a false patriot. His desire is to foment a "Revolutionary battle" by which his employer will be rendered powerless and from which he, Joel, will gain possession of the land Willoughby will not sell. If battle will not achieve Joel's purpose, his alternative is to replace Willoughby, "the only magistrate hereabout," with a "Committee of Safety" (151) acting in the name of the people for the interests of Joel Strides. Hiding behind the name either of the Continental Congress or of a popular committee, Joel has the safety of legality; he can escape responsibility by dividing it.

Joel's strategies reflect discredit only on American character and American ideals. If denouncing his victim as a Tory is unsuccessful, Joel will employ revolutionary cant: "I think the place could be carried in a few minutes, and then liberty would get its rights, and your monarchy-men would be put down as they all desarve" (481). It is only fitting that the American demagogue be the direct agent of the new revolution. To be sure, Willoughby was negligent in hanging the gates, but it was Joel who, given the command to hang them, failed to do so. Through a hole cut in the stockade by Joel, the deserting Yankees creep out. By means of a mine planted by Joel, the attackers rush in. Joel gathers the white attackers, and Joel plans the siege.

The darkness of Cooper's ending has no parallel in his fiction before *The Crater*. Regular American troops arrive a bit late for heroism, in time only to witness the carnage and carry away the survivors. Robert Willoughby and his bride emigrate to England, returning to the knoll only for a visit. After the Revolution, the once idyllic knoll is boarded up, reduced to a religious retreat for the Episcopalian minister. Significantly, Cooper reserves his bitterest strokes for his American patriot. Evert Beekman, rescuer from destruction, American colonel, and inheritor of the knoll, is ushered from the stage:

Beekman was never seen to smile, from the moment he first beheld the dead body of Beulah, lying with little Evert in her arms. He served faithfully until near the close of the war, falling in battle only a few weeks prior to the peace. His boy preceded him to the grave, leaving, as confiscations had gone out of fashion by that time, his uncle heir-at-law, again, to the same property that he had conferred on himself. (512)

In context, this quiet chronicling of Beekman's end is doubly effective. Viewing the treachery at the knoll, Beekman had echoed Harvey Birch by crying out "I shall ask for rigid justice" (496). Because there are no Washingtons in Beekman's world, Joel and his fellows, refusing to acknowledge any leader, simply melt away, unpursued and unpunished.

Poe objected to the stark horror of Cooper's ending:

The killing of Beulah, of Mrs. Willoughby, and Jamie Allen, produces, too, a painful impression, which does not properly appertain to the right fiction. Their deaths affect us as revolting and supererogatory; since the purposes of the story are not thereby furthered in any regard.[71]

Poe did not recognize that Cooper's presumed failure was actually his intent. *Wyandotté* leaves an unpleasant aftertaste because its "revolting," "supererogatory" brutalities are evidence of Cooper's desire to unburden himself of hatreds by admitting longstanding problems. Is not Captain Willoughby quite like Cooper in his later years? Are not they both men of divided political feelings, believers in a society in which the gentry supervise an agrarian hierarchy? Trusting to the civil laws as their sure defense, are not both of them deserted by their former supporters

[71] "Cooper's *Wyandotté*," *The Works of Edgar Allan Poe* (Chicago, 1895), VII, 8.

and left in somewhat isolated postures of defense while
the demagogues skulk to the attack?

Even if one waives the insoluble question of Cooper's
identification with Willoughby, *Wyandotté* clearly represents an immense change in Cooper's fictional presen-
tation of the American Revolution. Formerly manageable
doubts about the purity of American patriotism have
surfaced. The lowborn, ill-used, but patriotic hero of the
Revolution has disappeared entirely. *Wyandotté* has no
hero, only a protagonist. Whereas Mr. Wharton has
evolved into the honorable Willoughby, Harvey Birch,
the lowborn revolutionary, has devolved into the demagogue. The characters with whom we sympathize, Beekman excepted, are all neutral, divided in their loyalties,
or actively Tory. The villains of *Wyandotté* are Americans. Joel Strides and his conspirators are the Skinners
unleashed and victorious, with an important difference.
The Skinners were violent and open in their maraudings.
Joel Strides, far more clever than they, accomplishes all
with his tongue.

There are no glorious battles in *Wyandotté*, no declarations of American promise, no tributes to historical
leaders. The revolutionary war is viewed from a distance
as "a long and bloody civil war" (120). Its only visible
effects are death and defeat for Beekman as well as the
Willoughbys. There are no Americans like Captain Lawton to enforce poetic justice upon Joel and his accom-
plices. The only character is *Wyandotté* to speak glow-
ingly of liberty, equality, and triumph over the king is
Joel Strides. The only revolution has been to overturn the
best.

Wyandotté clearly associates the American Revolution

with the triumph of demagoguery. In the figure of Joel
Strides, the victory of American revolutionaries has even
become linked to the agitation of Anti-Rent "Injins,"
who by 1843 were looming ominously both in New York
and in Cooper's mind. The surest measure of the shift in
Cooper's conception of the war, however, is the change
he has wrought in historical fact. James H. Pickering has
revealed that, historically accurate though *Wyandotté*
generally is, the only Indian mercenaries active in Tryon
County during 1776 and 1777 were British, not American.[72] Cooper seems deliberately to have changed villainous Tories into villainous "pseudo-patriots."

At no point in his life did Cooper have a single, consistent view of the purpose or the political justice of the
Revolution. Nor are the problems of divided loyalty and
demagoguery, so apparent in *Wyandotté*, unimportant
in *The Spy* or *The Pilot*. Nonetheless, a shifting assessment is evident. To the Cooper of 1828, the American
Revolution signified the promise of a difficult struggle to
achieve political liberty and republican institutions. To
the Cooper of 1843, the Revolution posed only a seemingly insurmountable problem, how to resist the incursions of the demagogue. Revealing though the change
may be, it is a change in Cooper's conception of political
fact, rather than a change of political principle. Although
Lionel Lincoln and *Wyandotté* describe very different
revolutions, Cooper's changing feelings about American
character and American historical fact are not to be confused with his unchanging approval of the constitutional
republic that had been established in 1787.

[72] James H. Pickering, "New York in the Revolution: Cooper's
Wyandotté," *New York History*, XLIX (1968), 132.

2. First Notions of America

> Some few towns excepted, we are all till-
> ers of the earth, from Nova Scotia to
> West Florida. We are a people of cultiva-
> tors, scattered over an immense territory,
> communicating with each other by means
> of good roads and navigable rivers,
> united by the silken bands of mild gov-
> ernment, all respecting the laws, without
> dreading their power, because they are
> equitable. We are all animated with the
> spirit of an industry which is unfettered
> and unrestrained, because each person
> works for himself.
>
> ST JEAN DE CRÈVECOEUR,
> "What Is An American?"

DURING the 1820s Cooper wrote two works that directly attempt to determine the general qualities of postrevolutionary America. *The Pioneers* (1823) describes what Cooper saw in the America of 1793; *Notions of the Americans* describes what Cooper wishes to see in the America of 1828. In a pastoral and comic context, *The Pioneers* introduces problems of political justice and civil law that were to become far more serious in later novels about American frontier communities. Although *Notions of the Americans* often pretends that these problems do not exist, it defines an ideal polity and an ideal national identity that Cooper always desired to uphold. These two works are thus the standards against which any change of political conviction in Cooper's later works must always be judged.

To Cooper's darkening analysis of political justice and civil law in America, three novels, spaced over three decades, are of crucial importance: *The Pioneers* (1823), *Home As Found* (1838), and *The Crater* (1847). Critics have generally agreed that the dramatic power of *The Pioneers* derives from the skillful handling of the conflict between Leatherstocking and Judge Temple.[1] The crux of their conflict, the killing of one deer out of season, is a typically trivial and local event around which Cooper amasses much of his thought concerning the nature of political justice and the necessity of law on the American frontier.

Significantly, *The Pioneers* is the only novel in which Cooper creates two very different but equally admirable heroes, sets them in opposition to one another, and refuses to judge their comparative merits. Because men so principled as Natty Bumppo and Judge Temple oppose one another, it is logical to assume that Cooper's own political thought is torn between the individual's right to freedom and the community's need for order. In the opposition of Natty and the judge, Henry Nash Smith sees a "conflict of allegiances" within Cooper between "nature and civilization, . . . freedom and law." Mr. Smith argues that *The Pioneers* reveals a "genuine ambivalence" toward the merits of squatter's rights versus property rights, natural equality versus social stratification, natural piety versus institutional religion.[2] One would be

[1] Grossman, *James Fenimore Cooper*, pp. 31–32; Dekker, *James Fenimore Cooper*, p. 44; Henry Nash Smith, *Virgin Land* (New York, 1950), pp. 67–68. Donald Ringe's perceptive study of *The Pioneers* concentrates almost exclusively on Natty's dealings with Temple and his law (*James Fenimore Cooper*, pp. 32–37).

[2] *Virgin Land*, pp. 66–68.

foolish, indeed, to deny that Natty's values are as attractive to Cooper as the judge's more practicable views. Equal sympathy, however, does not necessarily entail inner conflict. Natty and the judge are not to be measured by the same standard, because they belong to different stages of settlement.

If we apply the *Second Treatise on Civil Government* to *The Pioneers*,[3] we find that Cooper's characterization of Natty Bumppo exactly corresponds to Locke's definition of the just man in a State of Nature. Judge Temple, however, exactly corresponds to Cooper's definition of the just man in a State of Civilization. *The Pioneers* records the evolution of the one state into the other. To Cooper, Natty's values are neither better nor worse than the judge's; they simply do not apply to the Templeton of 1793. As the life of the hunter yields to the life of the farmer, so must natural justice yield to civil justice. If Cooper's emotional sympathies go out to Natty Bumppo, his reason unequivocally sides with Judge Temple. *The Pioneers* forces the recognition that Natty's views of liberty and justice are feasible only in the wilderness.

In reading *The Pioneers* one must remember that the Leatherstocking is not yet Deerslayer or Pathfinder. Natty's resentment against civilization, his reliance on moral rather than civil law, are heroic, compelling and true within the context of the prerevolutionary wilderness. *The Pioneers*, however, describes a frontier that is rapidly being settled and institutionalized. The conditions of

[3] Although Cooper refers to Locke (*Letters and Journals*, IV, 199), I have been unable to prove that Cooper read the *Second Treatise*. I use Locke's ideas as a framework for discussing *The Pioneers*, not as a means of proving literary influence.

Templeton, as Cooper portrays them, argue that the change from a State of Nature to a State of Civilization is not simply to be condemned. Surrounded by the institutions of a village, Natty and Mohegan may still be heroic and compelling, but their views cannot be true in any meaningful sense. Within a settled society, they are magnificent anachronisms.

Although Cooper calls upon local and personal memories, he is writing a tale about the general conditions of American frontier society. The novel is titled, not "Templeton" or "Leatherstocking," but *The Pioneers*. Cooper later specified that his subtitle, "A Descriptive Tale," meant "descriptive as regards general characteristics, usages, and the state of a new country"[4]—America in 1793. As in *The Red Rover*, Cooper has used the device of the self-contained community which, because it is a melting pot, is a national microcosm. Templeton has its Englishman, Frenchman, German, Irishman, and Indian. During Dr. Grant's church service, Cooper notes that "half the nations in the north of Europe had their representatives in this assembly, though all had closely assimilated themselves to the Americans in dress and appearance, except the Englishman" (134).

Cooper's frontier town is ever expanding, in a perpetual state of change much like the entire nation in *Notions of the Americans*. Elizabeth Temple remarks upon the wondrous rapidity with which Templeton has grown and altered, rendering the familiar obsolete and the settled vulnerable. Cooper adds to our sense of flux by describing the round of the seasons, a cycle of cease-

[4] *Letters and Journals*, IV, 253.

less natural change.[5] As winter changes to spring and to summer, the promise of the American frontier town is gradually unfolded into pictures of full markets and ripening produce. In *The Pioneers*, the cycle of the seasons is not merely a pastoral convention; it provides an effective means of praising the virtues and promise of an American community.

At the outset Cooper offers us a glimpse of Templeton in 1823 in order to emphasize that his purpose is eulogy. Judge Temple and Oliver Edwards have turned the neutral ground into Cooper's ideal community, agrarian but fully civilized. Templeton presently lies in a land of "beautiful and thriving villages," "neat and comfortable farms" (13), replete with rich valleys and running streams. Cooper insists on tracing the fulfillment of the frontier village back to political rather than natural blessings:

> In short, the whole district is hourly exhibiting how much can be done, in even a rugged country, and with a severe climate, under the dominion of mild laws, and where every man feels a direct influence in the prosperity of a commonwealth, of which he knows himself to form a part. (14)

Like Judge Temple, Cooper insists that the pastoral village can only be grounded upon the rule of "mild laws" and the benefits of participatory republican institutions.

The judge's community possesses, in Cooper's eyes, an ideal social structure—democratic but not egalitarian. Because Templeton is in an early state of settlement, it knows no formal social distinctions. The members of the

[5] Thomas Philbrick has shown that the formal design of *The Pioneers* follows Thomson's *The Seasons* ("Cooper's *The Pioneers*," *PMLA*, LXXIX [1964], 579–593).

community, from Judge Temple to John Mohegan, gather convivially in the tavern on Christmas eve. Locks on personal property are almost unknown. Cooper is anxious to point out, however, that the removal of artificial distinctions between men only allows natural merit to be more apparent. Like the ordinary citizens described in *Notions of the Americans*, the common folk of Templeton respect their natural aristocracy. In church Judge Temple may sit apart, but his separation is not resented because it is not a political privilege: "this distinction was rather a gratuitous concession, made by the poorer and less polished part of the population, than a right claimed by the favored few" (132).

To Cooper communities such as Templeton were proof of the validity of the republican polity, because they were founded upon its principles. The flourishing frontier settlement exhibits the very essence of American values. In *The Wept of Wish-ton-Wish*, Cooper was to speculate upon the causes of settlement prosperity:

Necessity, promoted by an understanding of its wants, incited by a commendable spirit of emulation, and encouraged by liberty, early gave birth to those improvements which have converted a wilderness into the abodes of abundance and security, with a rapidity that wears the appearance of magic. Industry has wrought with the confidence of knowledge, and the result has been peculiar.

It is scarcely necessary to say that in a country where the law favors all commendable enterprise, where unnecessary artificial restrictions are unknown, and where the hand of man has not yet exhausted its efforts, the adventurer is allowed the greatest freedom in selecting the field of his enterprise. (242)

Necessity, emulation, liberty, industry, few but firm laws —these are the roots, not only of the social improvements Cooper describes, but of his republican faith. Yet, despite the expansive and confident tone of *The Pioneers*, these very qualities become the chief hindrances to improvement. With what ease necessity becomes an excuse for selfishness, emulation becomes envy, and industry turns into a prying business. In Templeton, liberty shades quickly into license and the law serves as a tool for the pursuit of gain.

The problem of justice in the neutral ground is defined differently in *The Pioneers* than in the revolutionary war novels. Questions of military control, political loyalty, and vigilante justice are now replaced by two connected problems, ownership of the land and the legal limits to be placed on man's use of nature. Because neither land ownership nor the citizen's use of natural resources is an issue which Templeton has yet resolved, the entire community assumes the qualities of an unformed neutral society, needing fixed principles.[6]

The difficulties begin, as always on Cooper's frontier, with the vexing problem of land ownership. He who owns the land has the right to institute civil laws based on the moral law, but who is the owner of the land? Cooper has created five characters in *The Pioneers*, all of whom have a considerable claim to "own" the land on Judge Temple's patent. The Indians, represented by John Mohegan, have a convincing natural right to its possession. Cooper calls the Indians the "original owners of the

[6] Dekker also argues that the setting of *The Pioneers* redefines the neutral ground of *The Spy* (*James Fenimore Cooper*, p. 46). Our emphases, however, are different. Dekker concentrates upon the lack of conservation laws rather than the uncertainty of land ownership.

soil" (88). When the Mohicans were dispossessed by the whites, Major Effingham gained legal title, but his deeds were sold, under apparently dubious circumstances, to Judge Temple during the war. Natty Bumppo possessed the wilderness by squatter's rights before Judge Temple ever saw it. Oliver Edwards Effingham, grandson of the major, has returned to Templeton in an attempt to recover his grandfather's lands and exact revenge upon the judge.

Five claimants may seem a bit extreme, but they present the full complexity of the problem as Cooper then saw it. Indian, dispossessed Tory, present holder of the deed and squatter—each recurs in the frontier novels, and each appeals either to natural, moral, or civil law as his justification. Throughout the Leatherstocking tales, Cooper is remarkably open-minded in fairly representing the merits of each of these appeals. Only the mean white, attempting to wrest the land from the titled possessor, is missing from the cast of *The Pioneers.*

The conservation laws, the immediate cause of the clash between Natty and the judge, arise from the settlers' inability properly to define their relationship with nature. Ironically, Natty Bumppo and Judge Temple both maintain that the bounties of nature may be consumed only according to a man's need; they subscribe to Cooper's doctrine of use. However, into the judge's patent have come other settlers, lawless plunderers like Billy Kirby, who good-naturedly axe the trees, butcher the pigeons, and kill the bass, primarily for the senseless pleasure of slaughter.

The disgust that both the judge and Natty feel at this outrage of natural law expresses itself in exactly opposite

ways. Natty dramatizes the moral law of nature. March-
ing up to the scene of the pigeon massacre, he kills one
pigeon and stalks defiantly away from the town sheriff
and the justice of the peace, who are busily engaged in
killing thousands. Whereas Natty refuses to force his
moral law upon any other man, Judge Temple, the magistrate, must decree civil laws to enforce the moral law in
which they both believe.[7] Natty's is an alegal and individual response that dissuades no one. The judge's is a
legalistic, communal response that is perpetually misused.

The great irony of *The Pioneers* is that it is Natty who
falls afoul of Temple's civil law and that the depredators
whom the law should be curbing not only go untouched,
but lead Natty's prosecution. The judge's law against
the seasonal netting of the Otsego bass is apparently not
yet in force; it restrains no one. His law against the seasonal killing of deer catches only Natty Bumppo. Cooper
includes no scenes of settlers praising or obeying civil
statutes. When the law is not defied, it is used, either by
Hiram Doolittle as a means of satisfying his curiosity, or
by Dickon for the purpose of a military show.

Conservation has necessitated the deer law, but neither
Natty nor the judge is primarily concerned about the particular deer or the particular statute. The deer law is an
issue between them because it has aroused a deeper question: are there limits to the authority which a just and
necessary civil law should have over the individual? Con-

[7] Leon Howard describes Natty as a believer in "natural liberty,"
a phrase which Howard defines as "the liberty to do as one
pleased" ("Introduction" to *The Pioneers* [New York, 1959], p.
xii). Natty, however, governs himself in accord with his understanding of moral law. Billy Kirby and Hiram Doolittle, in their
different ways, practice Howard's concept of "natural liberty."

versely, is there any justification for civil disobedience?

Natty's shooting of the deer and subsequent defiance of Templeton's magistrates draw out Cooper's faith in individuality and freedom. Even at the end of his life, Cooper was to argue for the social benefit of permitting unrestricted personal liberty in the early stages of settlement:

We certainly think that even the looseness of law, legislation, and justice, that is so widely spreading itself over the land, is not exactly unsuited to sustain the rapid settlement of a country. No doubt men accomplish more in the earlier stages of society when perfectly unfettered, than when brought under the control of those principles and regulations which alone can render society permanently secure or happy.[8]

Within the more abstract framework of *The American Democrat*, Cooper insists on strict limitation of political authority in ways that are strikingly like John Stuart Mill:

Individuality is the aim of political liberty. By leaving to the citizen as much freedom of action and of being, as comports with order and the rights of others, the institutions render him truly a freeman. He is left to pursue his means of happiness in his own manner.[9]

When Cooper speaks of preconditions of individual greatness, he declares that "all greatness of character is dependent upon individuality."[10] When speaking of preconditions of societal greatness, he states that "the very object of the institution [democracy] is the utmost practicable personal liberty."[11]

[8] *New York* (New York, 1930), p. 48.
[9] *The American Democrat*, p. 228.
[10] *The American Democrat*, p. 229.
[11] *The American Democrat*, p. 153.

Natty Bumppo practices Cooper's credo of individuality; he personifies the benefits of unhampered liberty. Judge Temple openly admits that Natty Bumppo is the exceptional frontiersman who has little need of laws designed for a Billy Kirby. Believing in a natural state in which all men are perfectly free and equal, Natty adheres to Locke's "Law of Nature," which demands "that being all equal and independent, no one ought to harm another in his life, health, liberty, or possessions."[12] More importantly, Natty exactly practices Locke's ideas about the proper use of natural resources in the State of Nature.[13] Believing that God gave all the world in common, Natty will appropriate to himself only so much of natural bounty as he can personally use. Once appropriated, however, the natural object, whether it be a deerskin or a hut, becomes personal property.

When Cooper evaluates the judge through Natty's eyes, he recognizes that the civil law is an impingement upon the rights of the natural man. The law now considers Natty an illegal squatter, yet Natty was not only the first white settler, but the first white possessor of the land. His hut, which the law will drive him to burn, is the original dwelling on Lake Otsego. Cooper insists on showing his reader that Natty Bumppo has prior property rights in accord with natural law. When Judge Temple first descended Mount Vision, years before the era of settlement, he encountered Natty Bumppo and was offered the hospitality of Natty's hut. Judge Temple's first

[12] *Second Treatise on Civil Government*, in *Locke on Politics, Religion, and Education* (New York 1965), p. 20.
[13] *Second Treatise on Civil Government*, pp. 28–35.

glimpse of Natty establishes a second and more crucial property right: "while I was lingering around the spot, Natty made his appearance, staggering under the carcass of a buck that he had slain" (259).

In fact, therefore, natural justice seconds Natty's claim that "There's them living who say, that Nathaniel Bumppo's right to shoot deer on these hills is of older date than Marmaduke Temple's right to forbid him" (24). Judge Temple himself admits that Natty "has a kind of natural right to gain a livelihood in these mountains" (121). Nor is Cooper entirely opposed to the right of the squatter to his kill. Natty explains natural law to the judge: "Game is game, and he who finds may kill; that has been the law in these mountains for forty years, to my sartain knowledge; and I think one old law is worth two new ones" (175).

At the outset of the action, Judge Temple is placed in an equivocal position, and Natty alone appears to care for moral right. A deer is running through the forest and three men shoot at it. Bumppo shoots the deer in the neck, Oliver Edwards kills the deer, and Judge Temple shoots Oliver Edwards. In his eagerness to kill a deer, the judge misuses a dangerous weapon. He seems indifferent to the legal right to the carcass as long as he can buy it. Thus, when the first deer is killed, it is Natty who follows moral law and the judge who appears as the depredator. Natty points out that the only civil law needing enactment is a statute prohibiting the judge's use of the smooth bore rifle (24). Long before the Leatherstocking slays a deer in the lake, the judge reveals that he has given Natty an endless right to shoot deer on the Otsego hills

(24). When Temple later sentences Natty for breaking the recent conservation law, he is clearly enforcing what is, in Natty's case, an ex post facto law.

Natty Bumppo violates the deer law, not because he wishes to defy a civil statute, but because he does not recognize the validity of the civil law at all. In Lockean terms, Natty has made no voluntary compact with Templeton society. He exists wholly within the State of Nature and is governed by natural laws. To the Leatherstocking, therefore, the civil law of Templeton is only another encroachment of an evil civilization. Its magistrates are a group of meddling snoops. He evidently believes that no civil law could effectively restrain the individual who wishes to break the moral law. When Edwards and the judge excitedly participate both in the massacre of the pigeons and the seining of the bass, his fears seem amply justified.

The offense for which Leatherstocking is found guilty, stocked, and imprisoned is not the killing of a deer but resistance of arrest and assault of an officer of the law. The underlying issue that forces open confrontation between Natty and Templeton's legal officers, however, is popular invasion of the right of privacy, a right that is as sacrosanct to Cooper's gentry as it is to the Leatherstocking. Because, unlike the gentry, Natty recognizes no distinction between a man and a man with a badge, he defies the law with violence rather than legally punishing its abuses. Leatherstocking drives magistrate Doolittle from "his property" with a rifle, threatens him with assault, and openly defies the search warrant. In court, however, he pleads not guilty to these very charges, acknowledging at the same time that he performed the actions of the charge.

If one argues from Natty's premises, his plea of not guilty is unchallengeable. Nowhere in the novel does Cooper state that the civil law has any jurisdiction over a hero such as Natty, who has prior natural rights, belongs to an earlier stage of civilization, and is governed by a superior moral law. In throwing Doolittle out of his cabin, Natty was only upholding the Lockean law of natural justice by defending both his liberty and his possessions:

And that all men may be restrained from invading other's rights, and from doing hurt to one another, and the law of Nature be observed, which willeth the peace and preservation of all mankind, the execution of the law of Nature is in that state put into every man's hands, whereby every one has a right to punish the transgressors of that law to such a degree as may hinder its violation.[14]

Because, in Templeton, Natty continues to believe and to act upon precisely these tenets of natural justice, he inevitably brings the civil law upon his head.

In *The American Democrat*, Cooper was to insist that his conception of liberty demands a toleration of the actions and thoughts of the individual who does not conform to the conventional notions of the community:

There is the safe and just governing rule, already mentioned, or that of permitting every one to be the undisturbed judge of his own habits and associations, so long as they are innocent, and do not impair the rights of others to be equally judges for themselves.[15]

[14] Locke, *Second Treatise on Civil Government*, pp. 20–21.
[15] *The American Democrat*, p. 152.

Natty surely cannot be accused either of violating another's rights, or of restoring to the "wasty ways" which both he and the judge deplore.

Natty's contempt for the administration of the law in Templeton is fully justified. Conservation laws have not yet proven an effective agent of restraint. The justice of the peace and the town lawyer have no interest in enforcing the deer laws for social benefit. Doolittle and Lippet simply use the deer law as a ruse for satisfying their curiosity about Natty's hut, discovering the location of Natty's mine, and seizing its nonexistent silver for themselves.[16] Templeton law condemns minor infringements, ignores major ones, and is used by its devious if absurd representatives for their own selfish and highly illegal ends. Why should the Leatherstocking submit to it?

To Natty Bumppo a civil law is worthless if not enforced by creditable men. To Judge Temple a just legal statute, because it is a just legal statute, is sacrosanct and must be obeyed. In *The Pioneers* Judge Temple sometimes suffers by the comparison, not because he is adhering to an evil law, but because his legalism leads him to protect his own corrupt officers. Judge Temple appoints Dickon sheriff only to discover that, by so doing, he loses control over Dickon's actions. Even at the end of the

[16] Unlike their fictional counterparts in Cooper's later novels, Doolittle and Riddel are wholly motivated by greed, not by envy of the gentry. Lawyer Lippet may devise a scheme for suing Judge Temple, but Lippet's motive is the dollar rather than any design to lift himself by discrediting the judge. It is significant that Lippet can arouse no popular support for his schemes. Aristabulus Bragg, an inhabitant of Templeton in later years, uses similar tactics with greater success.

novel, the judge remains insufficiently aware of the insidiousness of Doolittle and Lippet. Consequently, his frequent references to the protection and stability that the laws afford seem naive.

The Pioneers introduces the two contrasting types of judicial figures that were to recur in later novels. To Cooper a judge or a lawyer is nearly always the crafty, hypocritical Yankee or the principled gentleman, either Hiram Doolittle, Lawyer Lippet, or Judge Temple. Almost without exception, the active practicing lawyer is the devious Yankee, cunning in his combination of pure selfishness and appeal to popular slogans, subverting the legal framework of society while he pretends to serve it. The gentleman is rarely a practicing lawyer, but a judge or a semiretired advocate, a man of principle. The gentleman lawyer, although capable of quelling his Yankee underling, lives at a discreet remove from the field of treachery, and seems usually to be either unable to understand the Yankee, or unwilling to act against him. Doolittle and Temple are found, almost unchanged, in Timms and Dunscomb of *The Ways of the Hour*, written twenty-seven years after *The Pioneers*. More important than such consistency, however, is the fact that Cooper seems always to have viewed the lawyer, the upholder of the very framework of society, as either insidious or dangerously high-minded.

Both the insidiousness and the high-mindedness of the law are direct causes of Natty's presence at the Templeton Court of Common Pleas. The original wrong in a complex sequence of events was committed by the Justice of the Peace himself, when Hiram cut the leashes on Natty's hounds. Intentionally or not, Doolittle's action causes the hounds to hunt up the deer that Natty slays. Judge Temple, understandably anxious to preserve his "reputation for impartiality" (362), then grants Doolittle a search warrant with the weight of the Temple name, but without a thorough investigation of facts or motives. Hiram Doolittle thus possesses a legal right, but no just purpose, for pursuing his investigation. Natty Bumppo violates a civil conservation law, but Doolittle violates both a moral and a natural law by abusing his legal right of search. Speaking for Natty, Oliver Edwards redefines criminality in a moral rather than a legal context: "is it a crime to drive a prying miscreant from his door? Crime! Oh, no, sir; if there be a criminal involved in this affair, it is not he" (380).

All of the arguments from natural justice, prior right, individuality, and legal misadministration argue eloquently on Natty's behalf, and are not to be denied. Nonetheless, by the conclusion of the novel Natty's opposition to the civil law seems both inappropriate and simplistic. Simultaneously, Judge Temple, who first figures as a hunter with a hasty trigger, finally emerges as a civic leader of unquestionable integrity and strength. Cooper does not admire Judge Temple because he was modeled upon William Cooper,[17] nor because the judge speaks for James's Federalist heritage, nor because the judge has mastered the realities of frontier life. Temple

---

[17] In the *Brother Jonathan* letters, Cooper protested that few of the characters or events of *The Pioneers* were based upon local history or legend. The history of the Temple family, Cooper says, was entirely adapted from Proud's *History of Pennsylvania* (*Letters and Journals*, IV, 255).

exemplifies Cooper's definition of a just judge. His very presence in the novel gives the lie to Natty's unqualified attack on civil law.

The only means by which Judge Temple can maintain order and restraint, in an undefined and expanding society containing wasters and cheats, is by laws that are strictly enforced and commonly respected. After Temple sentences Natty Bumppo, he justifies his actions to his daughter:

Society cannot exist without wholesome restraints. Those restraints cannot be inflicted, without security and respect to the persons who administer them. . . . try to remember, Elizabeth, that the laws alone remove us from the condition of the savages; that he [Natty] has been criminal, and that his judge was thy father. (421–422)

In the *Second Treatise on Civil Government*, Locke had noted three deficiencies to justice in the State of Nature: the lack of established law, the lack of a single judge to decide the law, and the lack of magistracy to execute the law.[18] Judge Temple is endeavoring to bring all three to the neutral ground.

The judge's legalistic attitudes, restated in *Notions of the Americans* and *The American Democrat*, stem from his recognition that a frontier community has special need for the strict discipline of civil law. The judge concludes his charge to Natty's jury by saying "Living as we do, gentlemen, . . . on the skirts of society, it becomes doubly necessary to protect the ministers of the law" (407). To the man who has purchased legal title to the

[18] *Second Treatise on Civil Government*, p. 61.

land, established a prosperous community, and become its judge, Natty must represent the lawless squatter, an old friend allowed to rove unapprehended only as long as he remains harmless. When Leatherstocking defies civil law, however, Temple rightly asks Oliver Edwards, "Would any society be tolerable, young man, where the ministers of justice are to be opposed by men armed with rifles? Is it for this that I have tamed the wilderness?" (379).

In Cooper's eyes, one of Temple's most admirable qualities is his effort to govern his community by the rule of law, not by the bias of personal interest. Possessing the wealth and influence to do what he will, the judge nonetheless insists on dispensing the kind of impartial disinterested justice that so many of Cooper's heroes vainly seek.[19] Cooper arranges for Natty Bumppo to save Elizabeth Temple from a panther in order to illustrate that, for Temple, the law is no respecter of persons. At first our sympathy for Natty's plight is increased by the fact that he is sternly sentenced by a man whose daughter he has recently rescued. Later, however, this same fact only increases our sympathy for the judge. Temple's ideal of justice forces him to fine and imprison an old friend who saved his daughter's life. When Elizabeth objects that Natty should be freed because of moral innocence and a courageous rescue, the judge replies "it would sound ill indeed to report, that a judge had ex-

[19] Dekker suggests that Judge Temple is a development of Scott's wavering hero (*James Fenimore Cooper*, p. 55). However, except for the two occasions when Temple joins in the communal excitement of despoiling nature, the judge's actions and his ideas remain remarkably consistent. Certainly his principles of justice never waver either in theory or in application.

tended favor to a convicted criminal, because he had saved the life of his child" (421).

Natty Bumppo's harangues against law and civilization have great emotional impact because they are written in a vigorous, earthy dialect that contrasts favorably to the formal abstractions of Judge Temple. Natty's heart, however, is not to be confused with Cooper's reason. Natty is never willing to consider whether law is necessary in a social context. He is unwilling to admit that Temple's civil law is only a way of enforcing the moral law of use in which Natty himself believes. Whenever Natty's criticizes civil law, he refuses to distinguish between a just law badly administered, such as Temple's conservation law, and a civil law that is intrinsically unjust. This distinction is crucial. Natty wrongly assumes that, because magistrate Doolittle is violating his rights, the civil law is inherently evil. Judge Temple recognizes that, even though his laws are wretchedly administered, they must be maintained.

Natty Bumppo, who sees the civil law only as a constriction, cannot understand that for Judge Temple, as for Fenimore Cooper, the civil law is the only guarantee of liberty. The judge knows that laws are meant to preserve Natty's right to his game, not to threaten it:

Armed with the dignity of the law, Mr. Bumppo . . . a vigilant magistrate can prevent much of the evil that has hitherto prevailed, and which is already rendering the game scarce. I hope to live to see the day when a man's rights in his game shall be as much respected as his title to his farm. (175)

Although Natty flees from Templeton because of his resentment against the law, Judge Temple had hoped that, by setting up impartial laws, he could induce the

Leatherstocking to remain. After noting that Natty has
"a kind of natural right to gain a livelihood in these
mountains," the judge warns his household that "if the
idlers in the village take it into their heads to annoy him,
as they sometime do reputed rogues, they shall find him
protected by the strong arm of the law" (121). Weighed
against the outcome of the tale, the judge's statement is
obviously ironic, yet it indicates his hope that Natty's
rights in a State of Nature can coexist with the civil laws
of Templeton. Although this hope proves futile, it shows
that the judge values the best of the old ways no less
than Natty.

Marmaduke Temple exactly fits Cooper's idealized
sketch of the American County Judge for the Court of
Common Pleas: "these judges are usually men of education, and always men of character. They are frequently
lawyers, who continue to practise in the higher courts,
and they are often men of landed estate, yeomen of good
characters and influence, and sometimes merchants."[20]
In Cooper's eyes, Temple's lack of legal training is a
necessity of frontier life, not a personal criticism. Although the Judge gave both the land and the money for
the courthouse in which he presides (107), he refuses to
use his influence to establish irresponsible laws. He acknowledges that wealth was his primary motive in establishing Templeton (255), yet he has built a good society at great personal sacrifice. John Mohegan says of
Temple, "the brother of Miquon [William Penn] would
do justice" (442). And, at the beginning of the novel,

[20] *Notions of the Americans*, II, 156.

Cooper commends the Judge's "native clearness of mind," adding that Temple "not only decided right, but was generally able to give a very good reason for it" (37). Nowhere does Cooper say anything similar of Natty Bumppo.

The shift in auctorial authority from Natty to the judge begins with the three scenes in which the citizenry despoil the maples, pigeons, and bass. The law may not be able entirely to control the townspeople's destruction of nature, but the scenes clearly demonstrate that inner moral laws will frequently fail to restrain the most principled of settlers. Even Natty Bumppo, exemplar of the moral law, killed the all-important deer because he was too weak to resist a moment of temptation (326). Natty may kill only one pigeon during the communal massacre, but earlier in the novel he had boasted of former times when he had stood in the doorway of his hut and shot thirteen deer a day (21). When Leatherstocking, Temple, and Oliver Edwards all violate moral laws in which they firmly believe, stiffer civil laws, rather than none at all, seem necessary.

The scene of Natty's trial vindicates the judge's argument for civil law. A case that seems doomed to total misjudgment is suddenly decided in exact accord with true principles of civil justice. Both lawyers are comically incompetent. Neither the defense attorney, Lawyer Lippet, nor the prosecuting attorney, Dirck Van Der School, mentions any of the compelling arguments Cooper has provided either to excuse or condemn Natty's actions. After Judge Temple's charge, however, the jury returns an amazingly apt and sophisticated judgment. Natty is found not guilty of striking and assaulting Hiram Doolittle, but guilty of resisting the execution of a search warrant by force of arms.

The two charges arise from the same act. To Natty Bumppo, who cannot separate a man from a man with a badge, the judgment is ludicrously inconsistent. To Judge Temple and to the jury, however, Doolittle's faults as an individual must be clearly distinguished from Doolittle's action as an official magistrate. The jury decides that a just law must be upheld, even when it is abused by legal magistrates.[21] Cooper very evidently sanctions the court's decision. When Elizabeth Temple, acting upon the promptings of her heart, tells her father that "in appreciating the offence of poor Natty, I cannot separate the minister from the man," and that "it is immaterial whether it be one or the other," Cooper quietly remarks that his heroine has spoken "with a logic that contained more feeling than reason" (422).

The Leatherstocking of *The Pioneers* is a comparatively simple and garrulous old hunter, incapable of the philosophic abstractions he is to utter in later novels. Nevertheless, in the only language he does know, Natty argues forcibly against his sentence by referring to the original source of all differences:

Hear me, Marmaduke Temple . . . and hear reason. I've travelled these mountains when you was no judge, but an infant in your mother's arms; and I feel as if I had a right and a privilege to travel them ag'in afore I die. Have you forgot the time that you came on to the lake-shore, when there wasn't even a

---

[21] Or, in Donald Ringe's fine phrase, "Society demands . . . that the just man be punished that justice may prevail" (*James Fenimore Cooper*, p. 36).

jail to lodge in; and didn't I give you my own bear-skin to sleep on, and the fat of a noble buck to satisfy the cravings of your hunger? Yes, yes—you thought it no sin then to kill a deer! (409)

Compelling though the speech is, Natty can defend himself only by appealing to justice as it had existed in a State of Nature. His attempt to justify the slaying of a deer in 1793 on the grounds that he had slain deer for Temple's former benefit simply will not stand any test of reason. Throughout the trial, Natty remains comically unable to understand anything of legal procedure; he even refers to a breach of law as a "sin." Dressed as a natural hunter, Natty laughs silently at the court as he enters. Whereas Judge Temple sympathizes with Natty's viewpoint, Leatherstocking makes no effort to understand the Judge's more complex but equally moral codes of justice. Natty simply cannot consider the function of law in a social context.

Following Natty's trial and escape from the town jail, an event occurs which is all too easily dismissed as merely another occasion for a romancer's adventure sequence. Mount Vision, the hilltop from which Judge Temple had foreseen the glorious setting and future of his new community, is consumed in flames. The natural cycle, which had been used to unfold the promise of Templeton to summer fullness, changes to a parched brown. Cooper indicates that the destruction of Mount Vision is neither a providential judgment nor mere chance, but arises out of the actions of the townspeople. The pursuers of Natty Bumppo, by carelessly tossing their lighted pine knots into the dry underbrush, started the symbolic fire (457). The burning of Mount Vision is thus associated with civil officials who wrongly use the law to bedevil the Leatherstocking.[22]

After Mount Vision is consumed, the legal institutions created to maintain peace and restraint degenerate into lawlessness. Despite the justice of Temple's sentences, all prisoners escape from the jail. The only way of punishing the injustices of legal officials seems to be extralegal punishment. Doolittle's face is methodically battered by Ben Pump; his protruding backside is later winged by lead from Natty's rifle. The sheriff and his posse fight a pitched battle against Natty and Ben Pump, ostensibly to recapture fugitives from the law, but with the actual intent of investigating the mine. For the second time, the wrongs of a magistrate force Leatherstocking, who knows nothing of law, to resort to his rifle.

Farce is tragedy with fortuitous timing. Templeton's pattern of legal abuse followed by extralegal violence is finally ended by the courageous and timely intervention of Judge Temple. As in *The Spy*, social order can only be reestablished by the landowning gentleman:

Silence and peace! Why do I see murder and bloodshed attempted? is not the law sufficient to protect itself, that armed bands must be gathered, as in rebellion and war, to see justice performed? (480)

In the Templeton of 1793, the mere presence of the judge is sufficient to restore the rule of law, and the resort to violence is finally harmless, a source only of comedy.

---

[22] Thomas Philbrick interprets the fire as an emblem of fierce inner passions that have become increasingly uncontrollable as spring yields to summer ("Cooper's *The Pioneers*," p. 590). Although the fire surely is symbolic of unrestrained passion, Cooper insists on tracing its cause to one specific source.

Nevertheless, the question posed by the judge is disturbing; Cooper offers no answer to it. As the judge watches Natty combat Templeton's magistracy, he is witnessing a comic version of the legal entanglement, which in later novels was to become intolerable. The American frontier town has become a place in which just civil laws are opposed by both the godly individual who has little need for civil law, and by the overtly lawless for whom civil statutes were created. Yet the civil magistrates only use the authority of law to further their own lawless ends. While such abuses only render strict statutes the more necessary, the law does not seem sufficient to protect itself without the saving influence of the gentry.

Natty's conflict with the civil law of Templeton has made the valley which was once "a second paradise" (320) appear no longer endurable. By burning his hut, Natty renounces the marginal life and reasserts his right to freedom and privacy. His act is clearly symbolic of the end of any Lockean State of Nature within Templeton. Over the ashes of his hut, Natty delivers a diatribe to the sheriff's posse against "the troubles and divilties of the law," and the "wicked feet and wasty ways" of Templeton. In concluding, Natty describes himself with a simile which, from his viewpoint, is magnificently apt:

And now, when he has come to see the last brand of his hut, before it is melted into ashes, you follow him up, at midnight, like hungry hounds on the track of a worn-out and dying deer. What more would ye have? for I am here—one too many. (393)

Pursuing Natty's analogy, we find that all the connotations of shooting the deer are reversed. To Templeton and the judge, Natty is the hunter who has killed the deer and brought the law upon his head. To Natty, however, he himself is the deer that is being hunted by the hounds of the law and by a statute which, rightly conceived, seems only to work injustice.

Unless he would violate his conception of natural justice, Natty has no choice but to depart westward in retreat from the sounding axes, replenished with a new supply of gunpowder for the rifle which he uses to enforce natural law. Before departure, however, he indicates the effect of recent experiences upon his final renunciation. Natty, like Cooper, is prone to state that "the law of God is the only rule of conduct."[23] Measuring the law of God against the law of Templeton, Natty rightly finds the civil law deficient, but for the wrong reasons. Speaking of Mohegan's death, Natty says, "he's to be judged by a righteous Judge, and by no laws that's made to suit times, and new ways" (466). Natty's injuries have evidently led him to blame the judge rather than Doolittle, to confuse a law with its misadministration. Because Leatherstocking scorns all but immutable, divine laws, he totally disregards the exigencies of a frontier town in the late eighteenth century.

Cooper underscores Natty's misunderstanding. The Leatherstocking's last words to Elizabeth are a disguised criticism of the workings of her father's law:

I pray that the Lord will keep you in mind—the Lord that lives in clearings as well as in the wilderness—and bless you, and all that belong to you, from this time till the great day when the whites shall meet the red-skins in judgment, and justice shall be the law, and not power. (504)

[23] *The American Democrat*, p. 151.

Again, Natty wrongly assumes that Temple's law is unjust because it has been unjustly used. Observing only the workings of the law, rather than the law itself, Natty concludes that the civil law does not correspond to the divine law, and leaves civilization to seek the absolute in the forest.

Natty's October departure releases him from any social commitment into the wilderness, where Cooper will proceed to enlarge the old squatter into the mythical representation of the just man in a State of Nature. For the idealizing of the character, freedom from Templeton is necessary. Within *The Pioneers*, however, the release seems attained at a great price. Natty takes his great qualities outside of American society in order to maintain them.

The Pioneers begins as a pastoral but concludes as a tragicomic examination of the workings of civil law. Rather than ending in a eulogy of Templeton, as it had begun, *The Pioneers* concludes with a sense of a sad but necessary sacrifice. In *The American Democrat* Cooper was to specify the cause of such an inevitable loss:

Great principles seldom escape working injustice in particular things, and this so much the more, in establishing the relations of a community, for in them many great, and frequently conflicting principles enter, to maintain the more essential features of which sacrifices of parts become necessary.[24]

The qualities of Natty Bumppo must seemingly be sacrificed before Templeton can become a truly ordered or stable society. Natty Bumppo and Judge Temple, each of

[24] *The American Democrat*, pp. 109–110.

them representing a great but conflicting principle, cannot forever remain within the same social framework.

Even Elizabeth Temple recognizes that Natty's ways and principles of justice have no place in Templeton. Feeling that the Temple family has no right to possess the land as long as Natty and Mohegan are present, Elizabeth nonetheless knows that no return is possible:

> What can I do? what can my father do? Should we offer the old man a home and a maintenance, his habits would compel him to refuse us. Neither, were we so silly as to wish such a thing, could we convert these clearings and farms again into hunting-grounds, as the Leather-stocking would wish to see them. (308)

Like Natty, Elizabeth and Judge Temple know too well the prevalence of legal abuse. Unlike Natty, they recognize the necessity of restraint and adapt to change. The difference between the gentry and the libertarian hero is not in their principles, nor in their recognition of facts, but in the way in which they conceive their responsibilities. Temple becomes the legalistic judge, while Natty Bumppo retreats; Cooper condemns neither of them.

The ending of the novel resolves previous doubts and disputes in such a way as to justify Judge Temple's actions and thereby lessen regret for Natty's leavetaking. Oliver Edwards Effingham turns from hunter into gentleman farmer. The longstanding suspicion that Judge Temple climbed to prosperity and power by wronging Mr. Effingham is explained away. The issue of land ownership is conveniently and somewhat artificially resolved. We learn that the Delawares gave the Otsego lands to Major Effingham, thus extinguishing the Indian claim. Natty Bumppo, who had claimed a squatter's right to possession, was in fact only "a kind of locum tenens" (487) for Major Effingham. Mohegan and Major Effingham die at the end of the action and Natty departs for the west. The conflict between the two remaining claims is ended by the marriage of Elizabeth Temple and Oliver Effingham, a marriage which heals the supposed breach between Tory and revolutionary, and settles ownership of the patent upon the most legitimate holder of a civil deed. Templeton seems to have solved its problems by a satisfactory compromise that works solely to the advantage of the judge's values.

Cooper's ending reveals his personal commitment. Natty Bumppo represents for Cooper an older, equally admirable, civilization that must be superseded. The attraction of Natty's concepts of freedom and justice for Cooper never extends to his sanctioning them. The greatness of *The Pioneers*, however, is that Cooper does not obtrude his own preferences upon the reader. Because Cooper would not choose between the principles that Natty and the judge represent, he allows the facts of Templeton to dictate that, inevitably, Templeton must deprive itself of Natty. It is precisely the inevitability of the loss that makes Cooper's novel more than a precious record of a stage of American settlement. *The Pioneers* is one of those rare works in which an author has fully understood and successfully dramatized all the ramifications of a conflict that is crucial to his civilization's development.

"NOTIONS OF THE AMERICANS"

Neither the revolutionary war novels, the sea tales, nor *The Pioneers* had required that Cooper thoroughly examine the first principles of republican government. In preparing *Notions of the Americans*, however, Cooper extensively studied statistical and political sources about America. Among them was *The Federalist*, which Cooper considered "a text-book for the principles of the American government."[25] The more Cooper thought about a republican polity, the finer it seemed to him. Writing about America in Europe, Cooper was surrounded by what he considered to be the evil consequences of aristocratic oligarchy. His immediate purpose was to defend America from prejudicial accounts written by European travelers.[26] Under these impulses, a constitutional republic emerged in Cooper's mind as the ideal government. He became more aware of the effect of a nation's polity upon its civilization. Accordingly, it became more important to define true republicanism. *Notions of the Americans* is thus the first full definition of Cooper's political ideals. Despite its critical neglect, it remains the reference point by which all changes in Cooper's view of America must be measured.

[25] *Notions of the Americans*, I, 79. James Beard reveals that Cooper purchased and read *The Federalist* while working on *Notions* ("Introduction" to *Letters and Journals*, I, xxiv). Cooper's political and historical research presumably stimulated his serious interest in Jefferson's writings, an interest which first surfaces in 1829.

[26] Not until 1834 did Cooper acknowledge that his purpose had been to counter Adam Hodgson and Basil Hall: "In 1828, after a residence of two years in Europe, and when there had been sufficient opportunity to observe the disfavor with which the American character is viewed by nearly all classes of Europeans, I published a work on this country, whose object was to repel some of the hostile opinions of the other hemisphere, and to turn the

In *Notions of the Americans*, Cooper does not falsify his opinions; rather he suppresses with little difficulty those unsuitable to a paean to the American dream.[27] The massive bulk of the work, its documentation, and its political rhetoric, all attest to the sincerity with which Cooper wrote. Cooper's attempt to prove, by citation of fact or by simple assertion, that his dream had actually been realized, is the measure of his strength of belief.

Cooper's unbounded faith in the American republic rests squarely upon a few treasured concepts: a maximum of individual liberty, a minimum of governmental legislation, the checks and balances provided by the Constitution, universal manhood suffrage, the power of public opinion, and the reasonableness of the common man. As the Bachelor and Cadwallader traverse America, examining the nation by region, class and institution, they continually refer to these concepts, and find that they underlie nearly every visible evidence of American greatness. The travelers are also at pains to show that these concepts are not only interrelated, but interdependent. The ultimate source of American progress is political: "our prosperity is owing to our intelligence, and our intelligence to our institutions" (I, 264).

---

tables on those who, at that time, most derided and calumniated us" (*A Letter to His Countrymen*, p. 7).

[27] James Beard describes *Notions of the Americans* as "a classic statement (perhaps *the* classic statement) of the 'American dream'" ("Introduction" to *Letters and Journals*, I, xxiii). And Marvin Meyers treats Cooper's book as a representative Jacksonian eulogy of American culture and society (*The Jacksonian Persuasion* [Stanford, 1960], pp. 61–73). Meyers does not concern himself with the political aspects of the work.

From Cooper's faith in man's natural right to the maximum of liberty flows his conviction that national achievement can only be based upon a minimum of legislation and governmental interference.

It would seem that is the best and safest, and, consequently, the wisest government, which is content rather to protect than direct the national prosperity, since the latter system never fails to impede the efforts of that individuality which makes men industrious and enterprising. (I, 14–15)

Such assertions are confirmed by the peace and social stability which the travelers encounter everywhere. Cadwallader declares, "we have happily got the country into that onward movement, that there is little or no occasion for legislative impulses. As a rule, besides the ordinary grants of money, and the usual watchfulness over the proceedings of the executive, the less they [legislators] do the better" (II, 25).

Like Jefferson or Thoreau, Cooper had a deep emotional suspicion of political activity that frequently led him to wish all government out of existence. The relish with which Cooper turned to the sea novel, and his fondness for elevating solitary individuals to heroic stature, reveal his unacknowledged yearning simply to dismiss all problems of civil government. He seems always to have felt that "contact with the affairs of state is one of the most corrupting of the influences to which men are exposed."[28] When Cooper returned from Europe, he attacked governmental excess of power from two directions: "I see far less apprehension of executive than of legislative usurpation in this country. Still, I am willing

[28] *The American Democrat*, p. 119.

to admit that the president has too much authority for our form of government."[29] In Cooper's writings, only the judiciary, which protects individual rights and minimal government, is never accused of hunger for power.

It is a deliberate sign of national promise, therefore, that Cadwallader and the Bachelor see practically no evidences of governmental bureaucracy save at Washington. The Bachelor is astonished that the moral law seems sufficient restraint for the Americans:

In short, if one should draw somewhat literally on the ten commandments for rules to govern his intercourse with those around him, so far as I can see, he might pass his whole life here without necessarily arriving at the practical knowledge that there is any government at all. (I, 74)

At the end of the *Letter to General Lafayette*, written only two years later, Cooper was to indulge in a set of utopian prophecies for the future size of the national government. By 1835 all public debt will be abolished, the citizen shall pay no direct tax, and all government expenditures will be greatly reduced.[30] Beyond the little necessary to provide for upholding the laws protecting individual rights, the government will concern itself only with education, the clergy, and welfare for the immigrant poor.[31] Cooper's ideal government contracts toward nonexistence.

[29] *A Letter to His Countrymen*, p. 90.

[30] The *Letter to General Lafayette* proved oddly prophetic. In 1836 the government of the United States was out of debt and, by the end of the year, showed a budgetary surplus of almost $20 million. Jacksonian fear of growing government, however, led Congress to return the surplus to the states (G. G. Van Deusen, *The Jacksonian Era* [New York, 1963], pp. 106–107).

[31] *Letter to General Lafayette* (New York, 1931), pp. 42–50.

The guarantee of minimum government in the American republic is the series of checks and balances established by the Constitution. As Cooper surveys the legislative, executive, and judicial branches of the republic, he perpetually mentions the healthy limitations accruing from the reciprocal power among branches, and among different components of the same branch. The balance between House and Senate, state courts and federal courts, Congress and the president are all, in Cooper's eyes, guarantees of individual freedom. Cooper argues as vigorously as John Adams that liberty depends upon separation of powers.[32] The Constitution thus becomes the timeless and nearly unchangeable definition of limited government. To refer to its provisions is to appeal to absolute political truth.

Throughout his career, Cooper was acutely aware that, in a democracy, majority opinion, the will of the constituency, is the final source of power. Checks and balances have been established by the Constitution, but political integrity ultimately depends upon the force of an enlightened public opinion:

So admirable is the practice of checks and balances throughout all the departments of this government, and so powerful and certain is the agency of public opinion, that no political man-

[32] Cooper made a passing reference to John Adams in a journal entry of 1848. John Quincy Adams, recently deceased, is unfavorably compared to his father: "Old Adams is buried, and a good deal of old Adam with him, notwithstanding all their eulogies. He was a learned man, but his mind wanted a balance wheel. His father was much the abler man of the two" (*Letters and Journals*, V, 290). In commending the balance of John Adams's mind, Cooper may be thinking of Adams's insistence on balance of powers.

agement, except in cases that, by common consent, are thought to come fairly within the scope of political manoeuvrings, can easily be exercised. (II, 226)

When addressing his countrymen in 1834, Cooper was to insist—not with total pleasure—that the entire structure of the democratic republic rests ultimately upon the virtue of the constituency: "The highest authority known to the Constitution, in its spirit, is the constituency. It sits in judgment over all, and approves or condemns at pleasure. All the branches of the deputed government, executive, legislative, and judicial, are equally amenable to its decisions. It has retained the power of even changing the characters of its several servants." [33]

The cornerstone of Cooper's faith in the American republic is his high opinion of the constituency. By selecting the executive and the legislators, the electorate can, in effect, determine the civil law, alter the Constitution, and exert such pressure upon officials of government as to coerce their obedience to the popular will. In 1828 Cooper was convinced that the popular will of the constituency provided the surest bulwark of American democracy:

When there is much leisure, and all other means to reflect on life, apart from those temptations which hurry us into its vortex, the mind is not slow to strip it of its gloss, and to arrive at truths that lie so near the surface. The result has been, in America, to establish common sense as the sovereign guide of the public will. In the possession of this quality, the nation is unrivalled. (I, 170)

[33] *A Letter to His Countrymen*, p. 67.

"Common sense as the sovereign guide of the public will" is the most important phrase of the entire work. Throughout *Notions of the Americans*, Cadwallader and the Bachelor continually use such expressions as "American common sense" or "the practical reason of the American," or "the watchfulness of intelligent public opinion." A common sense, founded not even on the best of abstract theories, but on daily experience, is the essence of Cooper's view of democratic man. To allow the maximum of individual freedom is to give the freest play to common sense. Hence Cooper praises both the justice and the consequences of constitutional freedoms: "In the tossings and agitations of the public opinion, the fine and precious grains of truth gradually get winnowed from the chaff of empiricism and interestedness, and, to pursue the figure, literally become the mental aliment of the nation" (I, 172).

Notions of the Americans outlines a position on suffrage in a republic that Cooper was to cling to throughout the 1830s and 1840s. Confidence in the soundness of the constituency leads Cooper to praise extension of the franchise. Cooper accepts universal manhood suffrage, because it provides a further check against governmental abuses. He remains sharply critical of any attempt to represent property. The benefit of a trifling property qualification for voting is favorably considered, but not supported (I, 265). Above all, Cooper trusts that the widest extension of the suffrage only causes the intelligent electorate to choose the best leaders:

Now it is the distinguishing feature of our policy, that we consider man a reasonable being, and that we rather court, than avoid, the struggle between ignorance and intelligence.

We find that this policy rarely fails to assure the victory of the latter, while it keeps down its baneful monopolies. We extended the suffrage to include every body,[34] and while complaint is removed, we find no difference in the representation. As yet, it is rather an improvement. (I, 269–270)

Cooper's hymn to the republic is finally based on his conviction that "a majority will be sufficiently sagacious to know their own interests" (I, 270).

Because *Notions of the Americans* does not preach swift, stern enforcement of civil statutes, it appears to be the work of a less authoritarian writer than the author of either *The American Democrat* or *The Redskins*. In 1828, however, Cooper foresaw no need for legalistic warnings; the people recognize that law is sovereign. Cooper flatly states that "the only supreme authority in this republic is the law" (II, 220). Although Cooper declares that the people are the ultimate source of power, he can also assert, without inconsistency, that the law is supreme, because the people remain admirably deferential: "The Americans mingle with a perfect consciousness of their influence on the government, an admirable respect for the laws and institutions of their country" (I, 259). Cooper's Anti-Rent trilogy, written nearly twenty years later, was chiefly designed to reassert this same sovereignty of law.

The observations of the travelers only confirm Cooper's general assertions. The Bachelor discovers to his approval that Congress seats a sturdy yeoman by a gen-

[34] Cooper is referring to revisions of suffrage passed by the New York State Convention of 1821. Every white male citizen of twenty-one years and one year's residence was given the vote (Dixon Ryan Fox, *The Decline of Aristocracy in the Politics of New York* [New York, 1965], p. 251).

tleman of the manor, and the gentlemanly lawyer by his provincial counterpart. The member of Congress is "very commonly a plain, though always a respectable yeoman, and not unfrequently a mechanic" (II, 23) yet Cooper assures us that the democratic process evolves leaders of social station as well as inner virtue:

The surprise should be, not that the people choose so many men of a situation in life closely resembling that of the majority, but rather that they choose so few. There is a practical good sense in the mass of the community, here, that tells them a certain degree of intelligence and of respectability of character is needed in a representative of the nation. (II, 24)

The representative lawyer is not a gentleman of theory, but a common youth who, after completing college, trains in a law office for a number of years and then becomes a practitioner whose good common sense leads him to abolish the remnants of antirepublican law. Eventually, he becomes a legislator who frames statutes designed to "make men comfortable and happy" (II, 98). There are no such lawyers in Cooper's novels.

The workings of the American judiciary system are afforded high praise. For the common man, Cooper finds that "justice is comparatively cheap, and easy of access. Men have confidence in her decrees; and the fear of power, influence, and corruption, is unknown" (II, 211). The Supreme Court is characterized by "dignity and moderation." "The judges are amenable to public opinion, the severest punishment and the tightest check in a free community, and their corruption can be punished by impeachment" (II, 160). Thus popular opinion as well as checks and balances operate to guarantee the impartiality of American law.

Recognizing that a great deal of American civil law has yet to be codified, Cooper's reaction is to trust to the future lessons of practical experience. Like Jefferson, Cooper resents the wholesale importation of Blackstone and the British common law, and calls instead for a kind of natural, common law indigenous to America:[35]

As its institutions get matured by time, the power of the confederation is every day receiving strength. A vast deal of constitutional law, however, remains to be decided; but as new cases arise, the ability to make discreet decisions, grows with experience. (II, 163)

A species of natural law is growing up under this system, that promises to be eminently useful, inasmuch as it is adapted to actual necessity. I am a great venerator of those laws which are enacted by custom, since I entertain the opinion that the stamp of usage is worth a dozen legislative seals, especially in a community where men, being as free as possible, have every opportunity of consulting the useful. (II, 162)

In these quotations a perfect harmony between people, government, and law is theoretically constructed. The civil government, acting upon the daily experience of rational men, evolves a code of civil law which, being both just and useful, corresponds to natural law. Although new statutes will continue to be created, none of them will need repeal, because all are ultimately based on natural law. The statutes of Judge Temple fit this description, but no laws in any later novel are so ideally evolved.

Except for the diminishing danger of aristocratic prejudices, the only threat Cooper sees to such a harmonious

[35] The applicability of British common law to a republic was a crucial issue of jurisprudence in the 1820s. See Perry Miller, "Law Versus the Common Law" in *The Life of the Mind in America*, pp. 105–109.

system of government lies in the unlikely event of the people limiting their own powers:

They may enact laws of a more rigid character as the advancement or corruption of society shall require them, and they may possibly be driven to some slight curtailments of the franchise for the same reason; but this will, in no degree, change the principle of their government. By losing their intelligence, the people of the United States may lose the consciousness of their rights, and with it their enjoyment. But all experience goes to show how difficult it is to wrest vested rights from the communities. (II, 335–336)

Severity of civil law, limitations of franchise, and loss of personal right—all three are regrettable intrusions upon liberty and individuality. Cooper, however, makes a crucial distinction between the three. Severity of civil law and limitation of the franchise, though undesirable, are not incompatible with republican government because they are constitutional decisions that are made by the representatives of the people. If loss of popular intelligence ends in loss of popular rights, however, the Constitution is violated, and republicanism is gravely threatened. In later works, Cooper was to pursue the implications of these same distinctions.

In *Notions of the Americans* Cooper occasionally raises the troubling social questions of his later years, but problems are acknowledged only to be invariably dismissed. There is an admitted excess of mean, ill-educated country lawyers who concoct phony litigations in order to line their own purses. Cooper claims, however, that the difficulty is "already beginning to correct itself" and that the presence of such men has a positive advantage: "They serve to keep alive an active knowledge of their rights

among the people; and although much abused as petti-
foggers, they make, in common, exceedingly useful and
intelligent local legislators" (II, 212). Hiram Doolittle
and Lippet, much as they resembled the type, did not
have precisely this effect.

Notions of the Americans is essentially a hymn to the
land of the simple, virtuous, independent farmer. It presents a society in which the position of the natural aristocracy is assumed because it is unchallenged. The American republic may tend to level its people to a mediocrity,
but the mediocrity, it seems, is of the very highest level.
In America, the yeoman farmer does not yearn to pull
down Washington or Jay; he emulates them. As a result,
the yeoman is raised in understanding while the natural
aristocracy remains virtually in place. Political parties are
free from demagoguery because there are few governmental plums worth the exercise of one's self-interest.
Cooper argues that America is growing so rapidly that his
statistics will shortly be outmoded, yet the picture he
leaves of America is one of total stability and peace.
Change creates no social discontent. It simply sweeps
away lingering traces of feudalism, leaving an ever-
expanding democracy. In these ways, Cooper's notion of
America is oddly close both to Jefferson and to the early
political essays of Walter Whitman.

Cadwallader and the Bachelor travel down the Mohawk Valley to visit the site of Templeton. They find a
village without excitement or adventure, devoid of Indians or massacres of wild life. Instead there are green
fields, abundant harvests, a nestling village, and daylight
prosperity (I, 241–264). In short, they find the Templeton described in the first half of *The Pioneers*, a com-

munity which exemplifies the great merit of rural civilization combined with American democracy. The conflicts posed by *The Pioneers* do not recur; rather, the travelers view an expansive and habitable world that is hostile only to art.

If *Notions of the Americans* looks backward to *The Pioneers*, it also provides a necessary background for understanding Cooper's writings about Europe. Cooper's seven years abroad were devoted to a very self-conscious defense of precisely the conception of American republicanism outlined in *Notions of the Americans*. Cooper's method of defense, however, was not to praise the American polity, but to denounce its opposite.

3. The American Democrat in Europe

> Americans are, as Americans, the most
> self-conscious people in the world, and
> the most addicted to the belief that the
> other nations of the earth are in a con-
> spiracy to undervalue them. They are
> conscious of being the youngest of the
> great nations, of not being of the Euro-
> pean family, of being placed on the cir-
> cumference of the circle of civilization
> rather than at the centre, of the experi-
> mental element not having as yet entirely
> dropped out of their great political
> undertaking.
>
> HENRY JAMES, *Hawthorne*

IN 1834 Cooper recalled the purpose of the three ill-
received novels with which, presumably, he had terminated writing: "I determined to attempt a series of tales,
in which American opinion should be brought to bear
upon European facts."[1] *The Bravo, The Heidenmauer,*
and *The Headsman* are all set in the long ago of a small,
even a remote, European city state, but each of them is a
reflection of Cooper's immediate observations on political justice in revolutionary Europe. "American opinion,"
Cooper's notion of America, is the standard used in all
three novels to judge aristocratic oligarchy. At the same
time, however, Cooper's understanding of present European "facts" heavily influences his portrayal of the European past. By informing an ignorant America of the

[1] *A Letter to His Countrymen,* p. 12.

effect which European politics had had upon its peoples, Cooper hoped to free America from any present deference to aristocratic polities.

The European novels were not written by an author who intended to hymn the triumph of the revolutionary movements of 1830. Cooper was not describing, as Spiller thought, "the decline of the old order before the growing liberalism of the new."[2] Nearly all of *The Bravo* was written during the winter of 1830 and the spring of 1831 —after the liberal professions of Louis Phillipe had shown themselves to be a cloak for maintaining a narrowly based aristocracy. *The Heidenmauer* and *The Headsman* were published in 1832 and 1833, not in 1830. At the very moment Cooper began work on *The Headsman*, an aristocratic counterrevolution in Berne was threatening to overturn the political achievements of the two previous years.[3] Thus the three European novels were all completed at a time when Cooper was being forced to doubt the power of a popular revolt to resist the entrenched aristocratic oligarchies which were everywhere ruling Europe.

In 1828 Cooper had been quietly confident that Europe was progressing politically; he assumed that "the tendency is to natural rights, at the expense of artificial institutions."[4] The emergence of the July Monarchy and its repercussions in Belgium, Switzerland, Greece, Poland, and the German city states, led Cooper to believe

[2] *Fenimore Cooper: Critic of His Times*, p. 217.

[3] *Letters and Journals*, II, 321, 330–331; *Sketches of Switzerland*, part II, vol. II, 58–59.

[4] *Notions of the Americans*, II, 339.

that all European countries exemplified the same political condition:

The whole of this quarter of the world is divided into two
parties. They have different names, in different countries, but
their objects and tendencies are everywhere the same, subject
to modifications as depend only on local causes. One side is
struggling to reap the advantage of the revolutions, and the
other to arrest them.[5]

Everywhere in the events of 1830 Cooper saw a groundswell of popular revolutionary fervor surging up against
the entrenched abuses of aristocracy. Europe's first outbreak of truly democratic sentiment seemed to be threatening to overturn her entire feudal structure.

These views and expectations, at once more hopeful
and less complex than Cooper's view of the American
Revolution, were inevitably disappointed. By 1831 the
revolutions in nearly every nation had been checked or
had proven abortive: neither William I, the czar, nor the
feudal princes of Germany had fallen an easy conquest.
The Tories had thrown the Reform Bill out of the House
of Lords in 1831. To Cooper, however, the greatest disappointment was the betrayal of the revolution in France.
Louis Phillipe had shown himself to be more the king
than the bourgeois democrat; the Doctrinaires, party of
aristocracy, were resuming power.

Cooper seems never to have been as unaware of the
true intent of Louis Phillipe and the Doctrinaires as his
admired friend Lafayette. Nonetheless, the Paris of 1830
provided Cooper his first and most direct connection with

[5] *Letters and Journals,* I, 418.

the skilled secrecies of the political demagogue.[6] In discussions with Lafayette during the summer of 1830, Cooper had outlined, through specific measures for change in the French polity, the kinds of republican reforms he thought necessary for European aristocracies in general. France must become "a throne surrounded by republican institutions," rather than a monarchy that grants liberties. The hereditary Chamber of Peers is to be eliminated and replaced with a senate elected by a constituency of at least one million citizens. The aristocracy is to be deprived of political power while retaining noble title. Although Cooper rejects for France any representation of property ("the most vicious form of polity that has ever been devised"), he argues that a moderate property qualification for voting is desirable.[7]

The polity that would result from these changes corresponds closely to the republican polity described in *Notions of the Americans*. Historically, however, the July Monarchy was to yield few of these reforms. The Chamber of Peers ceased to be hereditary, but was still restricted to titular aristocracy. The suffrage was extended, but only to 200,000. Representation of property in the Chamber of Peers continued unchanged and only one-thirtieth of the adult male population elected the Chamber of Deputies.[8] Cooper's hopes, Lafayette's faith and the energies of the workingmen of Paris had all

[6] Cooper's fullest account of his experiences in Paris during 1830 is in *Sketches of Switzerland*, part II, vol. II, pp. 7–132.

[7] *Sketches of Switzerland*, part II, vol. I, pp. 29–39.

[8] R. R. Palmer, *A History of the Modern World* (New York, 1960), p. 456.

proven misguided; Louis Phillipe and the Doctrinaires had simply used their republican enthusiasms.

The events of 1830 and 1831 in France only confirmed Cooper's belief that the stability of any polity depends on its duly created institutions rather than its men. Cooper had been proven right in his belief that Lafayette "should have laid his institutions and seated his King on them, and not attempted to spin a web of republican simplicity with a royal distaff."[9] In later years, Cooper insisted that "The capital mistake made in 1830, was that of establishing the *throne* before establishing the *republic*; in trusting to *men*, instead of trusting to *institutions*."[10] After his return from Europe, Cooper was to continue to confide his political faith in American institutions rather than American personalities.

The course of the July Monarchy also has important social implications for Cooper's later writings. The heroic figure who for Cooper should be the pillar of social order had been deluded and stripped of power. When Lafayette's post as Commander of the Guards was abolished in December of 1830, Cooper witnessed the downfall of a patrician liberal he had long reverenced. Moreover, he saw the liberal gentleman succeeded by hypocrites of aristocratic persuasion who posed as republicans and who were supported by the moneyed interests of the upper middle class. Faced with so complex a situation, one not unlike Cooper's view of an American democrat confronted by the Whigs, Lafayette appeared to be excessively high-minded. Although Cooper pays tribute to

[9] *Letters and Journals*, II, 72–73.
[10] *Sketches of Switzerland*, part II, vol. I, p. 38.

Lafayette's "discriminating judgment," to his "Roman sternness," and to "the candour and simplicity of his opinions,"[11] Cooper also recognizes that "General La Fayette had been the dupe of his own good faith and kind feelings."[12] The liberal gentlemen of Cooper's later tales were to be just as principled as Lafayette, but not so innocent.

Cooper's distaste for European aristocracies grew in proportion to the stubbornness with which they maintained their power. Not only the *Letters and Journals*, but the travel volumes later based upon them, are consistently vituperative in their attacks on the French and English governments. To Cooper, neither nation possesses a clearly defined polity based on recognizable political principles. Both are hybrids created by the power compromises of centuries. Significantly, Cooper's anger is not directed against the king of either nation, nor against the institution of kingship; rather, it is the legislative and judicial institutions of both countries that are roundly denounced. In France and in England, Cooper saw the same invidious system—an illegitimate, but long-established and all-powerful nucleus of titled aristocrats maintaining control of the government by patronage rather than constitutional law.[13] Both parliaments represent the aristocracy to the virtual exclusion of all other classes and transact the affairs of government by unofficial committees or bureaus, which act solely for the interests of the ruling aristocracy, and from whose

[11] *Sketches of Switzerland*, part II, vol. I, pp. 114, 118, 8.
[12] *Sketches of Switzerland*, part II, vol. I, p. 26.
[13] *Letters and Journals*, I, 244; II, 287.

power there is no appeal.[14] Because, in each country, the judiciary is subservient to the legislature, legislative usurpation becomes a problem of aristocratic as well as democratic politics.

France and England were thus, to Cooper, monarchies only in name. As Cooper finds illegitimate aristocratic power veiled beneath a sham monarchy, true monarchy becomes increasingly attractive. Monarchy is not the buttress, but the check, to aristocratic privilege: "the most insidious enemy of monarchy is aristocracy."[15] In *Sketches of Switzerland*, Cooper suggests that absolute benevolent monarchy is the only truly harmonious polity because it is based on principles of divine order:

No one disputes, that the government which is controlled by a single will, when that will is pure, intelligent, and just, is the best possible. It is the government of the universe, which is perfect harmony.[16]

Because, however, Cooper recognizes that earthly monarchs rarely act upon divine laws, monarchy is never, even momentarily, considered as a political possibility. If power corrupts, as Cooper always believed, the only alternative to absolute monarchy is a protective republic, rather than the uncontrolled self-interest probable under an aristocracy.

Throughout his European years, Cooper continued to hope that increasing popular awareness of aristocratic cabals would drive England and France either to true re-

[14] *Gleanings in Europe: France*, pp. 321–322; *Gleanings in Europe: England*, pp. 174–176.

[15] *Excursions in Italy* (Paris, 1838), p. 46.

[16] *Sketches of Switzerland*, part II, vol. II, pp. 180–181.

form or, if necessary, to violent revolution. The lack of stability Cooper attributed to European oligarchies is reflected in a geometric figure he used to contrast the American and English forms of government. Both in *The Monikins* and *Gleanings: England,* he compared America and Europe to an inverted and an upright tripod. The American democracy rests on a wide, stable base of popular suffrage, from which the legislative, executive, and judicial legs all arise and balance one another. The English or European aristocracy, by contrast, has no base whatever, but is a top-heavy, unwieldy state weighing down upon its three spindly legs of king, Lords, and Commons.

Cooper projects his feelings about the course of the 1830 revolutions into the European novels. In all three tales there is a tension between Cooper's desire to assert that a new republican spirit is breaking over Europe, and his fear that this spirit will never be able to overcome the effects of centuries of aristocracy. Venice, Duerckheim, and Berne are all portrayed as differing variations of an aristocratic oligarchy seemingly on the wane. These representative European polities are all small, relatively powerless city states that are rotten from within, threatened by violence and popular insurgency. At the same time, however, they remain curiously able to resist any appreciable political progress. Precisely because their social order is so unstable, they are brutally repressive, and manage to perpetuate both aristocratic forms and aristocratic habits of mind. By portraying European political change as a doubtful possibility, rather than a triumphant certainty, Cooper sharpens the effect of his warning to American readers.

Nowhere in the European novels does Cooper suggest that human nature is different on either side of the Atlantic. The politically powerful aristocrats and bourgeoisie in the European tales, however, tend almost without exception to be deceptive, self-seeking, and unprincipled. Cooper wishes us to recognize that these qualities are the consequences of the polities under which they act. Gradenigo, Emich, Heinrich Frey, Bonifacius, and Peterchen all act for self, while maintaining a wily show of courtesies, because in Venice, Duerckheim, or Berne they have little alternative. There is no code of disinterested justice by which anyone's selfish impulses might be restrained.

The European novels are thus the most politically deterministic of Cooper's tales. Characters are defined by their relations to their surrounding polity. They can be divided into three groups: aristocrats who, exercising uneasy control of state, are living upon ancient entailment, common men that are victimized, and middle-class burghers who, climbing toward power, preach a muddled, derivative belief in hierarchy and force.[17] The aristocrat is usually corrupted, not because he possesses noble title, but because he governs a political system that is intrinsically unjust.[18] The upwardly mobile middle-class figures, Heinrich Frey and Peterchen, always remain comic because, although selfish and hypocritical, their

[17] In *Gleanings: England*, Cooper noted that "the new rich, as a body, are always found on the side opposed to popular rights" (195).

[18] Don Camillo Monforte of *The Bravo* and Baron de Willading of *The Headsman* are the only principled aristocrats in the three tales. Neither of them, Cooper emphasizes, has any part in the making of government policy.

aping of aristocratic ways is apparent to all, and they
lack ultimate power. Jacopo the bravo, Antonio, Balthazar, and Sigismund, the low-born men who are victimized, are peculiarly American figures, variants of Cooper's
democratic hero who are sacrificed to European politics.

This particular cast of character types is obviously designed for didactic novels denouncing European aristocracy. It is important to remember, however, that Cooper
is attacking aristocracy as a political, not a social institution. Cooper does not criticize Gradenigo, Emich, and de
Willading because they are aristocrats, nor does he condemn their government because they are run by men of
title. Venice, the Jaegerthal, and Berne are all condemned
because they are states in which a certain class of men
have created an aristocratic polity by restricting political
rights to their own class. That these men happen to possess noble title, and are thus aristocrats in a social sense,
is not considered blameworthy.

In all of these novels the true struggle is not between
monarchy and democracy, but between a government
that embodies constitutional rights in just laws, and
European "republics" that guarantee no individual liberties because they lack the proper statutes. *Sketches of
Switzerland* draws the distinction between the true and
false republic that is crucial to Cooper's European novels:

Political liberty does not exist in the nature of particular ordinances, but in the fact that the mass of a community, in
the last resort, holds the power of making such municipal
regulations, and of doing all great and sovereign acts, as may
comport with their current necessities. A state that set up a
dictator, so long as its people retained the practical means of
resuming their authority, would, in principle, be freer than

that which should establish a republic, with a limited constituency, and a provision against change.[19]

According to these standards, a monarchy set up by popular suffrage is freer than a "republic" in which political power is vested in a single class. "A republic, with a limited constituency, and a provision against change" accurately describes Venice in *The Bravo* and Berne in *The Headsman*. Both communities are the European foil to the widely based American republic. As examples of the false republic, Berne and Venice are intended both as an assurance and as a warning to Cooper's own countrymen—an assurance of the comparative purity of their democratic republic, and a warning against the danger of ever legally establishing the political power of the gentry. This was a position Cooper never abandoned, either for Europe or for America, until the year before his death.

Despite their many similarities in outlook and argument, the three novels do not attack the same political injustices. In each tale Cooper explores the inadequacies of a different European variant to the American republic. *The Bravo* deals with a totalitarian government that has no codified civil statutes. *The Heidenmauer* describes a province in which there is no governing power, no civil law, and no polity save anarchy. And Berne in *The Headsman* is an aristocratic polity which, unlike Venice, has civil statutes that are strictly regarded, widely enforced, but thoroughly antirepublican.

One consequence of all three polities, however, never changes. In the absence of constitutional laws that guar-

[19] *Sketches of Switzerland*, part I, vol. I, pp. 204–205.

antee personal property rights, European governments exist only as expedients for the illegitimate accumulation or illegitimate maintenance of property. Political maneuverings in Venice, Berne, and the Jaegerthal are power struggles, fought without the rules of law, for possession of property. Gradenigo, Emich, Bonifacius, and Peterchen all exemplify a generality of *The American Democrat*: "In modern aristocracies, the controlling principle is property, an influence the most corrupting to which men submit, and which, when its ordinary temptations are found united to those of political patronage and power, is much too strong for human virtue."[20] In the late 1830s and 1840s, Cooper's insistence upon American constitutional laws guaranteeing individual property rights is thus the obverse, not the reverse, of his criticism of property struggles in an aristocratic polity.

"THE BRAVO"

The setting of *The Bravo* reveals how Cooper's mind judged Europe according to cultural polarities. Venice is the exact opposite of the American neutral ground. In *The Bravo*, the formless promise of the American frontier is replaced by a dense, close, oppressive city decaying amid its wealth. The physical appearance of Venice is the perfect counterpart of its government. In Venice there is no freedom of action, no opportunity to see the divine law in nature. The city retains from the neutral ground only the inevitability of violence. Rather than reinforcing the qualities of its inhabitants, Venice determines these

[20] *The American Democrat*, p. 126.

qualities, suppressing the vital in the interest of conformity to a despotic aristocracy.

The novel is built around furtive journeys to and from St. Mark's Square, of which Cooper wrote "No other scene in a town ever struck me with so much surprise and pleasure."[21] As the novel progresses, St. Mark's Square embodies increasingly diverse qualities. A fusion of grandeur and decay, it is a place of leisure for the nobility but danger for the citizenry. The square seems the only place for open meeting, yet all communications there are fleeting and fraught with danger. The masks which all Venetians wear may assure anonymity, but most maskers in St. Mark's seem to be transacting state affairs.[22] From the square emanate the labyrinthine passageways of Venice, dark and twisting lanes that typify the nature of Venetian justice. Down them go the paid but unrecognizable agents of the aristocracy. Venice is a world in which "every fifth eye is that of a mercenary" (237). "The very marbles of the city give up their secrets to the state" (266).

Above all, St. Mark's Square leads toward that indefinable structure which is Venetian government. The doge's palace, the senate's chamber, and the prison form one continuous and inseparable complex. Architecture becomes symbolic of politics; there is no republican sepa-

---

[21] *Excursions in Italy*, p. 308.

[22] Donald Ringe connects Venetian policy to the custom of the mask: "Just as the state itself wears a mask to hide the reality from prying eyes, so also do the characters frequently go masked in the streets—a custom which alone makes life tolerable in Venice—and the rulers themselves are so well disciplined that their naked faces and avowed words conceal their inner thoughts behind a fair exterior" (*James Fenimore Cooper*, p. 59).

ration of powers in the Venetian building. Clothed in an outer show of architectural splendor and aristocratic pageantry, the interior of the complex is a maze of inseparable corridors. A series of ever-receding rooms is built for the ever-receding, but ever more powerful, series of councils. Beside this indefinable structure of government, yet detached from it, protecting the complex from directly facing the square, stands the cathedral. In *The Bravo*, religion is the buffer for the aristocracy.

Cooper later specified that "the government of Venice, strictly speaking, became the hero of the tale."[23] By "hero" he doubtless meant the chief actor, perhaps the determining force, of the entire narrative. The characters of *The Bravo* interact, not with one another, but with a nearly invisible government of which they are a part, or against which they have grievances. Maskers meet, hurriedly discuss the elusive, arbitrary policies of their government, and separate. Where the warmth of human feelings does exist—between Camillo and Violetta, Antonio and Jacopo, Jacopo and his father—that feeling consists very largely of a bond of sympathy between state victims.

Cooper unmasks the government of Venice in no uncertain terms: "Venice, though ambitious and tenacious of the name of a republic, was, in truth, a narrow, a vulgar, and an exceedingly heartless oligarchy" (166). Referring to Venice as "the self-styled Republic" (98), Cooper shows that the corruption of Venetian oligarchy depends on the fact that the aristocracy truly has no need to be more than verbally responsible to its citizenry. The

[23] *A Letter to His Countrymen*, p. 13.

aristocracy bestows graft upon all who support it and murders those who do not. It pays its patriots, sends its agents masked, and corrupts all who enter its service. Venice has a large, aristocratical senate, a Council of Three Hundred, a Council of Ten, and a doge, but all decisions are made by the Council of Three, men who are unknown and masked, men who, robed in black and crimson, pass forth unappealable decrees from the innermost chamber. Machiavellian though the Council of Three may seem, its workings closely resemble those of the French bureaus and English committees in Cooper's travel volumes.

Cooper deliberately keeps the truly heartless and powerful aristocrats as shadowy and nameless as possible. The three oligarchists that are fully characterized are not monsters of vice, but ordinary men who, once admitted to the sources of power, are turned into tools of a system they cannot understand. Soranzo and Gradenigo, senators of integrity and principle, illustrate the inevitability with which absolute power, especially in an aristocracy, corrupts those it does not destroy. Even the doge is finally revealed to be only a humane, ineffectual temporizer, a tool of the council which has coddled his ignorance and stripped him of power. A mere figurehead in the hands of the ruling aristocracy, the doge bears exactly the relation to the council that the English monarch bore, in Cooper's eyes, to the usurping nobility.[24] He represents the opposite of the firm executive power Cooper thought so essential to preservation of justice in a republic.

Cooper's means of attacking the oligarchy is to demon-

[24] *Gleanings in Europe: England*, pp. 173–174.

strate the workings of Venetian justice upon four of its
citizens: "I had it in view to exhibit the action of a narrow and exclusive system, by a simple and natural exposure of its influence on the familiar interests of life."[25]
Antonio and Jacopo are paired against Don Camillo and
Violetta in order to show that the injustices of an aristocratic polity bear equally upon the low but virtuous and
upon the very aristocracy whose interests it supposedly
is protecting. By examining the workings of justice
through its immediate effects upon a series of individuals,
Cooper judges European oligarchy by peculiarly democratic standards. Whether political justice is extended to
the individual becomes the chief criterion by which the
reader evaluates the aristocracy. The Council of Three
plainly employs any and all methods of injustice in order
to maintain power: narrow legalism upon an aristocrat,
murder for the low-born, and secret orders to a lower
court to erase a troubling scapegoat.

Cooper leads his reader to believe that Venice has but
one codified civil law, and that even this statue is mori-
bund, applied only when it is expedient. The aristocracy
has an ancient law prohibiting anyone with Venetian interests from holding or marrying outside the Venetian
state. Such a naturally unjust law preserves the self-
enclosed system of the oligarchy. Although the statute
protects Venice from outside influence, it also reinforces
the city's ingrown decline. Anxious to possess the Venetian properties of Violetta and Camillo, both of them of
Venetian nobility, the council invokes the law to pro-
hibit their marriage and deny them their property rights.

[25] *A Letter to His Countrymen*, p. 12.

Relying upon the letter of a dead law, the council then enforces it by seizure and kidnapping. The council succeeds in wresting the couple's Venetian properties to itself, yet, by driving the pair into exile, the state only deprives itself of the benefits of their services. Possessing the influence that accrues from noble title, Violetta and Camillo—and they alone—are able to withstand the tyranny of the aristocracy. The only method of survival, however, is flight.

Antonio and Jacopo serve as contrasting victims. Like Natty Bumppo in *The Pioneers* or *The Prairie*, Antonio is the aged and superficially simple commoner, a man of humble piety, competence in his natural environment, and forthright demands for absolute justice. His virtues are attributable to his closeness to the sea and distance from the city. Jacopo is astonishingly like Harvey Birch: an isolate, a martyr given to stoicism and bursts of self-pity, the scapegoat of his government, religiously devout, and dedicated to his dying father. Like Birch, Jacopo must always wear a mask and be cursed for a false identity. The heretic burial ground on the marginal sand bar is the counterpart of Birch's mountain hideaway.[26]

Yet the differences between Birch and Jacopo are equally significant. In the revolutionary war novels, the martyrdom of the democratic hero had two effects. Because the revolutionary hero was willing to maintain his principles in spite of mistreatment, his devotion and his principles acquired greater glory. Because he was mistreated and self-pitying, however, something was decidedly amiss either in him, in his cause, or in his sur-

[26] This comparison expands a suggestion made by Donald Ringe (*James Fenimore Cooper*, p. 61).

rounding society. In the European tales, the lowborn and
wronged martyrs—Jacopo, Antonio, Balthazar, Sigismund, Maso—become flatter, one-dimensional figures.
There is no problem of patriotism. The evils of aristocratic autocracy absolve the hero of complexity and reduce him to a pure victim with whom the reader is meant
entirely to sympathize.[27]

The injustices done to the two commoners are carefully constructed, not only to contrast to the lesser
wrongs done the two noblemen, but to parallel one another. Both Antonio and Jacopo become dangerous to
the aristocratic status quo, are tried by the Council of
Three, and are cold-bloodedly murdered by the state. In
each instance, the trial before the council is drawn out at
great length to reveal the depths of hypocrisy and soph-
istry that constitute Venetian justice. The members of
the council, at once crafty, garrulous, and indifferent to
all right, ostensibly refuse to pass judgment. They simply
allow Antonio and Jacopo to "incriminate" themselves,
temporize in a show of indecisive objectivity, and send a
surreptitious command to henchmen or to a lower court.
By prolonging the two trials, Cooper creates an effective
contrast to the unexpected rapidity with which Venetian

---

[27] Ringe finds *The Bravo* a greater book than *The Spy* because
its "deep insight into the moral complexities of a sophisticated
social organization" has "more significant ramifications for both
Europe and America that the ideal of simple patriotism affirmed in
the earlier tale" (*James Fenimore Cooper*, p. 61). Washington and
Birch, however, embody a quite complex definition of patriotism.
In contrasting European and American political merits, *The
Bravo* is more schematic than the novels of the American Revolution. Unlike *The Spy*, *The Bravo* is a thesis novel; its plot is
carefully shaped to argue the evil of aristocracy.

justice is actually executed. The drowning of Antonio and the beheading of Jacopo are acts of a moment: cruel, casual, and terrifyingly sudden.

The greatest horror of Venice is not the violence done the Cooper hero, but the permanence of its injustice. By victimizing Jacopo and Antonio, Cooper arouses our anger in order to refrain from releasing it. *The Bravo* concludes, not with the execution of Jacopo, but with the inevitable return to the status quo. Like the oligarchies Cooper saw in 1831, Venice is an aristocracy which may be dwindling, but is far from overthrown, and may indeed prove unchangeable. The wrongs done to Camillo and Violetta, the murders of Antonio and Jacopo, pass unredressed by the people. In a superb conclusion, Cooper describes how the beauty and the misery, the gaiety and the horror, merely resume: "Each lived for himself, while the state of Venice held its vicious sway, corrupting alike the ruler and the ruled, by its mockery of those sacred principles which are alone founded in truth and natural justice" (460).

The stagnation of Venice is the opposite of the endless social change which characterizes America in Cooper's fiction. As the setting seems to perpetuate itself without change, so does the government. In *The Bravo* Cooper repeatedly states his conviction that an oligarchy will brutalize its own people, and thus reproduce its own willing victims. An aristocratic polity perpetuates itself because it fosters the habit of deference, creates superstition and ignorance, employs shows of glitter and pageantry to dupe the people it seeks to oppress. Because Venice is a "republic," controlled by a supposedly responsible aristocracy, Venice must profess its justice with suspicious frequency; "necessity itself dictates to the oligarchist the policy of seemliness, as one of the conditions of his own safety" (170). The irony, however, is that the "policy of seemliness," based upon a clever combination of political cant, Catholicism, and a display of aristocratic pomp, is so successful.

Usually silent concerning the relevance or importance of his epigraphs, Cooper insisted, in three separate letters,[28] that "Giustizia in palazzo e pane in piazza," be included in all editions, and be included exactly. His primary intention was doubtless to direct his reader to the scene in which the fishermen, enraged by Antonio's murder, march threateningly on St. Mark's Square with the epigraph as their rallying cry. The groundswell of rebellion by the common people, and the suppression of the aristocracy, fuse in this scene that is so reminiscent of Cooper's political outlook during the early months of 1831. Within the mob, however, are qualities of the European mind which Cooper has denied to his common-sense American: a predilection to accept the sops of aristocratic cant and sham piety, weakness before a show of authority, and a lack of conceptual framework within which to express revolutionary republicanism. Having created these deficiencies, the aristocracy then uses them to quell the revolt with expected ease.

Cooper's insistence upon his epigraph surely had the additional purpose of directing the reader toward the central problem of distinguishing true from false justice. Certainly there is no "justice in the palace" and little "bread in the square." Cooper's characters continue to use

[28] *Letters and Journals*, II, 93, 102, 136.

the word "justice" until it rings with irony. Antonio's first words to the doge, "Justice!—great prince!" (116) are later paralleled by Gelsomina's plea to the doge for Jacopo's life, "Highness, I ask only for justice" (450). The doge's two replies, "Justice is the motto of Venice" (450) and "Justice and mercy are not always companions" (117), epitomize the "policy of seemliness" and the reality underneath it. Only Jacopo among Cooper's characters can possess the full awareness of the author, because only he is at once the symbol, tool, and knowing victim of the state. Using the deliberately undefined pronoun, Jacopo tells Antonio "They will pardon all but complaints against their justice. That is too true to be forgiven" (224).

Cooper elsewhere acknowledged that *The Bravo* was directed not only against ancient Venice, but contemporary France, and most specifically against the aristocrats who profited from professing republicanism in 1830. In *A Letter To His Countrymen*, Cooper stated that "the Bravo is certainly no very flattering picture for the upstart aristocrats of the new *regime*."[29] In a later preface he wrote "The work was written chiefly at Paris, where opportunity was not wanting to illustrate the subject by observing the manner in which the specious and designing trifled with the just hopes of the mass."[30]

Gleanings in Europe: France denounces the Doctrinaires in terms that could perfectly apply to the demeaning effect which the aristocracy of *The Bravo* has upon the people of Venice:

[29] *A Letter to His Countrymen*, p. 35.
[30] Second preface to *The Bravo* (London: Bentley, 1834). Quoted by Shulenberger, *Cooper's Theory of Fiction*, p. 42.

The party of the *doctrinaries* is the one that menaces the most serious evil to France. It is inherently the party of aristocracy; and, in a country as far advanced as France, it is the combination of the few, that, after all, are most to be apprehended. The worst of it is, that, in countries where abuses have so long existed, the people get to be so disqualified for entertaining free institutions, that even the disinterested and well-meaning are often induced to side with the rapacious and selfish, to prevent the evils of reaction.[31]

"The disinterested and well-meaning" could apply to Soranzo and Gradenigo as justifiably as to the French. One of the evils of aristocracy which Cooper declared *The Bravo* had exposed was "the manner in which the selfish and wicked profit by its facilities, and in which even the good become the passive instruments of its soulless power."[32] Rather than anticipating revolutionary triumph, *The Bravo* argues that, in Venice, aristocratic abuses have created a people "disqualified for entertaining free institutions."

Critics of the novel debate whether Cooper was attacking Venice, Europe as a whole, the Doctrinaires,[33] or the Whigs.[34] Nor is there any certainty exactly how Cooper intended his novels to be read in America.[35] If, however,

[31] *Gleanings in Europe: France*, p. 327.

[32] *A Letter to His Countrymen*, p. 13.

[33] James F. Beard, *Letters and Journals*, II, 4.

[34] Marius Bewley, *The Eccentric Design*, p. 61. This possibility seems especially slight. Cooper says nothing of Whiggery until his return from Europe. In the winter of 1830, Whiggery as an organized party did not exist. In arguing his case, Bewley provides a one-sided view of Gradenigo; there is more to the senator than his financial strategies.

[35] See Russell Kirk, "Cooper and the European Puzzle," *College English*, VII (1946), 199–200.

The Bravo had been confined to any specific contemporary significance, Cooper would not have created a novel quite so dark, intense, and memorable. *The Bravo* is not, ultimately, a denunciation of France, Venice, Europe, or Whiggery. The government of Venice is rather the imaginative composite of all the political forces Cooper most detested. Point by point the aristocratic oligarchy of Venice exemplifies the opposite of every quality attributed to the American republic in *Notions of the Americans.*

Venice is founded, not upon the principle of maximizing individual liberty, but upon a network of governmental agents, repression, and conformity. Rather than a minimum of protective governmental legislation, Venice does not even possess a body of civil laws to which the individual might appeal. Law is *not* sovereign, it *is* a respecter of persons, and its chief function is invasion of privacy. The American system of checks and balances has no place amid the total, arbitrary power of the Council of Three. The Venetian legislature has totally usurped all executive and judicial powers. The very building from which tyranny is dispensed is symbolic of a merging of separate functions of government.

Gullibility rather than reasonableness is the chief quality of the citizenry. In a Venetian context, individuality has no meaning. Public opinion is either created by the aristocracy, manipulated, or ignored. It cannot effect policies of government or in any way redress injustice. Popular suffrage is not only utterly foreign to such a polity; one suspects, given the nature of the Venetian commoner, that the vote would long prove ineffective as a means of reform. The decay and enclosure of Venice is the exact foil to the land of thriving rural settlements.

Throughout his career Cooper was often to return to the one reliable distinction he saw between all other types of government and the American republic: "It was the general and ancient rule that liberty existed as a concession from authority; whereas, here, we find authority existing as a concession from the ruled."[36] Venice is a fine example of the distinction; all of the evils of the Venetian government flow from the one fact that an aristocracy, vested with total power, will not find it in its interest to concede a liberty.

In final impact, *The Bravo* transcends its attack upon the injustice of European government—upon what Cooper described, in summarizing the effects of European despotisms on European courts, as "the secrecy of their proceedings, the irresponsible nature of their trusts (responsible to power, and irresponsible to the nation), and the absence of publicity."[37] Nor is the novel limited to its attempt to define the false republic. Rather, the governing principles of the Council of Three typify those of any and all governments which, as *The Bravo* declares, "set at defiance every other consideration but expediency, —all the recognized laws of God, and every principle of justice, which is esteemed among men" (170).

"THE HEIDENMAUER"

In setting *The Heidenmauer* is a deliberate contrast to *The Bravo*. Cooper is attempting to widen the scope of

[36] *The American Democrat*, p. 83.
[37] *Gleanings in Europe: France*, p. 136.

his attack on European political systems by shifting its focus. The stifling decay of Venice has been replaced by the open and sparsely settled valleys along the Rhine. *The Bravo* was timeless because the Venetian aristocracy perpetuated itself endlessly and without change. *The Heidenmauer* describes events of the early sixteenth century in order to convey the hope of progress aroused by a specific shift of government, temporal and religious. The qualities of the American neutral ground are thus recreated in sixteenth-century Germany, but the institutions that struggle for control of the neutral ground, being European, feudal, and thoroughly corrupt, allow little promise of social progress. The effect of turning from *The Bravo* to *The Heidenmauer* is, therefore, one of the unfolding of the close European environment, an unfolding that is arrested because of the anarchy produced by European political institutions.

Cooper's characteristic portrayal of large social forces through single individuals struggling for power in a symbolic setting is perfectly illustrated in *The Heidenmauer*. The neutral ground, suggestively called the Jaegerthal, is a valley bitterly disputed between its three hunters: Emich of Leiningen, the medieval Baron, Bonifacius, the medieval abbot, and Heinrich Frey, the medieval burgher. Each of these representative figures controls a dwelling which becomes the symbol of his institution. The Benedictine Abbey of Limburg and the Castle of Hartenburg are juxtaposed by being situated on facing hills, whereas Heinrich Frey, burgomaster of the town of Duerckheim, lower than either in setting and in power, is caught between the two forces. Berchthold, follower of the heretic Luther, does not yet have a dwelling, but must use and be used by Emich in the struggle between monk and baron.

By means of the three dwellings and four figures, Cooper damns European political injustice in a polity dramatically different from the autocracy of Venice. The perpetual warfare, open or clandestine, between baron, abbot, and burgher illustrates how, in the absence of a single, established governing force, the resulting vacuum of power will lead to the disintegration of social order. The absolute depotism of the Council of Three and the anarchy of the Jaegerthal yield the same results: popular ignorance, obeisance to corrupt powers, and hunger for property. Cooper describes the Jaegerthal as a region lacking both the "frank and just institutions" and "the majesty of the law" (188–189) that are inherent in a constitutional republic.

The need for firm republican law is pointed up by the failure of the Holy Roman Empire. An established hierarchy of emperor, elector, abbot, baron, and burgomaster theoretically exists in the valley (65). Though characters appeal to the hierarchical structure as a defense, the civil forces of the Empire are present only momentarily and withdraw from the abbey before it is sacked. Designed to create stability through reciprocal duties, the hierarchy produces petty jealousies of station that end in warfare. A chief criticism leveled at the Empire is its failure to separate church and state, its "unnatural union between secular and religious power" (103). Because Abbot Bonifacius is a political figure, principles of divine justice are misused or ignored. Because Count Emich must support the church, he becomes contemptuous of its powerlessness.

Gaining power in the Jaegerthal demands that one be able to adapt both to the neutral ground and to the Holy Roman Empire. The successful monk, baron, and burgomaster are all accordingly cut from the same mold. Each of them professes to follow the accepted ideals of conduct for his particular station, but each acts solely for economic gain. Although an elaborate display of surface respect is necessary to one's superior in the hierarchy, true deference would be suicidal. Bonifacius, Heinrich, and Emich all act for self, using penitence, faith, alcohol, mercenaries, bribery, superstition—anything that will serve their wary drive to dominate. At every point in the action, their principles give way to greed or to the need for defensive attack.

Cooper's condemnation of the social and moral consequences of a weak, aristocratic hierarchy is unequivocal. The meaning of the historical change he has invoked, however, is much debated. To Spiller, the sacking of the abbey by count and burgher shows "the effect of Lutheranism in liberating the mind of man from superstition, and the social order from corruption."[38] Kirk believes that Cooper was portraying only a substitution of "King Log for King Stork,"[39] and Bewley implies that the change was in fact a regression "from the world of the imagination to the world of profit."[40] Beard, however, refers to Cooper's "chronicling synoptically in *The Heidenmauer* the birth of European freedom."[41] Arguing a more moderate interpretation Dekker concludes that the tale illus-

[38] *Fenimore Cooper: Critic of His Times*, p. 220.
[39] "Cooper and the European Puzzle," p. 204.
[40] *The Eccentric Design*, p. 56.
[41] *Letters and Journals*, II, 121.

trates "the slow yet certain progress of civilization."[42]

These differing judgments surely reflect the tension between Cooper's desire to praise the political progress of Europe and his doubts that such progress had ever truly been significant. As in all three European tales, Cooper allows his doubt of progress to emerge more strongly as the novel progresses. The era and the plot Cooper chose for his tale allowed him to evoke at the outset his American reader's assumption of beneficial social change. During the early Reformation, Bonifacius and the Benedictines are decisively driven from the valley. After the abbey is destroyed, anarchy is finally ended by an alliance between count and town. When the Lutheran hero marries the burgomaster's daughter, and thereby gains respectability and power, the tale seems a Protestant's dream. The nobility, the middle class, and Lutheranism all gain at the expense of the Catholic Church.

Cooper may have evoked these stereotyped historical responses in order to challenge them. The abbey is not destroyed by principled, oppressed Protestants, but by greedy citizens indifferent to religion but alive to power. The three most sympathetic and principled characters in the tale, Ulricke, Odo the penitent, and Father Arnolph, are all staunchly devout Catholics. No novel trying to argue a case for progress would conclude with a benevolent and pious monk pointing to a cross on a remote mountain and sadly saying that the unapproachable cross is "the type of God's durable justice" (424).

If Cooper had been primarily interested in portraying

[42] *James Fenimore Cooper*, p. 135.

the shift of power, he surely would have ended his novel with his climactic scene, the sacking of the abbey. By extending the novel far beyond the destruction of Limburg, Cooper shows his reader the guilt and apprehension within the pillagers, the lingering susceptibility to Catholic superstition in Emich, and the near recapture of authority by the Benedictines.

In final effect *The Heidenmauer* is nearly the reverse of a straightforward tale celebrating the breakup of feudal hierarchy. Cooper has recorded the surface evolution of a Protestant society, in order to reveal how, underlying any change of government, there remains the unchanging nature of the European mind. Perhaps the early Reformation has been selected in order to demonstrate how thoroughly ingrained in feudalism the European mind has become, and how difficult it is, therefore, to eradicate the habit of deference. At the conclusion of his novel, Cooper states his purpose:

Our object has been to show, by a rapidly-traced picture of life, the reluctant manner in which the mind of man abandons the old, to receive new, impressions—the inconsistencies between profession and practice—the error in confounding the good with the bad, in any sect or persuasion—the common and governing principles that control the selfish, under every shade and degree of existence—and the high and immutable qualities of the good, the virtuous, and of the really noble. (464)

No mention is made of Luther, of the breakdown of feudalism, or of any triumph over a corrupt, degrading church.

The thirty-page introduction to *The Heidenmauer*, in which Cooper seems simply to be rehearsing the movement of his ménage from Paris to Duerckheim and re-

counting the source of his tale, is crucial to the larger
meaning of the novel's events. The introduction places
the Jaegerthal in its properly small perspective. From
contemporary Paris, which Cooper describes as the city
of all paradoxes, we move to an isolated valley, a province
whose "surface is about equal to two-thirds of that of
Connecticut" (xix). After witnessing the evidences of
Belgium's present revolt, Cooper simply introduces his
fireside tale of the long ago. The problem of connecting
the past of Duerckheim to the revolutionary present of
Paris or Belgium is posed, but its solution is left to the
reader. In retrospect, the connection might be that the ingrown habits of the feudal mind survive all European
revolutions and impede republican changes, in 1830 as
in 1530.

The introduction tells of Cooper's thoughts while resting on the top of the Teufelstein, overlooking the past
and present of Duerckheim. Only as the reader returns
to this scene after completing the tale does the irony of
Cooper's plot become fully apparent. The baronial line of
Emich of Hartenburg, whose triumph is the ostensible
subject of the tale, fell from power during the French
Revolution. The fall of the barony during the Napoleonic
Wars is not, however, a cause of rejoicing. Napoleon,
whom Cooper consistently denounced as a tyrant and
false liberator, is but one of a long line of conquerors.
Looking upon the Heidenmauer, Cooper ruminates on
the succession of triumphs which the walls have witnessed. The history of the Jaegerthal seems to illustrate
little but an endless sequence of waves of futile conquest,
from primitive hunter, to Roman, to Charlemagne, to
the Church, to the nobility, and to Napoleon. The gutted,

heathen walls, which provide the novel its title, have hardly any connection with the narrative. They are, however, a fitting symbol for Cooper's view of the historical course of European politics—change without progress.

"THE HEADSMAN"

Venice, a despotism without civil laws, had been followed by the Jaegerthal, a self-destructive anarchy of feudal institutions. *The Headsman* completes Cooper's judgment upon Europe by denouncing the third possible alternative to American republicanism. Like Venice, Berne is a false republic because it represents property and has no suffrage. Unlike Venice, however, Berne is governed by self-righteous burghers and by civil laws of aristocratic entailment which are rigidly defined, widely publicized, and strictly enforced.

The laws of Berne are not the focus of attack because they are rigid, nor because they are created by men of title. The holding of vast properties by the Swiss aristocracy is never criticized; the nobleman, Baron de Willading, is a fallible but decent person. Cooper's way of attacking aristocratic oligarchy is to seek out the most noxious example of aristocratic entail and perpetuate that entail through an unchangeable civil law. The Council of Three and the powers of Duerckheim retained the ability but not the will to change. Berne is a polity frozen in the legal abuses of its own past. By emphasizing the irony of the community's terming itself a republic, while unjustly enforcing ancient and aristocratic legal statutes, Cooper is in fact returning to the concerns that haunt his European experience: the difficulty of eradicating aristocratic principles, the abortive attempt to establish republican institutions, and the warning to his countrymen in the true republic.

After reading *The Headsman*, it is surprising to learn that Cooper was comparatively complimentary to the polity of Berne in his travel writings. A passage from *Sketches of Switzerland* describes Berne as a small but powerful canton, "the most important of the sisterhood," a center of commerce fiercely defended and tightly ruled. Although Berne, like Venice and Duerckheim, seems to breed a dread of inquiry and to shackle thought, Cooper approves the visible order of its government, its well-executed laws, and small taxation. Because of these qualities, all of which are common to Cooper's ideal republic, he calls Berne "the most just and most moderate of all the governments of this form [aristocracy] that have existed in modern times."[43]

Despite its merits, Berne remains to Cooper a bogus republic. Its ruling Bürgerschaft is an hereditary aristocracy combining two separable evils. Obviously, Berne is an aristocratic polity because it legalizes the power of the nobility. The aristocrats of the surrounding countryside have a legal right to join the Bürgerschaft for their self-protection. Once within the Bürgerschaft, the right of membership in that "republican" institution is hereditary. Berne is also an aristocracy in Cooper's strictly political definition of that term. Any wealthy man, of whatever class, may buy a seat in the Bürgerschaft; the few rule without recourse to the people. Both socially and

---

[43] *Sketches of Switzerland*, part I, vol. I, pp. 46, 52.

politically, Berne is a "venerable seat of aristocracy in the shape of the *Bürgerschaft*." Cooper remarks that "as these burghers were comparatively few and the right was hereditary, the government of the canton is strictly an aristocracy."[44]

The criticisms of *Sketches of Switzerland* are wholly applicable to *The Headsman*. A predominately middle-class government, Berne's republicans pay homage to the remains of its social aristocracy. The burghers uphold all laws of feudal privilege because the Bürgerschaft itself is maintained by such a law. The characters of *The Headsman* vacillate between aristocratic concepts that feed their self-interest and republican sentiments they know to be naturally just. Because they feel a lurking guilt over the government from which they profit, they insist the more rigorously upon the letter of its laws.

Cooper cites but one law of aristocratic entailment, allows it to represent the body of Bernese law, and builds his novel around it. At first glance, the fact that the office of executioner in Berne is hereditary, has legally fallen upon a fine man, and has caused him to be ostracized without recourse, seems a slight basis upon which to attack an entire government, let alone the gamut of European aristocracies. The law of hereditary headsmanship gains wider significance, however, because it is a parallel to the law of aristocratic entailment by which the Bürgerschaft perpetuates itself. The civil law fixes lucrative aristocratic privileges upon one burgher and the office of headsman upon another. Cooper continually returns to the damning

[44] *Sketches of Switzerland*, part I, vol. I, pp. 48, 52.

contradiction that the headsman, because he holds the most ancient and legitimate office in Berne, is the most accursed and shunned of its citizens.

Balthazar the headsman, like Jacopo, is the scapegoat of an aristocratic oligarchy, an assassin who not only carries out legal executions, but bears the entire public disapproval of them. Unlike Jacopo, however, the bravo of *The Headsman* has long held the legal sanction along with the moral disapproval of his state. The legality of the office of headsman increases our horror of aristocratic entailment, but also allows the victims outwardly to protest against a specific law in ways that Antonio and Jacopo never could have dared. Balthazar identifies himself to the burgomaster: "Herr Bailiff, I am by inheritance the last avenger of the law" (290). Sigismund, Balthazar's son, turns the language of aristocracy savagely upon himself: "I, too, have now a narrow monopoly of all the honors of our house!" (196). Later he bluntly states that "Our origin is a curse entailed by the ruthless laws of the land" (248). His sister Christine acknowledges the total power the law exerts upon her family: "We are what we seem in the eyes of others, because the law makes it so" (432–433).

The Headsman draws a crucial, subtle distinction between social and political aristocracy. Berne is a political aristocracy because the few rule, but the political aristocrats are middle-class burghers. Baron de Willading, the representative nobleman of the tale, does not actively participate in the Bürgerschaft and seems to exercise little power in Berne itself. Peter Hofmeister, an officious town merchant, has been appointed bailiff, presides over the Abbaye, and is an associate justice at the final trial. The nouveau riche, not the noblemen, represent the political aristocracy of Berne. Like the gentry in later American tales, the nobility of Berne are becoming peripheral figures who hold power in name but not in fact.

Cooper points out that the shift in political power ironically results in no change in political belief. Peter Hofmeister's politics are more aristocratic than de Willading's. Only a burgher and proud of it, Peter is nonetheless a sycophant to the nobility, bowing to the wishes of Willading and Grimaldi at every turn. Insisting upon authority and respectability to the detriment of justice, Hofmeister bustles importantly but avoids decision. He condemns education, literacy, and any semblance of political change, yet continues to profess republicanism. His conception of government is that its first and only obligation is to protect itself. Bloated with being Hofmeister, Bailiff of Vevey, Peter is, nevertheless, only Peterchen.

In those few moments when Peterchen is not amusing, he is thoroughly detestable. In the person of Hofmeister, the Berne Bürgerschaft precipitates the catastrophe of the novel. While presiding at the Abbaye des Vignerons, Peterchen is forced to pass judgment upon a young man who has refused to marry the headsman's daughter because her family origin has been publicly proclaimed. Ignoring the fact that Colis, the groom, has legally executed the marriage contract, Peterchen yields to the popular prejudice against Balthazar by allowing the groom to renounce the headsman's daughter. Peterchen then shuns responsibility by claiming a patently false justification: "If Jacques Colis will none of thy girl, I have not the power to make him" (299). Pandering to misguided public sentiment, Peterchen has committed injustice because of his own weaknesses.

Before the Abbaye is concluded, the bailiff commits a second injustice by freeing Conrad, an unruly commoner, from the charge of assaulting the law. In so doing, Peterchen only liberates a criminal to commit murder. Having twice yielded to the pressure of prejudice, popular and aristocratic, Peterchen closes the Abbaye with a eulogy of Berne as "a paragon of a community" (306).

We openly and loudly profess great truth and equality before the law, saving the city's rights, and to take holy, heavenly, upright justice for our guide in all matters of theory. (306)

A minute later, when speaking to Sigismund of the strength of aristocratic prejudice, Peterchen states, "while I adore justice, Herr Sigismund, as becomes a bailiff, I confess to both prejudice and partiality, mentally considered" (306). Peterchen's presence in the novel argues the need for that firm, disinterested sense of justice which Cooper finds so incompatible with an aristocratic polity.

The climactic scene of *The Headsman* is, almost inevitably, an extended trial. Peterchen's false judgments lead directly to the murder of Jacques Colis. The failure of earthly justice thus gives way to a contrasting trial in which Cooper forces his reader to expect, at last, judgments according to divine law. The murder is to be tried in an Augustinian convent amid Alpine grandeur, "the most elevated habitable abode in Europe" (390). The nature of the trial "had induced the monks to select the chapel of the convent for the judgment hall" (419). The Augustinians, whom Cooper portrays as pious men whose "convent has been founded in charity" (393), are declared at the outset to possess "civil jurisdiction in such cases as required a prompt exercise of justice" (384). In such a convent, removed in time, location and political affiliation from any taint of aristocratic law, the godly father Xavier shall try a case in which inherent class prejudices and aristocratic laws of entailment have presumably led to murder.

The divine justice we have been led to anticipate is immediately perverted. Into the judgment chapel creep unexpected civil authorities, Peterchen and the châtelaine of Valais, who proceed to usurp the place of the priestly judges and to frustrate all possibility of judgment according to divine law. The châtelaine intervenes to act as a judge—presumably because his authority is only slightly less illegitimate than Peterchen's. While describing the châtelaine's character, Cooper draws the inevitable comparison; the châtelaine is "a grave ponderous dignitary of justice, of German extraction, like [Peterchen]" (416).

Peterchen and the châtelaine conduct a trial that violates every right of a defendant. The reader quickly realizes that both men are anxious to find any victim whose guilt will not reflect discredit upon the baron or the Bürgerschaft. By delivering a prompt and distant judgment on a criminal, the ill effects of the law entailing the headsman may remain unexposed.

The châtelaine's first ploy is to harass Balthazar into an admission of guilt. The headsman is assumed to be guilty until he proves himself innocent. Failing in this attempt, the châtelaine then badgers Marguerite and Christine by forcing them to examine Colis' body. Obtaining no admission from anyone, the judge transfers his interrogation to Maso and proceeds by an equally unfair mode of questioning. False circumstantial evidence is cited as the proof by which Maso is to be hanged. The châtelaine and Peterchen, parading their mutual respect, concur that justice must be speedily executed. Conrad, the murderer, is dismissed and Maso ordered into irons. Through Marguerite, Cooper passes judgment upon the corruption of divine law that has occurred even at the remotest height of Valais: "The judgment-seat hath fallen to the lot of the corrupt and designing" (428). "Here is thy boasted justice! Thine own laws are brought in support of thine own oppression" (429).

Ironically, the rapidity with which Peterchen and the châtelaine wish falsely to prosecute Maso becomes the means of bringing forth the truth. Reduced to his last defenses, Maso reveals that he is the bastard of Grimaldi, who in turn is the doge of Genoa. Artificial though these revelations may seem, they serve Cooper's theme. Having condemned Maso as a convenient scapegoat, the two justices must confront the fact that their lowborn victim is actually the son of nobility. Maso, however, is realist enough to know that only these irrelevant revelations may gain him immunity. Peterchen and the châtelaine, true to the burgher's deference to the aristocracy, simply withdraw from all judgment, yielding Maso his freedom, not because Maso is guiltless (which he is), but because Maso is the doge's son. All semblance of a trial is speedily and conveniently forgotten. Justice proceeds on no other grounds than respect for social rank.

The parallel revelation, that Sigismund is no child of Balthazar, but the son of the doge of Genoa, is equally forced, but does not serve Cooper's theme. Sigismund, who had been cast as the lowborn, heroic figure, who had upheld a natural aristocracy and detested social title, marries the baron's daughter and quietly accepts all the favors of a social aristocracy. Sigismund's noble qualities, Cooper thus implies, have aristocratic rather than natural origins. An implausible discovery has been used to force a comic ending.

As the critics of the novel have repeatedly shown, the discovery of Sigismund's true origin can be defended neither on artistic nor thematic grounds.[45] It is important to recognize, however, that the ending represents a social not a political statement. Cooper's class beliefs have led him to turn the commoner into a nobleman, marry like to like, and buttress the social aristocracy; he even associates natural merit with noble title. But the ending does not in any way affect our feelings about the civil laws of entailment that unalterably settle upon Balthazar, Peterchen, and de Willading different political and social rights. Cooper's approval of social aristocracy is kept quite distinct from his disapproval of a political aristocracy. It is misleading of Dekker to argue that "despite the author's good intentions, *The Headsman* turns into an argument for a hereditary aristocracy."[46]

Whether deliberately or by chance, Cooper's incongruous ending allows him to conclude his novel without any promise of political change in Berne. Before the final revelation, both Adelheid and the baron had become guiltily aware that false laws of entailment had unjustly

[45] Grossman, *James Fenimore Cooper*, pp. 81–84; Ringe, *James Fenimore Cooper*, pp. 64–68; Dekker, *James Fenimore Cooper*, pp. 138–140.

[46] *James Fenimore Cooper*, p. 139.

stigmatized Sigismund. The ending eliminates the significance of their new awareness and makes any actions for political change unnecessary. Accordingly, the resolution of the novel returns Berne to the status quo. The office of hereditary headsman simply remains, unfilled but tolerated. Peterchen apparently retains his power with the blessings of all. Like *The Bravo* and *The Heidenmauer*, *The Headsman* raises the possibility of change within European aristocratic polities in order finally to deny it.

The Headsman clearly reveals that Cooper attacks European nobility only when nobility is granted special political privileges. Although Cooper's social values assimilate European aristocrats quite easily, his political values remain wholly republican, for Europe as well as for America. Cooper takes no exception to Europeans' retaining noble title, but politically he was convinced that "the hereditary principle, as extended beyond the isolated abstraction of a monarch, is offensive to human pride, not to say natural justice."[47]

ITALY

Upon his return to America, after writing *A Letter to His Countrymen* and completing *The Monikins*, Cooper devoted his energies to revising and reordering his European journals and letters into a set of volumes which would be, at once, a chronological portrait of the tour of his ménage, and the American democrat's assessment of Europe. The initial volumes on France and England are expectedly acid in tone and consciously republican in

[47] *Gleanings in Europe: England*, p. 185.

value. Like the three novels and the original letters, these volumes praise the natural and artistic beauties of Europe, reveal a respectful curiosity toward European nobility, but remain consistently critical of the political structure of the Old World. The concluding volume of the series, however, seems the work of a different author assessing a different continent by different standards.

Excursions in Italy is a work of personal nostalgia that turns into a cultural reevaluation. Like its three predecessors, it pulls America and Europe into two contrasting archetypes. No longer, however, does Cooper set aristocratic oppression against the free and growing republic. Rather we see Cooper's love for the sleepy indolence, the warmth, and the measured forms of Italian life. America, by contrast, is the plain land of the dollar.

Unlike Cooper's novels about Europe, *Excursions in Italy* declares that the European continent is progressing steadily toward enlightenment, its general level of intelligence advancing, its prejudices and oppressions fast disappearing.[48] Most importantly, the beneficial changes occurring in Europe are stabilized by popular respect for tradition and for the refinements which the past has everywhere left visible.

In a four-page contrast between Rome and New York we see most clearly the new alignment Cooper has made of the values of Europe and America.[49] Rome is one of the many capitals that give Italy its ordering centers of tone and elegance. New York, by contrast, is only the largest mart of a land composed of vulgar, commercial

[48] *Excursions in Italy*, pp. 49–50.
[49] *Excursions in Italy*, pp 270–274.

towns. Rome—settled, tasteful, looking backward to a great past—clings to the fineness of its traditions. New York, however, anticipates a doubtful future; its boasts can only be of prosperity, gain, and tasteless expansion. The Roman's sense of communal pride contrasts with the lonely self-seeking bred into transient New Yorkers.

Cooper was to project these rather Jamesian cultural standards into later social novels about America. His realignment of European values remains, however, a social not a political reevaluation. *Excursions in Italy* does not extend its praise of European culture to praise of aristocratic polity. Although Cooper's European years had given him a great appreciation for cultural values that America sadly lacked, they had also taught him how thoroughgoing a republican he truly was. Read as a whole, Cooper's European writings reveal that, in his judgment, an ideal nation would retain the cultural advantages of an aristocracy within political institutions that were fully republican. This was an intricate but fully consistent standard that Cooper was to continue to apply to America. In 1838, however, Cooper's countrymen were in no mood to make such subtle distinctions about Cooper's writings. Because Cooper was beginning to criticize American cultural deficiencies, they assumed that he was becoming politically "aristocratic." Conversely, because America seemed in many ways crude and provincial, Cooper looked back at his always beloved Italy with increasing nostalgia.

4. The Conservative Democrat in Templeton

> The moment the idea is admitted into so-
> ciety that property is not as sacred as the
> laws of God, and that there is not a force
> of law and public justice to protect it,
> anarchy and tyranny commence.
> JOHN ADAMS,
> *A Defence of the Constitutions of Gov-
> ernment*

THE FACTORS that led Cooper to become so critical of America upon his return are varied and interwoven. Exposure to European culture surely made him more conscious of American provincialism and American mediocrity. On the other hand, the America of 1833 was markedly different from the land Cooper had left seven years previously. Although he returned with a predisposition to criticize, he also faced unexpected national developments that in his judgment needed censure. The change, therefore, was both in America and in Cooper's attitudes toward America; the change was not, however, in the republican political principles by which America was being judged.

Between 1825 and 1840 New York State was undergoing something like a social revolution. The Templeton of *The Pioneers* and the agrarian dream of *Notions of the Americans* were rapidly disappearing. The comple-

tion of the Erie Canal and the beginnings of railroad em-
pires eased social mobility while they accelerated the pace
of life. Waves of European immigrants, many of them
poor, Catholic, and unable to speak English, were crowd-
ing into New York City and spreading slowly upstate
where they met immigrant Yankees moving west. Land
speculation in the late 1820s and early 1830s was fever-
ish; by 1830 Albany was the seventh largest city in the
country. Cotton mills and textile factories had by 1833
become an important part of the economy of the Mohawk
Valley. The trade union movement began to develop in
the early 1830s, at the same time that large numbers of
bank charters were issued. Old Federalists tended to
become Whig manufacturers while the agrarian gentry
declined in power. Six months after Cooper's return, during his first journey to Cooperstown, he confessed that
"Every hour I stay at home, convinces me more and
more, that society has had a summerset, and that the élite
is at the bottom!"[1] In upcountry New York even religion
was changing. Mrs. Abbot, Cooper's caricature of a fundamentalist in *Home As Found*, reminds us that by 1838
central New York State was already becoming the
"Burned Over District," much to the amusement of one
gentleman in Cooperstown.[2]

[1] *Letters and Journals*, III, 42.

[2] My summary of historical changes is drawn from the following sources: Dixon Ryan Fox, *The Decline of Aristocracy in the
Politics of New York* (New York, 1965), pp. 302–380; Samuel
Eliot Morison, "The Empire State, Citadel of Democracy, 1820–
1860" in *The Oxford History of the American People* (New York,
1965), pp. 485–499; Arthur M. Schlesinger, *The Age of Jackson*
(Boston, 1945), pp. 177–209.

These changes in New York State were, as Morison argues, a mirror of national changes. The growing political and economic power of manufacturers, cities, immigrant and labor groups was distressing to men of Cooper's social and cultural assumptions. Van Wyck Brooks describes the years from 1830 to 1850 as the era of Sam Slick and go-aheadism, an age of bumptious over-confidence in which disappearance of class lines was accompanied by vast expansion of commerce and transportation.[3] The depression year of 1837 reminds us, however, that it was also a time of over-speculation in paper credits and land values. One less dramatic change would surely have been equally significant to Cooper. In 1835 Chief Justice Taney succeeded Chief Justice Marshall, thus bringing the Supreme Court into an era in which the community's right to general welfare took precedence over the individual's right to property.[4]

We must also acknowledge, however, that when Cooper returned to face these changes, he was primed to find fault. He was convinced that his country had repudiated his European efforts because the majority of Americans either could not or would not condone true republican principles. In the muted and embarrassed acknowledgment of *Notions of the Americans*, in Cassio's review of *The Bravo*, in an anonymous review of *The Heidenmauer*, and in adverse criticism of his part in the Finance Controversy, Cooper rightly detected a persistent deference to aristocratic political thought, not only in the American

[3] Van Wyck Brooks, *The World of Washington Irving* (New York, 1944), pp. 399–425.
[4] Schlesinger, *The Age of Jackson*, pp. 324–326.

press, but in the populace.[5] In July of 1832, having just completed *The Heidenmauer*, Cooper acknowledged in an ironic outpouring to Horatio Greenough the emotions with which he contemplated returning to America:

> I think of going home in October, with Morse. In order to insure myself a reception that shall not be mortifying, I have serious thoughts of writing an essay on the beauties of Aristocracy, and on the blessings of exclusiveness in religion, politicks, and trade, the whole to finish with an eulogium on the private character of the House of Brunswick. By puffing it myself, in the Quarterly, and forming an intimacy with all the bitterest enemies of America and of American principles, it is not improbable that all I have hitherto done on the other side of the question may be overlooked.[6]

When both press and readers seemed willing not only to copy but to believe European or aristocratic reviews of his novels, Cooper concluded that the republic was betraying its most basic principles. The European novels had been written explicitly to eradicate from the American mind that very deference to aristocracy which now, ironically, was denying Cooper's novels their fair hearing.

Cooper's predisposition to detect an American aristocratic conspiracy against true republicanism found striking confirmation in the state of national politics upon his return. The evils of party conflict—between Democrat and Whig, Jackson and Congress—had ended the socalled "era of good feelings." The executive's right to use the veto, the executive's attempt to collect due naval reparations from France, and the executive's right to dis-

---

[5] See Dorothy Waples, *The Whig Myth of James Fenimore Cooper* (New Haven, 1938), pp. 75–78, 90, 100–102.

[6] *Letters and Journals*, II, 268.

miss his own appointee, were all being challenged by a congressional faction which, in Cooper's view, represented a composite of political evils. Cooper increasingly detested the Whigs because they represented to him the moneyed, commercial classes some of whom, like many of the Federalists, wished to confine political representation to propertied wealth.[7] Whigs were loose constructionists for the sake of party because they had censured the executive only to discredit Jackson.[8] They were deferential to aristocratic thought, weak in foreign policy, and motivated by political expediency rather than political principle. To Cooper, the congressional Whigs were the French Doctrinaires in another guise. *A Letter to His Countrymen* makes the connection explicit: "I knew that there existed at home a large party of *doctrinaires*, composed of men of very fair intentions, but of very limited means of observation, who fancied excellencies under other systems."[9] Upon returning from Europe in 1789, Thomas Jefferson had been horrified by the Federalists, whom he considered to be monarchists and Anglophiles, who were more aristocratic in their politics than Europeans, but who were, he thought, preparing to subvert a

[7] Cooper called the Whigs "much the falsest and most dangerous association of the sort that has appeared in the country in my day" (*Letters and Journals*, IV, 473). In 1835 he wrote Shubrick that Whiggery was an "UnAmerican principle" and that its "course, if successful, would completely subvert the most important feature of the Constitution" (*Letters and Journals*, III, 177). Cooper's tendency to see the Whigs as a reincarnation of the Federalists' longing for political aristocracy is clearly implied in *Sketches of Switzerland*, part I, vol. II, p. 158.

[8] *Letters and Journals*, III, 94–103.

[9] *A Letter to His Countrymen*, p. 15.

republican government.[10] Forty-five years later, James Fenimore Cooper, who had been reading Jefferson's letters in Europe, was to have very similar suspicions of the Whigs.

Cooper's initial defense against Whiggery was to write the A.B.C. Letters for the *Evening Post*. The ostensible purposes of these letters were threefold: to support Jackson's insistence upon naval reparations from France, to support Jackson's removal of funds from the Second Bank, and to condemn the congressional censure of Jackson. The underlying purpose of the A.B.C. Letters, however, was to insist upon strict construction of the Constitution. The A.B.C. Letters accused Congress of violating constitutional checks and balances when it overstepped its authority by censuring Jackson's withdrawal of funds. Cooper argues that article II, section II, clause II of the Constitution empowers the executive to remove as well as appoint such federal officers as Jackson's Secretary of the Treasury, William J. Duane. Jackson's decision to attack the Second Bank is defended, not on grounds of financial merit, but on grounds of constitutional legality. By refusing to cooperate with the president's demands for reparation, the Congress was blatantly disregarding the provisions of a legal treaty.[11]

The distinction between the obvious and the underlying purposes of these letters is important. Cooper is concerned with party warfare insofar as the Constitution is affected or violated. Unlike most Jacksonians, Cooper

[10] See Jefferson's letter "To the President of the United States," May 23, 1792.

[11] *Letters and Journals*, III, 61–139.

does not blame the monster Bank for sins against the republic. Throughout the 1830s, Cooper is comparatively silent about the most heated issues of his day: the Bank, hard money, the tariff, internal improvements, and slavery. He writes of these issues because larger considerations of respect for law and survival of the Constitution are at stake. Cooper is distressed by American concern with secondary issues when the underlying legal and political framework of the nation is endangered. His characteristic attitude toward this reversal of priorities is expressed in a letter of 1834 to a Yale classmate: "We have a vast deal of party politics without, I firmly believe I say truth, a single statesman in the whole country. I have not met a single man, since my return, who appears to me to have thoroughly examined the Constitution."[12]

Cooper's angry contempt for Whiggery and his consistent approval of the measures of the Democratic party logically led him to admire Andrew Jackson both in character and in principle.[13] Jackson's military achievements in the War of 1812 aroused Cooper's lifelong admiration for patriotic heroism. The bluntness of word and deed, the willingness to offend in defense of principle, and the moral finalities of Andrew Jackson appealed strongly to Cooper's love of plain dealing. As a representative of the common man, Jackson struck out at moneyed interests which Cooper had always detested. Cooper's beliefs in a strong executive, strict construction and frugal gov-

[12] *Letters and Journals,* III, 58.
[13] Cooper's most forthright commendations of Jackson are the following passages: *Letters and Journals,* I, 402, 411; II, 78; *Letter to General Lafayette,* p. 38; *Excursions in Italy,* p. 187 n.

ernment found their exemplar in Jackson. As a national leader, Jackson seemed to Cooper to embody the moral virtues of the old rural republic, a government of equal rights and severely restricted authorities.[14]

Although Cooper's support of Jackson was real and ungrudging, he never responded to Jackson as warmly as he did to Washington, Lafayette, Jay, or Jefferson. Unquestionably, Jackson's lack of gentlemanly breeding contributed to Cooper's refusal ever to idealize Jackson as a standard of political truth. Even more important, however, was Cooper's fear of the influence of Jackson's presidency upon the conduct of republican politics. The visible beginnings of the spoils system and rotation in office foreboded ill to the politics of principle. By readily accepting the machinery of party, Jacksonians seemed to Cooper to have dealt a heavy stroke to a manly independence of judgment. In *The Monikins*, these fears surface in direct, bitter satire. A less obvious measure of Cooper's reservations about the effect of the Old Hero is the demagogue of his later fiction, who mouths a debased version of Jacksonian ideas of popular virtue.[15]

Cooper's effort to separate Jackson the man from

[14] I have followed Marvin Meyers' view of Jackson rather than the adulatory, almost New Dealish portrait of Jackson by Schlesinger. Meyers argues that Jacksonianism is a reactionary, nostalgic movement (*The Jacksonian Persuasion*, pp. 3–32).

[15] Dorothy Waples oversimplifies in referring to Cooper as "one of Jackson's inordinate admirers" and in describing Jackson as Cooper's "old idol" (*The Whig Myth*, pp. 28, 25). Moreover, Waples repeatedly implies that Cooper adopted certain political stands in the 1830s because of his loyalty to the figure of Jackson rather than to Jackson's principles. Dekker's account of Cooper's reaction to Jackson is more balanced (*James Fenimore Cooper*, pp. 141–150).

Jackson the political phenomenon was the corollary to Cooper's own attempt to serve his country as an American democrat, not a Democrat. Cooper steadfastly denied any connection with the Democratic party of New York on the grounds that "No freeman, who really loves liberty, and who has a just perception of its dignity, character, action and objects, will ever become a mere party man."[16] In 1834 Cooper insisted that he was "not a party democrat, but a real democrat."[17] Four years later, he stated "It is a very different thing to be a democrat, and to be a member of what is called a democratic party; for the first insists on his independence and an entire freedom of opinion, while the last is incompatible with either."[18]

Even if Cooper had been willing to serve as a party spokesman, he would have faced a difficult decision of loyalty on the state level. In the 1830s, New York Democrats were deeply divided between Locofoco and Hunker factions. The Locofocos, the more radical and theoretical of the groups, were closely linked with immigrants and labor, vilified the Bank and John Marshall, and supported an elective judiciary. Cooper sympathized with none of these tendencies. Many of the Hunkers, on the other hand, supported state bank charters, internal improvements, and believed in loose construction; by 1840, a goodly number of the Hunkers were willing to vote Whig.[19] Cooper's few references to the division in the

---

[16] *The American Democrat*, p. 228.

[17] *Letters and Journals*, III, 59.

[18] *The American Democrat*, p. 227.

[19] My account of party warfare among the Democrats is drawn from the following sources: Dixon Ryan Fox, *The Decline of Aris-*

Democratic ranks reveal his thoroughly expected detachment from both groups.

Thus Cooper remained convinced that personal detachment from the political battlefield was the necessary
precondition both of individual liberty and of the search
for political truth. Because he believed, on a national
level, that Democratic policies were more fully in accord
with democratic principles, he felt it his duty to give the
issues of the party the support of his pen. As soon as
Cooper did so, however, he was treated by the Whigs as
a party spokesman. One of the ironies of Cooper's career
is that novels written in the service of disinterested truth
became, after 1835, vehicles for party warfare.

The thoughtless damning of Cooper's works during
the late 1830s only proves his assertion that the spirit of
party inevitably distorts truth. Considering himself the
true American democrat, Cooper continued to denounce
principles of political aristocracy that he found within
the Whig ranks. The Whig opposition, attempting to out-
democrat the Democrats for the 1840 election, characterized Cooper as an aristocrat with foreign airs. More
importantly, the Whig press accused Cooper of being an
aristocrat because of so-called unrepublican political
principles. Stone, Webb, Weed, and Benjamin, all of
them Whig editors, wrote a joint, open letter to Cooper
for the *New World* in 1840:

You have, with malice prepense, endeavored, by exaggerated
dialogues and extravagant caricatures, so to malign and vilify
the men and women of America, in their manners, customs,
and characters, that your books should be quoted by foreign

tocracy, pp. 381–408; G. G. Van Deusen, *The Jacksonian Era*, pp.
95–103.

monarchists and aristocrats as affording evidences of the jusness of their sneers and animadversions upon republican institutions and society.[20]

Such a statement shows how the Whig editors found it convenient to confuse vital distinctions. Cooper's attacks on American social demerits are treated as if they were slurs on republican politics. Because Cooper argues that, in a democracy, the gentry should be voted into power, Cooper becomes a political oligarchist. And, because Cooper argues that the gentry are usually the natural and social superiors of the common man, Cooper becomes an aristocrat who believes in noble title. By these three distortions, Cooper was charged with betraying the very principles he had long labored to uphold. An angry counterattack was inevitable. Cooper's accusors were, in his eyes, demagogues who used egalitarian cant and false charges to gain political power for the commercial classes and their close associates, Whig editors.

Dorothy Waples has convincingly demonstrated that the distortion of Cooper's position began with reviews of the European writings but became far more abusive when Cooper directly attacked the Whigs and justified Jackson in *A Letter to His Countrymen*.[21] Although Cooper had formally and publicly ceased writing in 1834, he published two unfinished projects, *The Monikins* and the travel volumes, only to have them greeted with the same pattern of reactions: intelligent defense by the *Evening Post*, contemptuous distortion by Whig papers, and neglect by the populace he was trying to reach.

[20] The letter is reprinted in Ethel Outland's *The 'Effingham' Libels on Cooper* (Madison, Wisconsin, 1929), pp. 228–231.

[21] *The Whig Myth*, pp. 73–78, 143–156.

Cooper resumed writing new books in 1837. Fittingly, the first work he published was a textbook on American political principles entitled *The American Democrat*. In his introduction Cooper contended that his intentions in writing the book were simply "to make a commencement towards a more just discrimination between truth and prejudice" (69) and "to present to the reader those opinions that are suited to the actual condition of the country" (71). It seems more likely, however, that Cooper's declared aims conceal his desire to deliver a warning to his countrymen by grounding them in true republican principles.

Four years before writing *The American Democrat*, Cooper had laid down his pen with these words:

I have felt a severe mortification that I am to break down on the question of distinctive American thought. Were it a matter of more than feeling, I trust I should be among the last to desert my post. But the democracy of this country is in every way strong enough to protect itself. Here, the democrat is the conservative, and, thank God, he has something worth preserving. I believe he knows it, and that he will be true to himself.[22]

Thus, Cooper's decision in 1834 to cease writing should be attributed, at least in part, to his continuing faith that the American republic would maintain its greatness without the assistance of republican authors. It is only logical to assume that Cooper's decision to resume writing reflects his realization that, in the America of 1838, the democrat was not the conservative, and that what was worth preserving was in fact being threatened by self-styled democrats.

[22] *A Letter to His Countrymen*, p. 99.

"THE AMERICAN DEMOCRAT"

Cooper's treatise is not so much an exposition of political convictions as it is an attempt to deal with political dilemmas posed to the perpetuation of Cooper's ideal republic by national events and personal observations of recent years. The work cannot be viewed, as it often has been, as Cooper's definitive statement of his political feelings. Because it was designed as a formal textbook, a didactic guide to government, *The American Democrat* declares its truths with ringing finality. Yet it remains, in Cooper's canon, a transitional and unsure assessment of the national condition. In order to define these political dilemmas and to determine whether the years of absence and return had at all changed Cooper's political convictions, it is essential to compare *The American Democrat* to its forerunner, *Notions of the Americans*.

At the outset one must beware of oversimplifying the comparison. The two books were written to different audiences for different purposes. *Notions of the Americans* is designed to refute prejudicial European accounts of America—most particularly those of De Roos, Adam Hodgson, and the forthcoming *Travels* of Basil Hall.[23] *The American Democrat*, addressed to Cooper's countrymen, is a catechism in the first principles of republican politics. *Notions of the Americans* does not portray an unqualified utopia nor does *The American Democrat* resort to an easy despair. Nonetheless, there is a decided change from eulogy to fault finding, a change that is as

[23] R. E. Spiller, "Introduction" to *Notions of the Americans*, I, p. v, n. 1.

much the measure of altered intent as of darkening feelings.

The American Democrat outwardly denies none of the assertions and arguments made in *Notions of the Americans*; in fact, the later work reasserts nearly every tenet of Cooper's republican faith. Rather than contradicting or retracting statements of his earlier work, Cooper reaffirms them with crucial shifts in emphasis. Although the components and principles of Cooper's ideal republic remain unchanged, the purposes for which the principles are reaffirmed are markedly different. Cooper reacts to the thrust of recent political developments, not by altering his republicanism, but by arguing that old principles work toward more restrictive ends.

The most evident change between the two works is one of tone. An ecstatic hymn has been replaced by troubled praise. The view of America as a land of virtuous, productive farmers unhampered by the trammels of government has given way to a definition of all life as "a state of probation in which the trials exceed the enjoyments" (232). The democratic republic, formerly the measure of political integrity and the seed of endless social progress, is by 1838 viewed as but the least imperfect of three alternative polities.

Cooper's familiar insistence upon maximizing individual liberty is nowhere more forthright than in *The American Democrat*. It is in 1838 that Cooper declares "The very object of the institution [democracy] is the utmost practicable personal liberty" (153). Furthermore, liberty continues to be associated with a republic of strictly delegated powers in which the majority rules through voting for representatives (111–118). In 1838, as in 1828, Cooper argues that "By leaving to the citizen as much freedom of action and of being, as comports with order and the rights of others, the institutions render him truly a freeman" (228).

In other passages of *The American Democrat*, however, we find Cooper emphasizing longstanding constitutional limitations on popular freedom, limitations which *Notions of the Americans* had scarcely acknowledged. By 1838, evidently, the troubles created by legislative usurpation, demagoguery, rotation in office, and leveling to mediocrity had, in Cooper's view, reached such a point that he longed to curb the exercise of individual liberty that he equally longed to maintain. Hence we find Cooper insisting that the American republic proceed along a narrow and difficult path between two principles neither of which he would relinquish:

Liberty therefore may be defined to be a controlling authority that resides in the body of a nation, but so restrained as only to be exercised on certain general principles that shall do as little violence to natural justice, as is compatible with the peace and security of society. (118)

In this quotation, government according to natural justice continues to be, as always for Cooper, the ultimate good, because it approximates divine law. The means of obtaining natural justice, however, has become less clear. Majority rule is now conceived as a possible threat to natural justice rather than its civil precondition. A suspicion Cooper is reluctant to acknowledge underlies this statement—that the enactment of natural justice may necessitate strong restraints upon the majority rule of a free people. And so, faced with this difficulty, we find Cooper beginning to redefine the meaning of liberty: "Although it is true, that no genuine liberty can exist without being based on popular authority in the last resort, it is equally true that it can not exist when thus based, without many restraints on the power of the mass" (117).

True liberty, in short, exists only in the exercise of restraints. Insisting upon this maxim much more strongly than Judge Temple, Cooper sets the limits of the legal powers of the majority:

The majority rules in prescribed cases, and in no other. It elects to office, it enacts ordinary laws, subject however to the restrictions of the constitution, and it decides most of the questions that arise in the primitive meetings of the people; questions that do not usually effect any of the principal interests of life.

The majority does not rule in settling fundamental laws under the constitution; or when it does rule in such cases, it is with particular checks produced by time and new combinations; it does not pass judgment in trials at law, or under impeachment, and it is impotent in many matters touching vested rights. (113)

Here we find Cooper clinging to the utmost of liberty and to majority rule, yet desiring to confine the powers of the majority to "questions that do not usually effect any of the principal interests of life."

The second paragraph of the quotation reveals a meaningful shift in the purposes for which Cooper continues to praise the Constitution. In *Notions of the Americans*, the Constitution had been glorified because it guaranteed the natural right of the citizen against the remote possibility of oppressive government.[24] No problem of the changeability of the Constitution arose. In *The American*

[24] *Notions of the Americans*, II, 12–14.

Democrat, however, Cooper is beginning to consider the Constitution as a bulwark of protection for the individual against the body of his own nation:

The power of the people is limited by the fundamental laws, or the constitution, the rights and opinions of the minority, in all but those cases in which a decision becomes indispensable, being just as sacred as the rights and opinions of the majority; else would a democracy be, indeed, what its enemies term it, the worst species of tyranny. (155)

Thus minority rights, which are presently threatened, have become of greater concern to Cooper than majority rights, which are not. Both, however, are to be upheld. As a result, Cooper is often forced into the extremely delicate position of defending majority rule, yet simultaneously praising the Constitution, because its laws inhibit the threats of the majority.

Cooper's divided leanings concerning the merits of majority rule lead him into another dilemma. On the one hand, Cooper wishes to present the Constitution and all existing bodies of civil law as static and unchanging, as fixed and permanent defenses against those who would turn public opinion into law. At the same time, however, Cooper's devotion to and knowledge of the American polity lead him to acknowledge and to honor the changeability of law: "it is a requisite of liberty, that the body of a nation should retain the power to modify its institutions, as circumstances shall require" (111).

If the true republic is to be maintained, the Constitution cannot be changed, but unless change is permitted, the very meaning of American liberty is lost. This paradox underlies the change from ringing assertion to reluctant qualification in the statement quoted previously,

"The majority does not rule in settling fundamental laws, under the constitution; or when it does rule in such cases, it is with particular checks produced by time and new combinations." The dilemma is apparent elsewhere: "The constitution contains the paramount laws of society. These laws are unchangeable, except as they are altered agreeably to prescribed forms, and until thus altered, no evasion of them is admissable" (163). Nearly ten more years were to pass before Cooper was to acknowledge the full horror that this very problem posed to the perpetuity of his ideal republic. In Cooper's cataclysmic novel, *The Crater*, Mark Woolston decides to remain knowingly passive while demagogues, taking advantage of Mark's adherence to his Constitution's changeability, overthrow the hierarchical, landed republic that Mark and his creator had held so dear.

In *Notions of the Americans* the American republic had not been equated with perfection, but there had been no inherent or incurable flaws in its practices or ideology. *The American Democrat* announces a startling and significant change in Cooper's thinking: "the peculiar sins of a democracy must be sought for in the democratical character of the institutions" (143). The dangers to American democracy that Cooper had foreseen in 1828 had all been extrinsic limitations upon democracy: increased severity of civil law, limitations of the franchise, loss of the individual's natural and constitutional rights.[25] By 1838, however, the chief dangers are intrinsic: popular disregard for civil statutes, demagoguery, and loose construction of the Constitution.

[25] *Notions of the Americans*, II, 335–336.

Cooper's heady national faith had always been founded on confidence in the corrective power of the public will. In *The American Democrat,* however, Cooper begins to single out an uncontrollable and false public opinion as the flaw most deeply ingrained within the nation: "It is a besetting vice of democracies to substitute public opinion for law. This is the usual form in which masses of men exhibit their tyranny" (130). Recognizing, as he always had, that the constituency was the ultimate source of power in America, Cooper strikes out at the ease with which democratic institutions allow public opinion to become civil law:

The condition of this country is peculiar, and requires greater exertions than common, in extricating the mind from prejudices. The intimate connexion between popular opinion and positive law is one reason, since under a union so close there is danger that the latter may be colored by motives that have no sufficient foundation in justice. (134)

Acutely aware that the virtues of the democratic polity are posited upon an enlightened populace, Cooper berates all those who would undermine popular intelligence: "In a democracy, misleading the publick mind, as regards facts, characters, or principles, is corrupting all that is dear to society at its source, opinion being the fountain whence justice, honors, and the laws, equally flow" (177).

Fear that public opinion would override law gave rise to two problems with which Cooper's mind and writings would henceforth be preoccupied. The first is a problem of causation. Cooper was continually to alternate between two conjectures. Was public opinion being corrupted because self-seeking demagogues were deluding an intelligent constituency? Or had a debased, selfish constituency created its own demagogues in order to follow them to power? Not until Cooper was sure of the true quality of the constituency could he determine whether increased legal strictures might ever be necessary. Throughout *The American Democrat* Cooper vacillates between libertarian utterances that assume a practical, rational populace, and darker forebodings assuming that the people are credulous, selfish, and ignorant.

There also arose the problem of the method of demagoguery. If public opinion were manipulated until existing statutes were openly defied, those statutes could be invoked in a court of law, and the demagogue, assuming an honest judiciary, would be quelled. What, however, if the very forms and institutions of democracy were used by the demagogue to subvert the law? These questions, present in embryo in *The American Democrat*, were to become crucial to Cooper's later social fiction. *Home As Found* and the Littlepage trilogy deal with open defiance of the law, *The Crater* and *The Ways of the Hour* with the second, and far more troubling, question of subversion.

Either way Cooper viewed the dilemma, the demagogue had become the Achilles heel of democratic government: "The true theatre of a demagogue is a democracy, for the body of the community possessing the power, the master he pretends to serve is best able to reward his efforts" (154). Or, again, "the people are peculiarly exposed to become the dupes of demagogues and political schemers, most of the crimes of democracies arising from the faults and designs of men of this character" (128). The problem Cooper faced in assessing the constituency is clearly illustrated by these statements. The second quotation presumes a deluded but innocent populace; the first, however, implies a clever willingness to be deceived.

The demagogue was becoming a figure of such ominous import to Cooper's view of America that he felt it desirable to insert into *The American Democrat* a sketch by which he could be identified:

The demagogue is usually sly, a detractor of others, a professor of humility and disinterestedness, a great stickler for equality as respects all above him, a man who acts in corners, and avoids open and manly expositions of his course, calls blackguards gentlemen, and gentlemen folks, appeals to passion and prejudice rather than reason, and is in all respects, a man of intrigue and deception, of sly cunning and management, instead of manifesting the frank, fearless qualities of the democracy he so prodigally professes. (155–156)

It is both important and characteristic that Cooper's demagogue turns social distinctions and social prejudices to political advantage. Exactly the same methods are used by the long series of egalitarian demagogues who attempt to upset the order of the landed gentlemen in Cooper's later fiction: Steadfast Dodge, Aristabulus Bragg, Van Tassel, Jason Newcome, Seneky Newcome, and Williams. The demagogue, like the Whig, deliberately confuses social and political rights.

With the emergence of the demagogue, the vexing question posed by *The American Democrat* becomes sharply defined. Given Cooper's commitment to republican institutions, what measures will he advocate to cope with the threatening powers of the demagogue? Throughout the book Cooper suggests four methods of defense. The most obvious is control of the demagogue by swift recourse to all existing civil statutes relating to property, libel, and minority rights. This solution, advocated constantly, need not be belabored. To adopt it meant no sacrifice of any principle of Cooper's republican faith, only a shifting toward a more legalistic habit of mind.

The second method of defense is the landed gentleman, always Cooper's measure of manly virtue and social order, who, he contends, will have the intelligence and moral fibre to resist the incursions of the demagogue. Here, however, a new difficulty arises. Cooper realizes that the landed gentleman will provide a defense only if such men retain both social position and political power. By 1838 there were signs, which Cooper could not help but acknowledge, that his revered figure was losing the necessary influence.

In outline the gentleman remains the same figure whom Cooper had so highly valued in *Notions of the Americans*, yet how different the tone with which Cooper now describes him. Compare the following passages, the first from *Notions of the Americans*, the second from *The American Democrat*:

> The American who has the advantage of early association with men of breeding, and who possesses the advantages of fortune and education, occupies a station in society that the gentleman, or nobleman, of no country of different political institutions can ever fill. He sees, and knows that he exists without a superior. He has wealth, and manner, and education, and beyond this, neither he nor any of his countrymen can go. (II, 293)

> There can be no question that the educated and affluent classes of a country, are more capable of coming to wise and intelligent decisions in affairs of state, than the mass of a population. Their wealth and leisure afford them opportunites for obser-

vation and comparison, while their general information and greater knowledge of character, enable them to judge more accurately of men and measures. (113)

The earlier passage is deliberate overstatement designed to convince the European reader. The author's tone can be assured to the verge of truculence because the gentleman in America occupies the high place he merits. The later passage is equally overstated, but the cause of overstatement is special pleading. Cooper has been forced to urge that the landed class be allowed to retain the political and social preeminence which, in *Notions of the Americans*, had been assumed. A later passage in *The American Democrat* expresses Cooper's longing somewhat less delicately: "Power cannot be extended to a *caste*, without *caste's* reaping its principal benefit; but happy, indeed, is the nation, in which, power being the common property, there is sufficient discrimination and justice to admit the intelligent and refined to a just participation of its influence" (150).

Perhaps because Cooper suspects that the landed gentleman may prove an insufficient defense, he considers, with evident reluctance, two changes in his ideal polity: limitation of the franchise and repudiation of instruction —two further defenses against the demagogue.

Universal manhood suffrage, which had seemed to Cooper one of the glories of the American polity, comes under criticism. Cooper now finds dangerous what had once seemed a great benefit—the likelihood that universal suffrage makes a government more responsive to the needs of the citizenry.

The first sign of a changing attitude is Cooper's concern with defining the word "people." In *Notions of the*

Americans the word had been used loosely to mean the general populace;[26] there had been no need for a more precise definition. *The American Democrat*, however, specifies the political meaning of the term:

> In a political sense, the people means those who are vested with political rights, and, in this particular instance, the people vested with political rights, were the constituencies of the several states, under their various laws, modifications and constitutions, which is but another name for the governments of the states themselves. "We the *people*," as used in the preamble of the constitution, means merely, "We the *constituencies* of the several states." (85–86)

Cooper's insistence on a legalistic definition of the word, like his insistence on states' rights vis-à-vis federal powers, is another means of lessening the threat of a widening majority.

Although universal manhood suffrage had never been essential to Cooper's definition of American republicanism, he had always praised it. Now, however, unless Cooper were to support limitation of the franchise, he faced the prospect of condoning greater power in the hands of undesirables less fit to govern. Faced with these alternatives, Cooper reaches no conclusion. He presents the advantages of limiting manhood suffrage, but refuses to advocate their enactment:

> The laws which control the great and predominant interests, or those which give a complexion to society, emanate from the states, which may well enough possess a wide political base. But towns and villages regulating property chiefly, there is a peculiar propriety in excluding those from the suffrage who have no immediate local interests in them. An undue

[26] *Notions of the Americans*, II, 23–28.

proportion of the dissolute, unsettled, vicious and disorganiz-
ing, collect in towns, and that balance of society, which, under
other circumstances, might neutralize their influence, is destroyed, leaving, as a consequence, the power to control their
governments, under a suffrage that is universal, in the hands
of the worst part of the community. (193)

Those whom Cooper considers unworthy of the franchise
are precisely the class that Cooper denigrated in works
ranging from *The Pioneers* to *The Ways of the Hour*, the
rootless "go-ahead" commoners (Cooper also called them
"birds of passage") who thrived upon stirring up excitement in stable country villages. To deprive this class of
the franchise, however, would achieve the same political
effect as the direct representation of property. Because
Cooper remains resolutely opposed to representing
property, he stops short of approving limitation of the
franchise.

Finally, Cooper considers curbing the demagogue by
denying the legitimacy of instruction, a term of the age
which referred to the obligation of an elected representative to vote the will of his constituency. In Cooper's discussion of this question, the same duality appears. On
the one hand, Cooper's commitment to the polity he calls
"confederated representative democracy" (160) leads him
to affirm the doctrine of instruction:

There is no doubt it is the intention of the American system,
that the will of the constitutional majorities, to a certain extent, should be properly regarded by the representative; and
that when the latter, who has been elected with the express
understanding that he is to support a particular measure, or
a particular set of principles, sees reason to change his opinion, he would act most in conformity with the spirit of the
institutions, by resigning his trust. (160–161)

In the succeeding paragraphs, however, Cooper so quali-
fies his initial approval of instruction that he seems to
deny it altogether. He states that "no constituency has a
right to violate the honest convictions of a representative"
(161) and soon concludes that "there is no pretence that
the obligation to regard the wishes of his constituents is
more than implied, under any circumstances; the social
compact, in a legal sense, leaving him the entire master
of his own just convictions" (162). Exactly where Cooper
stood upon the issue of instruction was probably not
quite clear even to him. *Notions of the Americans*, however, had not even raised the question; the rectitude of
the popular will had been assumed. Ten years later Cooper doubted the validity of instruction because he was
hoping to find a means whereby those who govern need
not be responsible to the errors of popular judgment.
Thus, in *The American Democrat*, Cooper's fear of the
congressional demagogue is complemented by his fear
of the people. On the one hand, Cooper warns us against
the legislator; on the other, against his constituency.

In *Notions of the Americans*, the American's individuality had been cause for glorifying political freedoms
and predicting the greatness of the American future (I,
169–172). The term "individuality," considered in a national context, had implied both the American's right to
be distinctive and the strength of his separate identity.
Cooper's firm commitment to American individuality is
reaffirmed in *The American Democrat*, but, as the treatise
unfolds, the concept is redefined and applied to a different purpose:

The principle of individuality, or to use a less winning
term, of selfishness, lies at the root of all voluntary human

exertion. We toil for food, for clothes, for houses, lands, and for property, in general. This is done, because we know that the fruits of our labor will belong to ourselves, or to those who are most dear to us. It follows, that all which society enjoys beyond the mere supply of its first necessities, is dependant upon the rights of property. (187)

The meaning of individuality has blended into the spirit of possession, and the spirit of possession has in turn been declared the basis for property rights. Extending the argument to its logical conclusion, Cooper argues that retention of property is as just a tenet of natural law as liberty of action: "we may infer that the rights of property, to a certain extent, are founded in nature. The food obtained by this toil cannot be taken from the mouth of man, or beast, without doing violence to one of the first of our natural rights" (187).

Leatherstocking had, of course, argued that, in a State of Nature, natural law dictated that use of God's bounty turned it into personal property. But Judge Temple had countered that, in a State of Civilization, the civil law is the only guarantor of one's natural right to the same property. Cooper had always believed that "the first great principle connected with the rights of property, is its inviolability in all cases in which the law leaves it in possession of the proprietor" (188). What is new in *The American Democrat* is not the argument for property, but the degree of insistence upon it. The protection of personal property rights by recourse to the civil law has become the most important test of the viability of the American republic. Republicanism in such later novels as *Home As Found*, the Littlepage trilogy and *The Crater* is measured, not by the constitutional political rights of the majority, but by the constitutional property rights of the minority. After 1837 Cooper seems to have agreed with Locke that the primary function of contractual government is the preservation of property.[27] In *The Pioneers* and *The Prairie*, Cooper had openly debated questions of land ownership before resolving them in accord with the civil law. For the Effinghams and Littlepages, however, a gentleman's deed certifies unquestionable, almost timeless ownership.

Cooper was at no time willing to extend the meaning of "all men are created equal" beyond the domain of political rights. His firmer insistence on social and moral inequality in *The American Democrat* must be attributed to the fact that by 1838 inequality was being challenged in a way that the author of *Notions of the Americans* had deemed impossible. In the earlier work, social inequality between gentry and yeoman did not need to be belabored because it was recognized and honored by all. Conversely, Cooper had argued that political equality allows each man those opportunities for self-betterment that would lead to a more enlightened and able constituency (II, 323). By 1838, however, Cooper's defense of political equality rests upon a significantly different basis:

[27] *Second Treatise on Civil Government*, p. 67. Although protection of property may have become Cooper's test for republican virtue, this narrowed criterion is not incompatible with Cooper's refusal to represent property. Confining the vote to the propertied has no connection with demanding that the republic protect property rights. Dekker misleads when he argues that, in *The American Democrat*, there is "always a powerful tension, verging on contradiction, between his [Cooper's] absolute commitment to the defense of property and his conviction that it ought not to rule" ("Introduction" to *The American Democrat*, p. 36).

All men have essentially the same rights, an equality, which, so far from establishing that "one man is as good as another," in a social sense, is the very means of producing the inequality of condition that actually exists. By possessing the same rights to exercise their respective faculties, the active and frugal become more wealthy than the silly and ignorant; the polished and refined more respected and sought, than the rude and vulgar. (137)

Whether equality of rights conforms to natural justice now seems secondary; the primary advantage of political equality is that it leads to social inequality. In Cooper's eyes, the republican polity no longer allows opportunities for the self-benefit of everyone; it separates the wheat from the chaff.

In addition to Cooper's uncompromising defense of political equality and property rights, there are other ways in which components of his ideal polity are reaffirmed for shifting purposes. When Cooper praises his ideal of minimizing governmental legislation, the emphasis is no longer on the blessings accruing from a scarcity of statutes, but on the strict enforcement of those that presently exist. Checks and balances continue to be celebrated as the essence of limited government, yet their purpose seems no longer the checking of excess power so much as the balancing of powers to prevent change.[28] *The American Democrat* advocates restoring the constitutional balance of powers by use of the presidential veto

[28] Contrast Cooper's insistence on balance of powers with the thrust of the following passage from the *Letter to General Lafayette:* "*Checks* abounded in their [the Americans'] institutions; but a *balance* was avoided, as the certain means of a hazardous contest. In every instance, they placed the people as arbiters in the last resort" (39–40).

against Congress, but Cooper's yearning for a strong executive does not quite square with his former ideal of a nearly invisible government.

The qualities of individuality, common sense and manly independence, qualities which the Bachelor so often had noted in the American character, have shaded almost imperceptibly into selfishness, gullibility, and license. Cooper may reassert his notion that "The principal advantage of a democracy, is a general elevation in the character of the people" (121), but, a few pages later, he admits that "the tendency of democracies is, in all things, to mediocrity" (129). Truth is no longer winnowed out by the clash of opinion; it is stifled by the majority disposition to defer to the wrong. Cooper's earlier faith in future laws that would result from the daily experience of American life[29] shifts to a reliance on the long-existing body of civil statutes. *Notions of the Americans* had decried the probability of political management because the enlightened constituency was vigilant (II, 226). In *The American Democrat*, however, the demagogue clearly takes his inevitable place as the most formidable threat to republican institutions.

The American Democrat, written as a "sort of higher school book"[30] for New York State, is the work in which Cooper defines what he had meant by his aphorism "Here, the democrat is the conservative."[31] As Cooper's faith in democratic man wavers, he praises strict enforcement of the civil laws and property rights of the old order. His reliance upon republican institutions

[29] *Notions of the Americans*, II, 162.
[30] *Letters and Journals*, III, 317.
[31] *A Letter to His Countrymen*, p. 99.

grows as his faith in republican man fails. Moreover, he sees advantages to limitation of the franchise, a stronger executive, repudiating instruction, and curbing majority rule. He does not, however, advocate any of these measures, nor does he argue for any laws repressive to the liberties or at variance with the institutions in which he has long believed. Cooper is not willing to condone the repressive actions that might save his ideal republic from the demagogue. *The American Democrat* arrives at no new political convictions; it only shows us Cooper's realization that, in 1838, the true democrat is he who wishes to conserve the republic. In this sense, and in this sense only, can we define Cooper's American as a conservative democrat.

On July 22, 1837, Cooper issued his handbill against trespassing on Three Mile Point. That very evening, the townsmen declared a meeting of the citizens of Cooperstown to pass popular resolutions censuring Cooper for asserting his right to his property. A letter to Shubrick indicates that Cooper had completed *The American Democrat* by September 4, 1837, only slightly longer than one month after the controversy arose.[32] It is, therefore, possible, but quite doubtful, that the Three Mile Point controversy appreciably influenced *The American Democrat*. All the more remarkable, therefore, is the following passage in Cooper's treatise:

The end of liberty is the happiness of man, and its means, that of leaving the greatest possible personal freedom of action, that comports with the general good. To supplant the exactions of the laws, therefore, by those of an unauthorized publick, is to establish restraints without the formalities and

[32] *Letters and Journals*, III, 287.

precision of legal requirements. It is putting the prejudices, provincialisms, ignorance and passions of a neighborhood in the place of statutes; or, it is establishing a power equally without general principles, and without responsibility. (199)

The passage corresponds exactly to Cooper's view of the symbolic blow dealt to the authority of American civil law by his townsmen's actions in July of 1837. Even more importantly, it indicates how firmly Cooper held to his belief that the maximum of liberty could be guaranteed only through respect for the civil law. Freedom continued to be misunderstood as well as abused. Accordingly, when Cooper wrote *Homeward Bound* and *Home As Found*, he intended to demonstrate that public opinion could as easily endanger liberty as uphold it. *The American Democrat* phrases the same point somewhat differently: "There is getting to be so much publick right, that private right is overshadowed and lost. A danger exists that the ends of liberty will be forgotten altogether in the means" (229).

"HOME AS FOUND"

Inept as a novel, *Home As Found* is a valuable social document, not only because it is the first American novel of manners, but because it unsparingly criticizes certain recurring faults in the national character. Cooper and the Effinghams probe the most sensitive spots in the American psyche: the passion for social equality, delight in change for the sake of change, deference to public opinion, absorption in transitory crises, a colonial complex that finds release in chauvinism, and an aping of the nouveau riche who are mistaken for "aristocracy." The continued excoriation of national sins is done without pity and frequently without humor by members of a family who are allowed to remain immune from the faults they criticize. Cooper sometimes commits a more grievous error by editorializing upon national faults rather than dramatizing them. The unattractive self-righteousness of the Effinghams should not, however, lead readers to conclude that the Effinghams are politically or socially illiberal. From the outset, Cooper insists that it is the Effinghams who defend liberty and America which has become intolerantly egalitarian.

In *The American Democrat* Cooper had argued that it was a public duty of gentlemen of private station to protect the legal rights of the individual (149). In a republic the American gentleman is the disinterested upholder of individual liberty (149–150). The gentry in Cooper's later fiction all act out this conception of their class duty through resisting illegal, illiberal attacks upon property. To a man, these gentry subscribe to Cooper's definition of political liberty in *Home As Found*: "The power which was given to the people collectively, was only so given to secure to them as perfect a liberty as possible, in their characters of individuals" (255). Although this concept of liberty is perfectly consistent with Cooper's earlier works, the gentry who practice it in later novels become less attractive due to a change in the terms of conflict. The gentry's own liberties are now being attacked rather than the liberties of the people. Because defense of liberty now means defense of self, the gentry sometimes seem to be selfishly obsessed with property rather than devoted to republican principle. We should remember, however, that Cooper intended to represent the disinterestedness of the gentry, even when he failed to do so.

In *Homeward Bound* Eve Effingham evaluates the effect of Europe upon her family and herself: "My greatest fear is, that in acquiring liberality, I have acquired nothing else" (11). The liberality of which she speaks is, for Cooper, the essential trait of her class:

Liberality is peculiarly the quality of a gentleman. He is liberal in his attainments, opinions, practices and concessions. He asks for himself, no more than he is willing to concede to others. He feels that his superiority is in his attainments, practices and principles, which if they are not always moral, are above meanness, and he has usually no pride in the mere vulgar consequence of wealth.[33]

For the Effinghams as for Cooper, this notion of liberality entails specific social and political principles: the supremacy of law over public opinion, the right of privacy, the freedom to be superior, sacredness of personal property and social inequality. The Effinghams find all of these to be violated, in opinion or in fact, upon their return. Because the Effinghams and their creator equate their liberality with the first principles of republicanism, they believe the nation has retrogressed both politically and socially. In the preface to *Home As Found*, Cooper identifies the "predominant thought" of his novel: the American nation is "in arrears to its own avowed principles" (viii).

In order to establish that movement forward in time has been a movement backward in principle, Cooper forces his reader to compare Templeton present to Templeton past. *Home As Found* was consciously planned as

[33] *The American Democrat*, p. 150.

the sequel to *The Pioneers*. Considered together, the two books were to record the development of the American village: "The scene of *Home As Found*, is transferred to the Templeton of *The Pioneers*, in order to show the difference which half a century has made in the appearance and usages of an American village."[34] The changes within Templeton were to typify the changes in American society between 1793 and 1837: "The scene of *The Pioneers* is used in *Home As Found* in order to show what are the ordinary changes of American society, by connecting the two books."[35] Cooper links the two novels by structural similarities as well as character reminiscence. Both novels are built around two plots that are but loosely connected to one another. The first concerns the fortunes, marital and pecuniary, of the young Effingham heirs; the second concerns a conflict between Templeton's citizenry and its civil laws, a conflict in which general qualities of American political justice are defined.

Cooper deliberately leads his reader to assume that the Templeton of 1823 has grown in size without sacrificing its rural virtues. The Effingham entourage reenacts the crucial scene in which Judge Temple had first viewed the unspoiled beauty of Lake Otsego. Returning from twelve years in Europe, the entire party climbs Mount Vision in order to look upon long-remembered Templeton. Mount Vision, newly green, shows no trace of its former burning. The Effinghams see a village which is "generally beautiful and map-like," displaying "a general air of neatness and comfort" (147). Templeton's buildings are either "painted white" or show "the better taste" of

[34] *Letters and Journals*, III, 351.
[35] *Letters and Journals*, IV, 84.

"graver and chaster hues of . . . grey stones" (147). The Effinghams seem to be returning to the thriving agrarian world of *Notions of the Americans*.

After the scene atop Mount Vision, the remainder of *Home As Found* is devoted to the disillusionment of the nearer view. Beautiful to the eye, Templeton has declined in inner character. The good will between a Judge Temple and his townsmen no longer exists. Class lines have hardened and jealousies of social station have become pronounced, partly as a consequence of growth, and partly as a consequence of increasing vulgarity among the provincial inhabitants. In 1793 Judge Temple went to the village tavern to drink with his settlers, but in 1837 the barber of Templeton refuses to go to Judge Temple's hall to perform his public trade.

The comparative rigidity of class lines has brought no sense of permanence. Rather it has made Templeton the village of false democrats who resent the superiority of their own gentry. The power of public opinion, formerly a guarantee against error or tyranny, now threatens to turn social prejudices into law. Templeton's population is no longer either congenial or heterogeneous; all former distinctions of national origin are leveled, yet the town is sharply divided between the old settlers, descendants of 1793, and grasping transients from Down East.

Characteristically, Cooper has created certain individuals to represent the leading features of Templeton. Mrs. Abbot, Wenham, Howel and the barber, however, bear discouragingly little resemblance to the Hollisters, Ben Pump, or Major Hartmann. Good-natured decency has given way to shiftiness and prejudice. What has been lost is of a price beyond recall:

"Alas!" said John Effingham, "The days of the 'Leather-stockings' have passed away. He preceded me in life, and I see few remains of his character in a region where speculation is more rife than moralizing, and emigrants are plentier than hunters." (266)

Both Effingham and Cooper either have forgotten, or have chosen to forget, that misuse of the law of Templeton drove Natty to quit the American town. The hero who had never borne more than a marginal relation to the original Templeton has become the very measure of its past. The Commodore, himself a relic of the "days of the Leather-stockings," offers a mock serious association of great significance: "He was a great man! They may talk of their Jeffersons and Jacksons, but I set down Washington and Natty Bumppo as the two only really great men of my time" (229). Upon the Effinghams' return, they find that the busts of Washington and Franklin have vanished from the hall (177).

By 1838, therefore, Cooper had found that neither of his two greatest heroes, the libertarian gentleman nor the natural man of principle, truly belonged within Templeton. Without them the American town may prosper but will risk moral decay. The commodore dreams that all of Templeton will arrive in hell before the devil can reach Templeton. Even that temperate gentleman, Edward Effingham, has moments of bitterness. Overlooking Templeton from Mount Vision, he expresses Cooper's growing doubts about the march of civilization: "I fear this glorious scene is marred by the envy, uncharitableness, and all the other evil passions of man! . . . Perhaps it were better as it was so lately, when it lay in the solitude and peace of the wilderness, the resort of birds and

beasts" (152). Like both Effinghams, Cooper's disgust
with the state of civilization drives him to idealize the
hunter in a state of nature. It is no coincidence that Natty
becomes Pathfinder and Deerslayer shortly after Cooper
published his distaste for what he had found at home.

In *Home As Found*, unlike *The Pioneers*, attitude toward personal property has become the most important
test of American character. Both Cooper and the Effinghams measure change by the vocabulary of property.
Land speculators in New York inflate prices to cheat the
customer and encourage social rootlessness, if not chaos,
by their unending resale of acreage. America's new taste-
lessness is measured by its buildings; the Greek Revival
homesteads along the Hudson only resemble "mushroom
temples which are the offspring of Mammon" (133). The
new subdivision of American opinion is defined by the
seven spires of Templeton. Unknowingly, Aristabulus
Bragg defines the new American mentality by telling Mr.
Effingham of the townspeople's suggestions for changes
in the Effingham homestead:

In the way of houses, Mr. Effingham, I believe it is the general
opinion you might have done better with your own, than to
have repaired it. Had the materials been disposed of, they
would have sold well, and by running a street through the
property, a pretty sum might have been realized. . . . It would
have been no great matter to get another [home] on cheaper
land. The old residence would have made a good factory, or
an inn. (36)

All such observations lead directly toward the Three
Mile Point controversy, Cooper's central attempt to re-
evaluate the problem of justice through analysis of attitudes toward property changes.

Three Mile Point occupies only forty pages of *Home As Found*, yet Cooper has stated that "it was precisely on account of this affair that *Homeward Bound* and *Home As Found* were written."[36] The conflict between Effinghams and villagers over ownership of the picnic spot is all important, yet practically inconsequential. It is the focal point of the novel, yet Cooper deliberately minimizes its effects. He wishes to present the controversy, not as the cause of the Effingham's distaste for America, but as the primary illustration of the social forces presently at work in the nation. Three Mile Point is of ultimate national significance precisely because it is so small, so utterly common. Accordingly, Cooper strove to record the facts[37] of Three Mile Point, as accurately as was possible, within his fictional framework: "it was my wish to put the real case, as near as might be, on record, where it might stand as a refutation of the thousand lies that had been told about it."[38]

Like the shooting of a deer, the ownership of Three Mile Point is a small, legal conflict around which Cooper builds a discussion of political justice in America. Mr. Effingham cares little more for Three Mile Point than Judge Temple cares for the carcass of the buck. Yet both men, being sympathetic voices for their author, will defend to the utmost the principles which these objects embody. In both novels the rewards of the legal conflict are nothing but everything is at stake. Temple's arguments and Effingham's actions are based upon identical

---

[36] *Letters and Journals*, IV, 269.

[37] Appendix A provides an outline of the facts and chronology of the Three Mile Point controversy.

[38] *Letters and Journals*, IV, 85.

convictions concerning the rule of law and the right to property. Yet the motives and social attitudes of Edward Effingham and Aristabulus Bragg are markedly different from those of Judge Temple and Natty Bumppo. The changes of time have realigned the forces of conflict.

No longer can Cooper be concerned with the heroic man who honestly and with some justification believes his natural rights are threatened by a civil statute. The man of natural justice has been replaced by lesser folk who cite republican sentiments in an effort to upset justice. By 1838 none save demagogues argue that the civil law is a restriction upon individual liberty, because the facts of Templeton plainly reveal that the civil law is, in truth, liberty's only protection. The change in the quality of Templeton's citizenry strengthens Cooper's vindication of the opinions of Judge Temple. Because the virtues of Natty Bumppo are absent from civilized life, the Effinghams and the civil statutes embody the entirety of truth. Judge Temple discussed the relation of natural right to civil law in Templeton, but Mr. Effingham simply spreads his deed to Three Mile Point on the table.

There is no essential difference in the kind of law that Judge Temple and Edward Effingham invoke. The conservation law and the law concerning evidence of land title are both based upon Cooper's conception of natural justice. Both statutes restrict and define possession of property; both apply equally to all citizens. Judge Temple's law was intended to protect both the availability of game and each man's right to it. Although the property laws to which the Effinghams appeal work to their advantage, they equally protect the right of any man to enjoy his property.

The change is not in the particular law, nor in Cooper's decision to uphold the just civil law against those who resist it. If Cooper seems more legalistic in *Home As Found* than in *The Pioneers*, the cause is the passage of time in the community rather than any change in Cooper's political principles. In asserting that the people own Three Mile Point because they have long used it, the townspeople are reasserting a law of justice that pertains only to the natural state. They reassert the natural law of use, however, long after the natural law has ceased to have any jurisdiction in Templeton. Natty Bumppo had had natural rights that seemed to precede Judge Temple's statute. The townspeople of *Home As Found* can claim no natural right to the point because civil laws of possession had deeded it to the Effingham family long before their arrival. The townspeople, in short, attempt to treat Three Mile Point as if it were a neutral ground for which they can legitimately contend. To the Effinghams and to Cooper, however, laws based upon natural justice have long since declared that Three Mile Point is very personal ground indeed.

The Effinghams are more severe in judgment than Judge Temple because the threat to law has grown markedly. Not only are the people more vulgar and envious; they are now willing to believe the lies of demagogues. The press has come to Templeton, thus threatening both the individual's right to his character and the public's right to correct information. The chief problem in *The Pioneers* was the misuse of law by Hiram Doolittle, who was motivated solely by curiosity and greed, but who never dared to oppose the power of Judge Temple. By 1838, however, a significant portion of Templeton's townsmen are ready to deprive the gentry of their legal property by force of public opinion.

The greater severity of the threat to justice is exemplified by the character of Aristabulus Bragg. Like Dickon, Aristabulus is a good-natured, self-important man who oversees the estate of the landed gentleman. Whereas Dickon was Temple's loyal cousin, Aristabulus is not only no relation, but a Yankee, a country lawyer and the town land agent to boot. This insidious combination of roles leads Aristabulus to divided loyalties. Hired to be the Cerberus for the Effingham household, Bragg is tempted to rise by encouraging the popular claim to Three Mile Point. Dickon had only provided comic relief. In *Home As Found*, however, the gentleman's steward is ready to deprive his employer of his property.

Significantly Aristabulus never emerges as a true danger to the Effingham's position. Caught between his desires and his duties, his ambition and his "profound deference" (250) for Mr. Effingham, Aristabulus temporizes throughout the controversy. Later Yankees such as Jason Newcome were to be far more resolute in their concealed attacks on their employers. Unlike Jason, Aristabulus cannot take advantage of the law because he thinks in terms of existing public opinion rather than future political action. Bragg seems curiously unaware both of his own opportunities for demagoguery and of the just principles of the controversy. What never occurs to the Yankee lawyer is the simple but crucial legality of the controversy, the fact that Mr. Effingham possesses an accredited deed to the point and therefore has the legal right to publish any trespassing notice he sees fit. Equally blind to the distinction between a permission and a right,

Aristabulus never understands that the public has used Three Mile Point only because of Mr. Effingham's liberality.

Although there is no question that Effingham's cause is just and his actions legal, his method of dealing with the public wins few converts to his principles, either among the townspeople or Cooper's readers. Mr. Effingham is willing to show his deeds to Bragg, but not to the public. Bragg's objection, that Mr. Effingham might have chosen a more adroit way of handling the controversy (252), has much weight. The trespassing notice is curt. The Effinghams seem to withhold their evidence intentionally in order to provoke the townspeople to reveal the ease with which they mistake public opinion for civil law. When Bragg tells Mr. Effingham that "the public ought to know of this bequest of the late Mr. Effingham," Effingham simply says "I deny that there exists any such obligation" (244). He supports his denial only by asserting that a simple notice against trespassing is the "usual" mode of dealing with public encroachment. Judge Temple would surely have taken the same action, but he also would have appeared personally before the public to convince them of their folly.

Since *The Pioneers*, the gentleman has changed in authority and character without changing in his principles. Judge Temple had been the driving force of his community; he had built Templeton, brought its laws to passage, and enforced them. His descendants in *Home As Found*, however, detach themselves from the community and rely upon laws they have not made. Although the townspeople are forcing the gentry from power, the just disdain of the gentry drives them to become increasingly aloof. Marmaduke Temple had been the judge of his community; neither the Effinghams nor the Littlepages retain any legal authority.

John and Edward Effingham illustrate the problems Cooper faced in retaining the landed gentleman as his spokesmen in the later novels. Principled, educated and intelligent though they be, the Littlepages, Hardinges, and Effinghams remain inactive to the verge of purposelessness. Because the gentry are being forced to the periphery of American life, they can but superintend their estates. Recognizing that a manly independence is the only way to truth, they become uncomfortably aware that manly independence leaves them powerless. They speak the truth, but their truths are only observed, not tested through participation. Because such figures elicit rational assent without personal admiration, the reader all too easily allows his dissatisfaction with the gentleman's character to spread to a dissatisfaction with the gentleman's principles.

Throughout his career Cooper asserts that the simple American gentleman, Jefferson's natural aristocrat, is the superior of all titled European nobility. Cooper never abandoned this argument; one finds it in *Tales For Fifteen*, *Notions of the Americans*, *The American Democrat*, *Home As Found*, the Wallingford novels, and *The Ways of the Hour*. In Cooper's later novels, however, it becomes debatable whether Cooper's American gentlemen can truly be included among the natural aristocracy of America, as Judge Temple surely could. The Effinghams and the Littlepages live upon inherited wealth on a landed estate. They have natural merit, but they use it only to criticize. Lacking noble title, they are a social, though not a political, aristocracy. As gentlemen they continue to uphold liberty for all, but the function of political liberty is to preserve distinctions of merit that they do not quite exemplify.

Among Cooper's novels only *Homeward Bound* and *Home As Found* divide the American gentleman into two characters who disagree with one another. Edward and John Effingham represent Cooper's changeable feelings during the troubled years of the late thirties. Although Edward Effingham retains Cooper's social position in the town, Cooper was justified in maintaining that he and Edward could not simply be equated. Benign, optimistic, and self-contained, Edward offers temperate and assuring statements which Cooper very much wished to believe. His angrily cynical cousin utters denunciations which Cooper wished not to believe, but which were to recur in later writings. Through John Effingham, Cooper can exorcise his national demons without having to subscribe to them.[39]

Cooper's account of the Effingham heritage in *Homeward Bound* reveals a shifting evaluation of his own upbringing:

The Effingham family had started Federalists, in the true meaning of the term; for their education, native sense, and principles, had a leaning to order, good government, and the dignity of the country; but as factions became fiercer, and names got to be confounded and contradictory, the landed branch [Edward] settled down into what they thought were American,

[39] Grossman accurately summarizes the relation between John Effingham and his creator: "Jack is not Cooper's licensed mouthpiece, and neither Eve nor the reader ever fully believes him, but he manages always to be authoritative in his gloomiest forebodings" (*James Fenimore Cooper*, p. 119).

and the commercial branch [John] what might properly be termed English Federalists.[40]

Cooper carefully distinguishes between a "true" agrarian Federalism and the commercial, almost Whiggish, Federalism of John Effingham. Cooper's growing approval of "true" Federalist principles, however, is based upon social benefits only. Throughout the book the Effinghams refer to Europe and to England as standards of social and cultural value by which to judge American deficiencies. Politically, however, all three of the Effinghams—John, Edward, and Eve—remain staunchly republican despite their differing degrees of faith in the effect of republican institutions. No matter how critical of America they may be, none of them ever proposes any measures for change in the national polity.

Toward the end of *Home As Found*, John Effingham summarizes the observations of return (427–429). One by one he lists the faults which he has seen in Templeton and in the nation: provincialism, leveling to and worship of mediocrity, lack of national direction, absence of a capitol, flattery of public opinion, and submission to political party. Effingham's criticisms are Cooper's as well. More importantly, each of these national tendencies are faults because they destroy liberty and individuality. The cause of national demise, Effingham concludes, is violation of the moral law: "Man is worse than the beasts, merely because he has a code of right and wrong which he never respects" (429).

Never again was Cooper to write of his country or of

[40] *Homeward Bound*, pp. 65–66.

mankind in terms so unrelievedly black as those which
Effingham had used. The consequence of fully crediting
John Effingham's opinions was a price Cooper was not
willing to pay: "Harkee, Ned, . . . I should prefer the
cold, dogged domination of English law, with all its
fruits, the heartlessness of a sophistication without parallel, to being trampeled on by every arrant blackguard
that may happen to traverse this valley in his wanderings
after dollars" (258–259). In *Home As Found*, as in *Notions of the Americans*, importation of the British common law is firmly rejected.

John Effingham unwillingly considers repression;
Noah Truck openly advocates it. Captain Truck's politics form a wry comment upon the law of the neutral
ground that had so ravaged Westchester in *The Spy*.
Truck believes in "the law of the strongest . . . only
reduced to rules" (323):

I shall just own the truth, and make no bones of it. I have
been captain of my own ship so long, that I have a most
thorough contempt for all equality. It is a vice that I deprecate,
and, whatever may be the laws of this country, I am of opinion
that equality is nowhere borne out by the Law of Nations:
which, after all, commodore, is the only true law for a gentleman to live under. (323)

The plain-dealing captain expresses Cooper's growing
desire to bring the discipline of a naval hierarchy from
the quarterdeck to the shore. Truck and Cooper, however, are not to be confused. The captain's politics would
solve the nagging problems posed by the liberty of the
land, but would do so by destroying that liberty altogether. Even on land Truck trusts solely to Vattel and

not to the United States Constitution.[41] Because Truck
is vehemently antirepublican, he remains for Cooper a
figure of sheer phantasy, a man who, despite his percep-
tions, is comically out of his element. The democracy of
the land and the autocracy of the sea are separate
worlds.[42]

Templeton, however, does not yet need to be subjected
either to the dogged law of England or to Truck's "law
of the strongest . . . only reduced to rules." The Three
Mile Point controversy ends in a vindication and a triumph of the Effingham claims; the laws of property are
fully upheld. In 1837 Templeton is still a world in which
Cooper can assert that "public opinion, in order to be
omnipotent, or even formidable beyond the inflictions
of the moment, must be right" (255). By publishing the
townsmen's set of resolutions, Effingham shames the
public into a realization of its errors. By showing the
public that its resolutions contain libelous statements,
Effingham has forced the public to recant.

Cooper's resolution is not fully credible. Dodge's article on the Three Mile Point controversy has been published throughout the country, yet seems to have elicited
no response. In actuality Cooper was to resort to the

[41] Kay Seymour House remarks that "Captain Truck's beloved
Vattel is for him the same universally valid system based on
natural law that the Constitution is for the gentry" (*Cooper's
Americans*, pp. 201–202).

[42] In a review of *Clark's Naval History of the United States*, a
review written before *The Pilot* was conceived, Cooper had written that "Liberty and equality may have their merited estimation
in the minds of our citizens on shore—but we apprehend that
neither of these particular deities, are admitted to an abiding place
on board a vessel of war" (*Early Critical Essays*, ed. James F. Beard,
Jr. [Gainesville, Fla., 1955], pp. 4–5).

courts for seven years to defend his character against
newspaper charges arising from the controversy. The
Effinghams, however, do not prosecute Dodge for libel,
because in *Home As Found* the rebuke given to popular
opinion renders a recourse to the courts finally unnecessary. Yet a doubt remains; would the people of Templeton, as Cooper has characterized them, be likely to
submit so meekly after John Effingham had published
their resolutions?

Bragg and Dodge are defeated. In *Homeward Bound*
Dodge had remained a masterfully comic figure because
the Effinghams had read his designs immediately, and
because Captain Truck had wielded the power to prevent
Dodge from ever becoming dangerous. At the conclusion
of *Home As Found* Dodge rather conveniently disappears. Bragg is forced to leave Templeton. Unable to
temporize indefinitely, he at last declares his ambitions
by proposing to Eve Effingham, who very quietly induces
her father to fire the land agent. Bragg, like his prede-
cessor Doolittle, heads westward where his go-aheadism
will have greater opportunities and a wider range.

The ending of the novel thus restores Templeton to
tranquility and comparative purity.[43] Even Bragg admits
that the majority of lawyers still must emigrate to the
west in order to do a brisk business in turning over properties for profit (31). The only outgrowth of the machina-

[43] *The Chronicles of Cooperstown* provides an additional view
of Templeton in the year 1838. Here, too, the fundamental decency of the American village is reaffirmed. Three Mile Point is
briefly mentioned, but Cooper asserts that the community is already returning to its "ancient deportment" and concludes that "on
the whole, the feeling of the community is sound" (*The Chronicles
of Cooperstown* [Cooperstown, 1838], p. 92).

tions of Steadfast Dodge is to so enrage the commodore that he acquires enough of a social conscience actually to vote—against Steadfast Dodge. Eve has found that she can retain her faith in the American republic. John Effingham noticeably fails in his longstanding attempt to convince Edward that national pessimism is justified.

In 1838 Cooper maintains that, underneath all the newly found flaws in the American village, the heart of his community is still reliable. John Effingham's anger at the total collapse of the moral law proves unfounded. The technical hero of the two novels, Paul Powis Effingham, reasserts a long-treasured article of Cooper's faith:

I have everywhere found, not only the same nature, but a common innate sentiment of justice that seems universal; for even amidst the wildest scenes of violence, or of the most ungovernable outrages, this sentiment glimmers through the more brutal features of the being. The rights of property, for instance, are everywhere acknowledged; the very wretch who steals whenever he can, appearing conscious of his crime, by doing it clandestinely, and as a deed that shuns observation. All seem to have the same general notions of natural justice, and they are forgotten only through the policy of systems, irresistible temptation, the pressure of want, or the result of contention.[44]

Because man's moral sense survives, even the criminal finally recognizes that natural justice sanctions the laws of property. Aristabulus Bragg and Steadfast Dodge prove to have more than a glimmering of the principles of natural justice. When rebuked, they show their clear regard for the rights of property. Because they retract,

[44] *Homeward Bound,* p. 443.

no changes in the republican polity—such as those John Effingham feared—are necessary.

The Pioneers had concluded with the westward departure of the isolate hero and the restoration of civil order; Judge Temple had retained firm personal control of his community. *Home As Found* concludes with the westward departure of the village demagogue and a similar restoration of civil order. In the sequel, however, a strange vacuum of power remains in Templeton. The Effingham entourage departs for Italy.[45] Although civil liberties have been reestablished, there seems to be no one in Templeton ready to defend them.

Whether the Effinghams will remain permanently in Italy Cooper does not say. Nor does he explicitly state that the Effinghams are returning to Europe because they are disillusioned with the state of Templeton's civilization. Whatever the motivation of departure, however, it is evident that the Effinghams' world is contracting and turning inward. At the end of *The Pioneers*, Elizabeth Temple had married Oliver Effingham. At the end of *Home As Found*, Eve Effingham marries Paul Effingham.

Soon after Cooper brought the Effinghams to Templeton, he set into his narrative a lengthy analysis of the three separate stages through which a new settlement develops into an established community (187–192). The passage provides Cooper an opportunity to summarize

[45] The Effinghams are only acting out Cooper's personal desires. In 1838 Cooper wrote to Horatio Greenough in Florence: "My heart is in Italy, and has been ever since I left it. . . . Were I a single man, I would be with you in sixty days. There is very little attachment to home, in my family" (*Letters and Journals*, III, 329–330).

the changes Templeton had undergone between 1793
and 1837. Cooper declares that the first stage, "the pastoral age, or that of good fellowship" (190), has been
"imperfectly recorded in another work" (191). Admittedly, Cooper is correct in reminding us that Judge Temple's community had been built by neighborly good will
which had resulted from social necessity. However, to
totally gloss over Doolittle, Kirby, and the unsightly
aspects of Templeton by referring to 1793 as a "period
of fun, toil, neighborly feeling, and adventure" (188) is
to make an understandable, nostalgic oversimplification.
The man who condemns recent changes is likely to romanticize the past.

Home As Found, Cooper states, describes the second
period of settlement, in which "we see the struggles for
place, the heart-burnings and jealousies of contending
families, and the influence of mere money" (188). Vulgarity is as unavoidable as "gradations of social station
that set institutions at defiance" (188). The experience of
the Effinghams is wholly true to Cooper's description of
the second stage.

However troubled and difficult the second stage may
be, Cooper assures us that it is but temporary. The time
of contention will be succeeded by "the third and last
condition of society" in which "men and things come
within the control of more general and regular laws"
(189). If Cooper ever did contemplate a volume describing Templeton in the third stage, he never mentioned his
intention. One can hardly imagine his honestly planning
such a work. A settlement that gradually attains the
peace of "general and regular laws" cannot be found in
any novel after *The Pioneers*. The third volume of the

Littlepage Manuscripts, *The Redskins*, deals with precisely that time in history when Mooseridge and Ravensnest should have entered the third stage of settlement; instead of "general and regular laws," however, *The Redskins* was to exhibit nothing but social lawlessness.

5. Moral Law in the Wilderness: The Indian Romances

> What good man would prefer a country covered with forests and ranged by a few thousand savages to our extensive Republic, studded with cities, towns, and prosperous farms, embellished with all the improvements which art can devise or industry execute, occupied by more than 12,000,000 happy people, and filled with all the blessings of liberty, civilization, and religion.
>
> ANDREW JACKSON, *Annual Message*, 1830

COOPER WROTE six novels that may be called frontier Indian romances: *The Wept of Wish-ton-Wish*, the last[1] four Leatherstocking Tales, and *The Oak Openings*. Spanning Cooper's career from 1826 to 1848, these six romances all possess certain qualities which set them apart even from such novels as *Wyandotté* and *The Pioneers*. All are set on the very fringe of the border between white civilization and Indian savagery. Either a family has moved westward to the fringe (the Heathcotes, Bushes, Hutters, Warings), or the isolate hero, Natty Bumppo, returns eastward to meet the vanguard of white civilization—momentarily. All but *The Prairie* deal with an historical war and describe battle sequences. The war-

---

[1] "Last" in the order of composition: *The Pioneers* (1823), *The Last of the Mohicans* (1826), *The Prairie* (1827), *The Pathfinder* (1840), *The Deerslayer* (1841).

fare, which is always interracial and nearly always colonial, is finally resolved by the sudden intervention of
distant, but controlling military forces.

In reading the Indian romances it is essential to remember that Cooper is writing of a period that precedes
the first stage of settlement described in *The Pioneers.*
Each of these works is an historical novel as well as an
adventure romance, and each describes an era that precedes by at least twenty-five years its date of composition.[2] The opinions about law and political justice
advanced by Cooper's frontiersmen apply to the unformed American frontier, but not to the settled, postconstitutional society amid which Cooper is writing.
Natty Bumppo may express Cooper's yearning for the free
forest life, but the author of *The American Democrat* is
a writer who also recognizes, very clearly, that Deerslayer
is an anachronism to which he is paying a nostalgic
tribute.

Because Natty Bumppo and the Indians are so com-
pellingly vivid, whereas Cooper's civilized heroes are stiff
bores, readers have wrongly assumed that Cooper is seriously debating the merits of savagery against the merits
of civilization. Whenever the author directly reflects upon
this question, he declares that the march of civilization
must and should replace the life of the savage. In *Notions*

[2] As Cooper grew older, he tended to move the date of the
frontier romances further backward in time. *The Pioneers* (1823)
describes an era that is just around the corner from memory.
The Prairie (1827) takes place in 1803. *The Wept of Wish-ton-
Wish, The Last of the Mohicans, The Pathfinder* and *The Deerslayer* deal with periods between 1660 and 1763. Only in *The
Oak Openings* (1848) does Cooper return to the comparative
present of 1815.

of the Americans, Cooper justifies Indian removal on
humane grounds; because the Indian represents a lower
stage of human development, his inevitable demise
should occur as bloodlessly as possible.[3] Like Crèvecoeur,
Cooper always assumed the superiority of an agrarian to
a hunting culture. There was a great deal of the physio-
crat in Cooper, but nothing of the primitivist. Natty
Bumppo is described as "a noble shoot from the stock of
human nature, which never could attain its proper elevation and importance, for no other reason, than because it
grew in the forest."[4] And Roy Harvey Pearce has convincingly proved that "in The Leatherstocking Tales, as
in the society out of which they rise, the savage is taken
at once as anterior and inferior to the civilized, not, as in
our society, merely a different, somewhat less complex
order of the civilized."[5]

Within the immediate context of the action of a border
tale, the Indian poses vexing problems of moral justice to
Cooper and to his frontiersmen. Cooper readily admits
that, according to natural laws of use, the Indians are
the rightful possessors of the American land. The barbarous greed of many of Cooper's white frontiersmen,
and the eloquence of many a wronged but noble savage,

[3] *Notions of the Americans*, II, 277–288. The Bachelor describes
the Indians as "a stunted, dirty, and degraded race" (281) and concludes that "As a rule, the red man disappears before the superior
moral and physical influence of the white" (277).

[4] *The Prairie*, pp. 141–142.

[5] Roy Harvey Pearce, "Civilization and Savagism: the World
of The Leatherstocking Tales," *English Institute Essays* (New York,
1950), pp. 92–93. Mr. Pearce amplified his argument in *The Savages
of America* (Baltimore, 1953), pp. 199–212 and in "The Leatherstocking Tales Re-Examined," *SAQ*, XXXXVI (1947), 524–536.

argue that Cooper and many of his readers felt a need to expiate white guilt. Cooper also reveals his divided feelings concerning the merits of Indian codes of law. In all the border romances, these codes demand the duty of revenge, the legality of scalping, fidelity to tribe, and, above all, individual honor. Cooper respects Indian law because it upholds communal standards and fosters individual integrity. Cooper's Indians, unlike many of his whites, honorably obey their own principles. Nonetheless Cooper insists that Indian law must be superseded because it is barbarous and un-Christian. Whenever a Magua or a Rivenoak protest that revenge is a natural law, Natty Bumppo replies that nature exhibits higher laws than slaughter.[6]

Within the larger context of American history, however, Cooper knows that questions of Indian conquest, tribal differences, and the validity of Indian law are not of ultimate, continuing importance. Without forgetting white injustices and white slaughter, Cooper recognizes that, for the nation as a whole, the problem posed by the Indian will steadily diminish in importance. The larger question of political justice that is argued in these novels is the kind of justice that the white man is bringing to

[6] These interchanges bear an interesting similarity to a passage in chapter 18 of *The Scarlet Letter*. During Hester's meeting with Dimmesdale in the forest, a flood of sunshine illuminates Hester immediately after she has removed the letter from her breast. Hawthorne disapprovingly calls this occurrence a "sympathy of Nature —that wild, heathen Nature of the forest, never subjugated by human law, nor illumined by higher truth." It seems that, for Hawthorne, nature sanctions lesser moral truths, whereas for Natty Bumppo, if not for Cooper, only nature is capable of teaching the highest values, could men but perceive them.

the wilderness. In the total configuration of Cooper's border romances, the Indian per se is not as important as the white man's treatment of him. If, on the frontier, the white man can preserve the virtues of Christian civilization, Cooper's assumptions about the progress that accompanies the passing of the Indian will appear justified. If, however, the white man reverts to savagery, the march of progress will become the march of injustice.

Cooper evaluates the conquering white civilization by the way its representative individuals dispense justice. The means that the individuals employ depend upon peculiar conditions of the wilderness. All of the white settlers in these six romances are wholly within the Lockean State of Nature. Each has absolute liberty of action and absolute equality with all around him. Like Locke, the frontiersman believes that, in a State of Nature, every man has the right to execute the law of nature. Because there is no civil law on the frontier, Cooper's borderers must turn their definitions of the moral law into civil action. The amoral on Cooper's frontier plunder, kill and move onward without thought. Other frontiersmen, however, will pause at length and in the midst of the wilderness to discuss the relation of the moral to the civil law. Some feel it necessary to construct rudimentary courts to dispense civil justice according to their conception of moral law. Not all of them, however, agree with Locke's definition of fundamental natural law: "no one ought to harm another in his life, health, liberty, or possessions."[7]

The laws by which the frontiersmen act are derived

[7] Locke, *Second Treatise on Civil Government*, p. 20.

from their environs. In each frontier romance, the setting is recognizably different, yet remains a variant of the neutral ground. The forest is both the temple of God and an arena for slaughter, depending upon the man who enters it. Cooper's forest is an Eden filled with devils of red skin. Descriptions of its calm, silent beauty erupt into scenes of hideous brutality, then as quickly subside. To Natty Bumppo, the neutral ground is God's handiwork constantly subjected to the mutilation of settlement. To Tom Hutter or Hurry Harry, the forest is a mine waiting to be plundered. To more gentlemanly whites, it is a beautiful, unknown world in which they feel both exiled and incompetent. And the author, it seems, would convince us that the forest is an endless expanse of barbarism that is steadily being reclaimed by the ordered graces of civilization.

In each of these novels the neutral ground releases both the bestiality and the piety in man. The frontier restores one man to Adamic purity but unleashes suppressed violence in another. Because success in the forest is solely dependent upon physical prowess and mental cunning, Cooper believes that the forest permits settlers to dismiss moral considerations. Yet he also considers the forest to be the source of individuality and true manliness. The forest evokes all of Cooper's yearnings for utter freedom, but also reveals his acute awareness of the inevitable perversion of freedom. The appeal of the free life is expressed through the forest, but the setting indicates nothing so much as the necessity of just and severe civil laws.

None of Cooper's settings is more constantly in a state of change than his forest, yet none remains so utterly constant in its workings and effects. When transient human brutalities cease, the grand seasonal cycle merely resumes. The contrast of human atrocities to continuing cycles of natural order points out the incongruity between nature's law and man's actions. The cyclical theory of history implied in Cooper's handling of setting thus conflicts directly with Cooper's belief in the linear progress of American society. "The ruins of time" is not easily squared with the "westward march of progress."

In his social fiction, Cooper expelled the two troublesome extremes of American society from the eastern settlements to the west. Doolittle and Bragg, Birch and Bumppo—the isolate hero and the go-ahead sharpster were the two types that, for different reasons, could not remain within the civilized confines of the American village. In the border romances, these two types are balanced against a different kind of borderer, the thoughtless, crude despoiler whose bravery is complemented by his honesty. All three of these kinds of frontiersmen confront the problem of the Indian, and are judged by their conduct toward him. The dilemma that these frontiersmen face is insoluble. If the white borderer adheres to the values of his Christian heritage, he brings a redeeming civilization to the wilderness, yet his Christian principles render his civilization an easy prey to Indian violence. To yield to Indian laws of vengeance, however, is to revert to the most savage principle of justice in a State of Nature; white civilization is advanced by sacrificing white principles to red.

Natty Bumppo, as we shall see, exemplifies the dilemma most fully. Natty respects Indian codes because, as a cultural relativist, he believes that Indian "gifts"

are only natural. He is convinced that the good Indian is
the one who follows his "gift" of retaliatory scalping,
and the bad Indian is he who neglects his "gift." In applying the concept of "gifts" to white frontiersmen, however, Natty is not so forthright. A Christian's "gifts"
include reason, mercy and honesty, yet Natty argues that
white deceit ("sarcumventions") and white killing are
fully justified by the conditions of the wilderness. Leatherstocking continues to insist, as "a man without a cross,"
that his values are wholly Christian, yet he acts in unacknowledged accord with Indian laws. Cooper, however, does not charge Natty either with hypocrisy or
contradiction. Natty knows that, in the wilderness, the
uncompromising Christian will not survive. He believes
that the higher law of Christianity must supersede the
Indian code, yet adopts the Indian code as the only way
of bringing it about. Unlike Cooper, Natty is utterly contemptuous of civilization, yet through Natty's words we
can glimpse the perplexing problem Cooper faced. Cooper
is forced to trust that a Christian civilization will finally
be established despite the un-Christian violence that has
been necessary to build it.

In this chapter I shall concentrate on three of the frontier Indian romances that grapple most directly with the
problem of defining morally just conduct in the State of
Nature. I believe that the central theme of all these novels
is not interracial warfare, nor racial contrast, but the
difficulties white frontiersmen face in dispensing justice
in the American wilderness. In all six of the border romances, Cooper emphasizes the failure of the white pio-
neer to form and to adhere to codes of moral law that
are both practicable and just. Although Cooper asserts

that white law must supersede Indian law, he is unable
to portray any workable code of white justice that is
clearly superior to red. Cooper shows us that, in the
wilderness, recourse to Indian laws of retaliation is inevitable. Yet this very fact implies that just civil codes,
formulated in statutes and enforced by courts, are the
only check upon man's natural lawlessness. If a settler
might have known that he was protected by law, bloody
vengeance would not have been necessary. The Indian
romances do not argue the desirability of the natural life.
They argue that, because most men fail to act within the
bounds of just moral laws, civil statutes are essential.

"THE WEPT OF WISH-TON-WISH"

Because of misleading statements by T. R. Lounsbury and
Leslie Fiedler, critics continue to concentrate their analyses of *The Wept of Wish-ton-Wish* upon the secondary
questions of miscegenation and Puritan intolerance.[8]
Only Donald Ringe has perceived that, if *The Wept of
Wish-ton-Wish* is considered in its entirety, the novel
displays a consistent depth of meaning and a rare degree
of artistic wholeness. Ringe argues persuasively that the
organizing theme of the book is the distinction between

[8] Lounsbury claimed that Cooper's novel revealed his bigoted
misunderstanding of the Puritans (*James Fenimore Cooper* [Bos-
ton, 1883], pp. 74–75) and Fiedler confined his comments upon the
novel to those characters who illustrate the hopelessness of racial
conversion (*Love and Death in the American Novel*, pp. 200–202).
In differing ways, the studies of the novel by Grossman, Kay Seymour House and George Dekker pursue the same interests.

"true and false religion."[9] Because Ringe does not consider the book in the context of Cooper's other frontier tales, however, he stops short of making the fullest claims for the novel. If we set aside the stiffly heroic portrait of Columbus in *Mercedes of Castille*, which remains wholly a sea novel, King Philip's War is the earliest period of American history Cooper ever treated. At the very roots of American civilization, Cooper discovers that the Puritan is unable to inhabit the wilderness in accord with his own moral law. When social expediency conflicts with Christian law, the Puritan will violate the law. Within two generations of Puritans, Cooper traces a very clear erosion of the American character and the American community. The Puritan's betrayal of his own theocracy is an event which reverberates throughout the remainder of the frontier tales. Satisfying in its artistry, *The Wept of Wish-ton-Wish* is also crucial in theme.

Divided chronologically into two sections of equal length, the novel describes the life of a single settlement in the 1660s, and then again in 1676. Each of the two sections traces the rise and fall of the idyllic community established by Mark Heathcote. In 1676 as in the 1660s, a fledgling community of pastoral civilization, outwardly like the original Templeton, is established. In both sections a fugitive regicide of the English Civil War, named Submission, arrives to warn and defend the dwellers of the valley against an attack of the Narragansetts. The civil authorities, officers of the crown or of the Connecticut Colony, appear in both sections to demand civil obligations of the Heathcote family, obligations which

[9] D. A. Ringe, *James Fenimore Cooper*, p. 51.

conflict with the bibilical moral laws that govern their settlement. In the 1660s and again in 1676 the settlement is nearly destroyed by Indian attacks, but the Heathcote leaders survive to rebuild. In each section, a crucial decision between Christian forgiveness and heathen revenge is demanded of the head of the Heathcote family. The structure of *The Wept of Wish-ton-Wish* is thus one of considerable subtlety; its final meaning depends entirely on the implied parallels between its two halves.

The destruction wrought upon the settlement in the valley of Wish-ton-Wish takes place against the contrasting background of white triumph during the larger war. Through his frequent references to King Philip's War, Cooper emphasizes that we are witnessing the first step of the Indians' extermination at white hands, an act of bloody dispossession which prefigures all of those to follow. The preface informs the reader that King Philip's War ended Indian power in New England and caused the crucial displacement of the Mohegan tribe (vii). *The Wept of Wish-ton-Wish* is thus the novel in which Cooper assesses the truth of all the claims of unjust dispossession later advanced by his Mohican chieftains: Tamenund, Chingachgook, and Uncas.[10]

Unable to practice his unspecified doctrinal beliefs within the Bay Colony, Captain Mark Heathcote[11] has

[10] Cooper did not distinguish the Mohegans of Rhode Island from the Mahicans of the upper Hudson River Valley. He is historically inaccurate in assuming that his "Mohicans" are the remains of the Mohegan tribe (Paul Wallace, "Cooper's Indians," *NYH*, XXXV (1954), 428).

[11] Susan de Lancey's grandmother was the daughter of Colonel Caleb Heathcote. In "A Glance Backward," Susan Cooper states that Angevine Farm had been owned by Colonel Heathcote in 1704

moved his family to a fertile valley bordering on the Connecticut River, twenty hours north of the Hartford settlement. Like Natty Bumppo, Mark Heathcote retreats westward from the settlements in order to maintain a higher morality. Mark desires "to raise his own tabernacle in the wilderness" (23), and identifies himself as "a submissive sojourner in the wilderness of the world, and an humble servitor in the outer temple" (35). A firm believer in individual liberty, distrustful of Divine Right and all Stuarts, Mark is an intriguing combination of deep submission to God's decrees and a very active practicality. Stern and humorless, he is both military captain and man of God. Cooper may be amused by Mark's superstitions and military ways, but he is warmly sympathetic to the piety, purposes, and character of the old Puritan.

The community Mark constructs is not merely an "oasis amidst an ocean of wilderness" (164). Heathcote has turned a portion of the neutral ground into a self-contained civilization that has overtones of a utopia, a utopia based, not on the values of a Puritan theocracy, but on the social and moral ideals of James Fenimore

---

and that the old Heathcote house and Heathcote graves were very much in evidence in 1818 when Cooper moved onto the land. Susan de Lancey's family home at Mamaroneck was called Heathcote Hill. See Susan F. Cooper, "A Glance Backward," *Atlantic Monthly*, LIX (1887), 199–206.

The location of the settlements are distinctly separate in fact and in Cooper's fiction, but Cooper could not have written *The Wept of Wish-ton-Wish* without his wife's family in mind. When one considers the consistently respectful attitude Cooper assumed toward his wife's family, the sympathetic portrayal of Mark's family seems all the less surprising. Perhaps the entire tale is based on a family legend, or a portion of Heathcote history.

Cooper. Mark is a godly man who happens to be a Puritan; he is not the one to quibble over doctrinal distinctions. The great principle on which he has constructed his community is no more sectarian than the Ten Commandments. He concludes every one of his frequent prayers with one great petition, "that no descendant of his should ever take life from a being unprepared to die, except in justifiable defence of his faith, his person, or his lawful rights" (23). Upon the fulfillment of that command depends the continued moral purity of his settlement.

Wish-ton-Wish is a social utopia as well. In a removed and fruitful valley, blessed with a river and rich soil, Heathcote's community exemplifies all the rural virtues praised in *Notions of the Americans* and *The Pioneers*. The Heathcotes themselves represent Cooper's ideal of family life. Mark is the benevolent patriarch of a household in which strict domestic discipline and parental respect are always observed. Apprentices and handmaidens fashion tools and clothes for the benefit of all. Cheerful hearth fires are everywhere. Even political conditions are ideal without being unhistorical. As the novel opens, a new royal charter has just been obtained for Connecticut, guaranteeing "peace and freedom of conscience" (41). Submission tells Mark that "none now dwell under the Crown of Britain with fewer offensive demands on their consciences, or with lighter calls on their political duties, than the men of Connecticut" (41). With a charitable policy toward the Indian, no discordant elements within, and the setting for an ideal life, the settlement of Mark Heathcote seems beyond criticism. Three important characters, Mark Heathcote, Submission, and

Meek Wolfe, all refer to the community as Bethel—the place of God, the sanctuary.[12]

The Puritan mind endows the narrative of *The Wept of Wish-ton-Wish* with a more universal significance than the conflicts of Cooper's other frontier novels. Only Mark Heathcote, after settling a wilderness, declares "Hither have we been led by the flaming pillar of Truth" (236). When the Narragansets brutally and unexpectedly level Heathcote's settlement, the Heathcote mentality attributes the destruction to providential intervention. Mark believes that the wrath of God, working through diabolic agents, has justly punished Heathcote sins. Before the attack erupts, Mark has forebodings of its significance: "We have, of late, had in this Colony tragical instances of what the disappointed malice of Azazel can attempt; and it would be vain to hope that the evil agencies are not vexed with the sight of my Bethel" (151).

Because of such statements, *The Wept of Wish-ton-Wish* becomes a clearly symbolic novel. It is the author who describes the Heathcote settlement as if it were Bethel, and he who gives it the suggestive name of Wish-ton-Wish. On the simplest level, therefore, Cooper views the Narragansett attack as the onslaught of all the forces of unreason destroying civilization. Characters named Content, Submission, Faith, and Charity are literally defending their citadel of moral civilization against sieges

[12] *The Wept of Wish-ton-Wish*, pp. 151, 415, 429. In Genesis 28: 10–22, Jacob is visited by the Lord in a dream. Upon awakening he renames the place of his dream Beth-el, or "the house of God": "Then Jacob awoke from his sleep and said, 'Surely the Lord is in this place; and I did not know it.' And he was afraid, and said, 'How awesome is this place! This is none other than the house of God, and this is the gate of heaven.' "

of the heathen, who have come from the vast and encircling wilderness. Simple as such an archetype may be, Cooper's handling of it does not become banal, because the chapters in which we watch the Heathcotes being driven back, step by step, to their innermost defenses, form one of Cooper's most exciting and convincing sections of great narrative prose.

Although their community is decimated, the Heathcotes survive. After the family rearises,[13] Mark faces the decision of responding to the destruction of his settlement. He had extended only charity to the Indians who have leveled his dwellings. To yield to the temptation of revenge might seem, under the circumstances, an understandable act of just retribution, but it would explicitly violate Mark's command that no Heathcote may kill except in "justifiable defense of his faith, his person, or his lawful rights." Revenge would also reduce white civilization to the moral level of savagery. The decision that Mark makes is an act of Christian heroism which binds up the wounds of his community:

I ask not vengeance on the deluded and heathenish imitators of the worshippers of Moloch. They have ignorantly done this evil. Let no man arm in behalf of the wrongs of one sinful and erring. (232)

Hath no one a voice to praise the Lord? The bands of the heathen have fallen upon my herds; the brand hath been kindled within my dwellings; my people have died by the violence of the unenlightened, and none are here to say that

[13] Ringe argues that the well into which the Heathcotes have retreated symbolizes providential protection of the Heathcotes' familial virtues and allows Cooper to picture the community as regenerating itself, like the phoenix, from its own ashes (*James Fenimore Cooper*, pp. 51–52).

the Lord is just! I would that the shouts of thanksgiving should arise in my fields! (235)

By insisting that all the surviving members of his family and his community first forswear revenge, and then praise God for a just retribution, Mark confirms his right to rule as patriarch. He continues to uphold the moral law on which his community is founded.

Passing over fifteen years, Cooper reopens his narrative in 1676 by describing a thriving New England settlement of forty dwellings. Unlike the original settlement, however, the new community is inherently flawed despite its appearance of peaceful prosperity. The social structure of the settlement has altered ominously. A religious patriarchy has yielded to secular government. Temporal and spiritual authority, formerly combined in the figure of Mark Heathcote, have now been subdivided. Religious leadership has fallen to the Reverend Meek Wolfe, who contrives to cite Christian mercy as the justification for revenge upon the Narrangansetts. Mark's son Content has become captain of the trained bands. Eben Dudley, former servant of Mark Heathcote, is now the ensign, second in command. Both men are thus made into officials who determine the rudimentary civil laws of the valley. As civil officials, their loyalty is to the settlement rather than to the moral command that underlies it. Content Heathcote has inherited the position of greatest power, but his wavering, secular values contrast sharply to Mark's forthright piety. The decline of the community shows that Cooper's distaste for Puritanism is a dislike only for the hypocrisy of later generations, when the Puritan's zeal had outlived his religious conviction.

Cooper distinguishes the two settlements by a telling contrast between their responses to the colonial authorities. In the first section, the right of unfettered individual freedom, guaranteed by the charter, was immediately violated by officers of the crown, who shamelessly pried into every corner of Mark's dwelling in search of Submission the regicide. Having invaded a gentleman's privacy, the officers attempted to pressure Mark into loyalty by displaying a seal of state and a warranty. Mark, however, neither revealed the whereabouts of Submission nor promised any aid against future Indian threats. Although Mark recognized the dangers of Indian attack, his Christian values determined his decision to coexist with the Indian, rather than to join the colony in efforts to extirpate him.

The second section begins shortly after the historical defeat of Conanchet's Narragansetts in November of 1675. Cooper explicitly denies that the slaughter of the Indians by the whites was just (300). Stating that "Right or wrong, the Colonists gravely decided that the war on their part was just" (299), Cooper indicates that, when the colony demanded the aid of the settlers of Wish-ton-Wish, the colony received it. Unlike his father, Captain Content Heathcote yields his trained bands to colonial reprisals against the Indian. Content's character is laid bare by a subtle juxtaposition. Cooper flatly declares "In this expedition most of the men of the Wish-ton-Wish had been conspicuous actors, under the orders of Content" (301). Two paragraphs later, Content tries to evade responsibility by denying past participation. He refers to "that violence, of which, bounden by our social cove-

nants, we have unhappily been unwilling spectators"
(301).

Content Heathcote's weakness invites forthright vengeance from the Narrangansetts, who believe that retaliation is their moral duty. The Indians' decision to revenge
or to forgive rests upon Conanchet, a Narragansett who
has been taught both the red moral law and the white.
Educated in the religion of Mark Heathcote, Conanchet
admires his white benefactors and assimilates their beliefs, yet remains committed to his Indian heritage. Believing in Mark Heathcote's creed that there shall be no
killing except in justifiable defense, Conanchet has witnessed the massacre of his tribe by white settlers, among
them the Heathcotes.

The difficulty of Conanchet's decision is compounded
by a personal motive. When Conanchet had first been
discovered outside the Heathcote stockade, he had come
to Wish-ton-Wish to avenge his father's death, single-
handed, upon the entire white race. The murder of Miantonimoh, Conanchet's father, by Pequod Indians who
were employed and abetted by whites, is described as
the spark that set off King Philip's War.[14] Thus, in Cooper's novels, the original wrong committed between the
races is very specifically white.

In the second section the onset of King Philip's War
focuses the issue of differing racial morality upon two
decisions of intense seriousness. Both Conanchet and the
Heathcote settlement are tested by the moral principle of
Mark Heathcote. During the days of battle, first Conan-

[14] See pages x, 81, 292, 359, 361, 440.

chet and then Content have the desire and opportunity to "take life from a being unprepared to die." The pressures of war allow them to take that life with personal impunity. In neither instance, however, could the execution be called a "justifiable defence of . . . faith, . . . person, or . . . lawful rights" (23).

The significance of the two judgments is immeasurably heightened because Content and Conanchet must decide upon the lives of one another. In the Indian attack of 1676, the wronged Narragansetts again devastate the community of Wish-ton-Wish, but on this occasion the Heathcotes are not saved by their own ingenuity. Conanchet spares the lives of the family which had befriended him. The response of the white survivors, however, is fully and exactly to reenact the original racial sin. Obeying the colonial power a second time, Content Heathcote, Eben Dudley, and Meek Wolfe allow their Pequod mercenaries to murder Conanchet, son of the slain Miantonimoh. There are no practical necessities sufficient to in any way excuse this savage action. In *The Wept of Wish-ton-Wish*, sin descends from one white generation to its successor; white civilization is victorious at the price of its moral degradation.

Simply by juxtaposing the two judgments, Cooper's condemnation of the moral decline of his representative settlement acquires great dramatic force. Conanchet, the spiritual son of Mark Heathcote, is the Indian who obeys Mark's command of Christian justice. Content, the natural son of Mark Heathcote, is the white who disobeys his father's dearest principle. Conanchet's inherited impulse to revenge himself upon the Heathcotes has risen to an act of mercy. Content's Puritan piety, however, has degenerated into an expedient revenge. The Bethel of the valley of Wish-ton-Wish can survive any attack of savagery, but fails morally due to its own inner corruption.

The conclusion of *The Wept of Wish-ton-Wish*, like that of many other Cooper novels, concerns the future history of the settlement. A dark and somber tone prevails, befitting a tale that has described the fall of a humane patriarchy, with theocratic overtones, to a secular government in which power is subdivided among the vengeful. We learn that Wish-ton-Wish, its growth stunted, has nearly passed from human memory. Cooper suggests, however, that the death of Conanchet has led to communal resurgence. Many years after Conanchet's death, a thriving rural village rises over his bones (471). Spiritual authority within the restored community has shifted in a hopeful direction; Meek Wolfe has been replaced by Meek Lamb.

Conanchet evidently must die in order that the community which killed him be rebuked and purified. Despite the horror and injustice of Conanchet's death, Cooper views his loss as a sad but inevitable sacrifice. God's providence has clearly willed the triumph of the white over the red race. Submission's speech to King Philip ends the debate between the rights of white and red:

But know there is one who is master of all here on earth, as he is King of Heaven! It is his pleasure that the sweet savor of his worship should arise from the wilderness. His will is law, and they that would withstand do but kick against the pricks. Listen then to peaceful counsels, that the land may be parcelled justly to meet the wants of all, and the country be prepared for the incense of the altar. (429)

Amid a world in which assimilation of red to white is so evidently impossible, even a Conanchet remains one who "kicks against the pricks." He dies, not as a Christian, but as "the last Sachem of the broken and dispersed tribe of the Narragansetts" (461). Although Cooper acknowledges the price civilization pays for its triumph over savagery, he continues to justify the change.

The Wept of Wish-ton-Wish has the ethical depth, though not the literary finish, of tragedy. Conanchet and Mark Heathcote are characters of sufficient complexity and integrity to merit tragic stature. The situation in which they are placed, the dilemmas that they face, are of the highest importance. The conflicts drawn between savagery and civilization, biblical law and Indian law, are clearly outlined and convincingly resolved. Content, Mark, Meek Wolfe, and Conanchet themselves create the rises and the falls of their Bethel. The consequences of their deeds, good and bad, follow as remorselessly as in a novel by George Eliot.

An action in one section of the novel acquires greater significance from its parallel in the other. Because judgment is reached by juxtaposing analagous actions, authorial didacticism is unnecessary. The lives that are lost and the buildings that are burned are not merely part of an exciting battle. In the valley of Wish-ton-Wish, blood is shed to answer the questions, "What is the good life?" and "How should one lead it?" The title of the novel appears ludicrous and heavy-handed—until one realizes that, in four words, Cooper has suggested both the hopes of settlement and the eventual tragedy wrought by man's betrayal of a moral law.

"THE PRAIRIE"

By setting *The Prairie* in 1803 and beginning with a discussion of the Louisiana Purchase, Cooper forces his reader to consider the action of the tale in national terms. One year after publishing the novel, Cooper indicated the importance he attributed to Jefferson's act: "The purchase of Louisiana was the greatest masterstroke of policy that has been done in our times. All the wars, and conquests, and cessions of Europe, for the last hundred years, sink into insignificance, compared with the political consequences that are dependent on this increase of territory."[15] Within the novel itself, the prairie becomes a vast neutral ground in which representative American characters vie for power. Sioux, Pawnee, scientist, trapper, frontiersman, and middle-class whites are all present on the prairie. The presence of Inez and Middleton, ridiculous though it may be as an historic probability, shows Cooper's desire to portray all important social forces in his cast of characters. The marriage of the indolent Spanish Catholic to the Protestant officer suggests a national mingling of cultures.[16] Cooper emphasizes that by 1803 Ishmael Bush, not Natty Bumppo, is the charac-

[15] *Notions of the Americans*, II, 346.

[16] Joel Porte has indicated the importance of this seemingly irrelevant marriage: "old wounds must be healed, and Protestant and Catholic must reunite, so that America can move forward with both energy *and* beauty into a progressive future in our fallen world" (*The Romance in America* [Middletown, Conn. 1969], p. 50). I am deeply indebted to Porte's excellent study of *The Prairie*.

teristic American frontiersman. The narrative is awk-
wardly interrupted in order to inform the reader that the
explorations of Lewis and Clark are occurring simultaneously with the immigration of the Bush clan (144). Cooper accounts for Bush's character by explaining that
Ishmael typifies the American borderer: "brave, . . .
proud, . . . vindictive, . . . irreligious," "without restraint,"
and "beyond the reach of the law" (79).

In the first scene, Cooper defines the issues of his
novel. The grand, still figure of Natty Bumppo brings
Ishmael Bush's immigration onto the prairie to a momentary halt. "The man without a cross" confronts the bar-
barian frontiersman who believes that retaliatory vengeance is a moral law. This dramatic juxtaposition raises
national questions: Who shall inherit the new American
land, and by what principles shall it be governed? Thus,
like many other frontier romances, *The Prairie* is a grand
debate on the merits of Christian justice and retributory
justice as means of bringing civilization to the American
continent. In its setting, however, *The Prairie* is atypical.
The conditions of the prairie, unlike those of the forest,
force Cooper to admit that the lex talionis is natural law.
Rather than assuming that Christian justice is everywhere superior to retaliatory justice, Cooper considers
whether, on the prairie, Ishmael's law of retribution may
not only be inevitable, but peculiarly just.

In *The Prairie* the American land is still a neutral
ground, but it is no longer an Eden. The dreary, barren
monotony of the unending plains is presented as the consequence of a previous moral failure. The waste and
moral callousness of the American borderer seem to have
evoked a divine chastisement which has inflicted upon

the frontiersman the barrier of the prairie itself. Natty Bumppo surely speaks for Cooper's latent feelings about the evil consequences of civilization, when he describes the prairies in *The Pathfinder*:

I mean the spots marked by the vengeance of heaven, or which, perhaps, have been raised up as solemn warnings to the thoughtless and wasteful, hereaways. They call them prairies; and I have heard as honest Delawares as I ever knew, declare that the finger of God has been laid so heavily on them, that they are altogether without trees. This is an awful visitation to befall innocent 'arth, and can only mean to show to what frightful consequences a heedless desire to destroy may lead.[17]

In context, the Pathfinder's words seem comically naive, yet Cooper had confirmed them in *The Prairie*; the plains, once fertile, have been judged by God and have fallen barren (296–297).

For the American borderer, the new land proves to be ancient, unyielding and untenable. Seeking Eldorado, the Bush clan find only the prairie (12). Natty's wearied distaste for the Old World and the Old Morality (294) is partially explained by his nostalgic associations of the garden of Eden with the eastern forests. The Old World, as he insists, is all about him, but Natty's thoughts continually revert to his eastern past. Putting the best face upon the present that he can, Natty says, "here may natur' be seen in all its richness, trees alone excepted. Trees, which are to the 'arth, as fruits are to a garden; without them nothing can be pleasant, or thoroughly useful" (313).

Cooper's generalizations about the cultural signifi-

[17] *The Pathfinder*, p. 103.

cance of the prairie arouse contradictory feelings of hope and disillusionment. In many passages, Cooper typically praises the "march of civilization" (79). America illustrates all stages of settlement, from the barbarous primitivism of the prairie, to the decent, agrarian settlements of the Alleghenies, to the refinement of the eastern seaboard "where wealth, luxury, and the arts are beginning to seat themselves" (79). The future progress implied for the prairie by these waves of increasing civilization is sharply countered, however, by Cooper's description of the prairie itself. The emigrants who push westward are traveling over the ruins of previous, unnameable civilizations (297–298).[18] The interracial and intertribal warfare that forms the immediate action for the tale is merely self-destructive. The Pawnee and the Sioux, the clan of Ishmael, and the trapper with his band of respectable whites battle one another with no effect at all upon the dreary land over which they are fighting. Metaphorically, Cooper describes them as combatant fleets who move over the oceanic desolation of the prairie. By the end of the novel, the law of nature clearly seems to be cyclical rather than progressive. Natty Bumppo delivers a magnificent discourse on the inevitable fall and decay of the great oak (298); the final death of the old trapper, who is often likened to a tree, only provides a further illustration of the oak's law.

The neutral ground of the prairie is ultimately controlled, neither by the Sioux, who are slaughtered; by

[18] Cooper is echoing his contemporaries' belief that the burial mounds of the Mississippi Valley proved the existence of a civilization that preceded the Indians. See Bryant's "The Prairies," 11. 42–86.

Bush, who leaves; by the trapper, who dies; nor by the distant and fading Pawnees. Beasts of prey, visible during every battle, rule the prairie and practice its natural law, the law of the strongest. Over the surface of the plains hover the inevitable buzzards, ready to inflict upon the bodies of borderer and Indian what these men are too ready to inflict upon one another. The primordial bestiality of Cooper's prairie tacitly demonstrates the need for the graces of civilization and the restraints of civil law.

Because the prairie turns men into birds of prey, the buzzard serves Cooper as a metaphor as well as a fact. When a vindictive Indian crone moves toward Hard Heart with a knife, Cooper says that she "skirred away in the direction of her victims, like a rapacious bird that, having wheeled on poised wings for the time necessary to insure its object, makes the final dart upon its prey" (406–407). Although Natty scorns civilization, he is also acutely aware that the prairie turns the men who struggle to possess it into animals. Observing the Bush clan, the Pawnees, and the Sioux all primed for battle, Natty says: "Do you see yon birds watching for the offals of the beast they have killed? Therein is a moral which teaches the manner of a prairie life. A band of Pawnees are outlying for these very Sioux, as you see the buzzards looking down for their food; and it behoves us, as Christian men who have so much at stake, to look down upon them both" (256).

Against the background of the prairies, Cooper contrasts the two moral codes which conflict for its possession. Ishmael Bush considers the natural law of the prairie a sufficient justification for adopting and enacting its code of "an eye for an eye." The old trapper, however, condemns prairie law and clings to his identity as a Christian. Whereas Bush resembles a patriarch of the Old Testament, enforcing the lex talionis upon his clan, Natty resembles a Christian hero of the New, urging his principles upon all who will listen. Recent critics believe that *The Prairie* shows us the gradual evolution of the Old Law into the New.[19] In their view, Natty Bumppo administers a telling rebuke to Bush's principles, just as he had initially blocked Bush's westward movement. For these critics, the chastening of Ishmael Bush implies the purging of the American frontiersman; it is an act that foretells a truly Christian, civilized America.

This view of the novel raises perplexing questions. The purgation of Ishmael is briefly implied (452), but is never declared to be a permanent certainty. Natty Bumppo, representative of the "New" Christian order, is an aged man who passes away at the novel's end. Nowhere does Cooper state that the prairie will soon be ruled by frontiersmen of Christian justice. Instead, Cooper deepens our recognition that settlers of the prairie will inevitably revert to natural laws of vengeance. Natty clings to his Christian values only because he remembers his Moravian upbringing and falls back upon the natural piety he had absorbed in the eastern forests. Ishmael Bush, however, is the realist who practices the law of the prairie itself.

[19] Joel Porte, *The Romance in America*, p. 47; William Wasserstrom, "Cooper, Freud and the Origins of Culture," *The American Imago*, XVII (1960), 423–437; Robert H. Zoellner, "Conceptual Ambivalence in Cooper's Leatherstocking," *AL*, XXXI (1960), 406–411.

As Henry Nash Smith has shown,[20] Bush and Bumppo are curiously similar to one another. Like Natty, Bush is a squatter and a fugitive from the law of eastern settlements. Both men are scornful of civil laws and both deliver grumbling complaints against fetters on individual freedom. Natty agrees with Ishmael that, in determining land ownership, the natural law of use takes precedence over any legal deed (74). Natty is as much an Ishmael and a patriarch as Bush; conversely, Bush is as physically competent as the trapper. Ishmael's honest, stubborn adherence to his principles is equal to Natty's. Both men are proud to be illiterate, yet each has an awesome regard for the truth of the Book. From the Bible as from their surroundings, however, Bush and Bumppo have extracted widely differing principles.

Natty resorts to Killdeer as a necessary departure from the law of the Moravians and of his personal forest divinity. The Bush family, first settlers of a wilderness, observe the natural law of the prairie, elevate it into a moral law, and confirm it by citation from the Old Testament. Whereas Natty possesses the self-control to guide himself by Christian principles whenever possible, Bush seizes upon the lex talionis as a rationale for his own sluggish aggressions. For Natty, authority is self-imposed moral laws; for the Bush clan, authority is a tenuous, patriarchal tyranny.

Because both codes arise from natural surroundings, Bush must be considered to be the grotesque perversion of Natty Bumppo rather than his opposite. Just as their similarities in character result in different moral prin-

[20] "Introduction" to *The Prairie* (New York: Holt, Rinehart and Winston, 1950), pp. xvii–xviii.

ciples, so their similar pasts indicate different attitudes toward the law and the Indian. Although both men are fleeing from civil justice, Natty has left civilization because he scorned a court to whose judgment he had submitted. Ishmael, however, is a fugitive who had killed a sheriff's deputy. This pattern of contrast in similarity is carried down to historical detail. Both Bush and Bumppo had fought under Mad Anthony Wayne during the revolutionary war, and both had irregularly left Wayne's service. Despite Ishmael's love for killing Indians, he had deserted from Wayne's army because of "too much tattooing and regulating" (76). Natty had been proud to fight under Wayne's orders, until he discovered that Mad Anthony's warfare against the Indians was not motivated by moral justice (77).

Because the Bush clan both accepts and acts upon the prairie's law of vindictive retribution, the family suffers its consequences. Asa Bush, source of so much sorrow, kicks the obdurate prairie and states, "The rifle is better than the hoe in such a place as this" (91). Before the outbreak of conflict, Ishmael declares to the trapper the moral law by which he hopes to settle the prairie:

There'll come a time, stranger, right soon, when justice will have its dues, and that, too, without the help of what is called the law. We ar' of a slow breed, it may be said, and it is often said, of us; but slow is sure; and there ar' few men living who can say they ever struck a blow, that they did not get one as hard in return, from Ishmael Bush. (76)

When the Sioux commit the first wrong by stealing Bush's horses, Ishmael announces that he will retaliate "by taking hoof for hoof" (107). Like Natty, Ishmael believes that "when the law of the land is weak, it is right the law of nature should be strong" (113). The action of the tale, however, proves that Bush's law of nature, retaliatory vengeance, is far too strong. Ishmael's two attempts to set up a citadel of civilization are overrun, his chattels are kicked over the prairie, his treaty with the Sioux is betrayed, Ellen and Inez flee to join the old trapper, and his eldest son is shot. Natty's conviction that the prairie acts as a divine retribution on the moral codes of the American borderer is confirmed by Cooper's plot.

Bush's willingness to engage in immediate retaliation is effectively contrasted to the actions of Natty Bumppo. Because Natty observes the increasingly frequent resorts to violence, participating only when necessary, his enemies wrongly consider him harmless and allow him freedom of action. Natty offers disinterested succor to the helpless, whereas Bush acts only for his clan. By encouraging revenge, Bush is partly responsible for the tragedy that befalls his family. Cooper contrasts the effects of Bush's law of vengeance with Natty's desire to act as a Christian. Having adopted Hard Heart as a son, Natty nonetheless refuses to approve or transmit Hard Heart's policies of blood revenge. Bush's lex talionis only causes misery for his family. Natty's humanity to the Pawnee earns him an honorable resting place amid the best of Indian culture.

Until the ending of the novel, Bush and his codes of justice clearly suffer by comparison to the old trapper and Christian law. Accordingly, critics have condemned Bush without closely examining the meaning of Bush's final actions. Chase calls the Bush family "the real villains," "mean-minded materialists" who "have no trace of reverence for nature or man."[21] Ringe calls Ishmael a "completely selfish" man "who has confused liberty with license, who takes the law into his own hands,"[22] and Kay Seymour House goes so far as to state that Ishmael "embodies the great American nightmare of the early nineteenth century."[23] These descriptions more aptly refer to Abiram White than to Ishmael. By ignoring Cooper's very mixed attitude toward Bush's final court, the complexity of Cooper's divided opinions concerning frontier justice is easily oversimplified.

It is Ishmael Bush, not Natty Bumppo, who restores social order at the end of *The Prairie*. Because Ishmael belongs to society, even in its lowest form, he can bring rudimentary forms of civil justice to the barbarous wilderness. Natty, by contrast, has no place in society and can devise no concept of civil justice. Toward the beginning of the novel, Ishmael had stated "I have come five hundred miles to find a place where no man can ding the words of the law in my ears" (95). It is not only ironic but a tribute to Ishmael that he recognizes the necessity of holding a court to redress the wrongs supposedly done him by Natty and his young followers. The squatter who had scorned the civil law becomes the self-appointed judge of the frontier:

I am called upon this day to fill the office which in the settlements you give unto judges, who are set apart to decide on matters that arise between man and man. I have but little knowledge of the ways of the courts, though there is a rule

[21] Richard Chase, *The American Novel and its Tradition*, p. 61.

[22] Donald Ringe, *James Fenimore Cooper*, p. 47.

[23] Kay Seymour House, *Cooper's Americans*, p. 298.

that is known unto all, and which teaches that an 'eye must be returned for an eye,' and 'a tooth for a tooth.' (426)

Ishmael Bush achieves what few of Cooper's frontiersmen ever even attempt. He openly delivers impartial justice according to a fixed and stated principle of moral law.

Bush's court thus raises complex issues. Ishmael brings to the wilderness Cooper's cornerstone of social order, the civil law. The particular law that Bush enforces, however, is based upon a precivilized conception of justice. Even more perplexing is the fact that, although Cooper condones neither the tyranny nor the governing "rule" of Bush's court, he does acknowledge the grim justice of its dispensations. The cause of Asa's death is correctly determined. The two young couples are granted their just release. Even Natty Bumppo, whom Bush had dearly wished to punish, is allowed his freedom. Bush gains stature because the justice he provides is truly disinterested. He adheres to his conception of principle even after he recognizes that following that principle is no longer in his self-interest.

Nonetheless, the ironic outcome of Bush's court is that it forces disclosure of the tragic consequences of Bush's own code. By teaching retribution to his family, Bush has induced his son Asa to strike Abiram White—after Abiram had accused Ishmael of lawlessness. Abiram, Ishmael's brother-in-law, shoots Asa in the back. Defending himself before Ishmael, Abiram ironically pleads, "I did no murder; I gave but blow for blow" (438). Because Abiram has "shrieked" out this excuse, we presume that he honestly believes it. For Abiram, the consequence of adopting the lex talionis is that he can no longer distinguish between retaliation and murder. Ishmael presumably understands what has happened in Abiram's soul, and its effect upon his own family, yet he doggedly adheres to his law and hangs his wife's brother. The clansman who had ridiculed the law has decided that maintaining his principle of justice is of greater importance than clan loyalty.

The troublesome question of Cooper's own attitude toward Ishmael's action still remains. As a Deist and a gentleman, Cooper could not sanction Bush's decision to hang Abiram. Consequently, Cooper projects his conscious disapproval of Bush's vengeance through Bush's unconscious guilt. Sensing that something is greatly wrong with the lex talionis, Bush tries to deny his responsibility for the hanging. Having left Abiram on a rock ledge with a noose around his neck, Bush tells him "You shall be your own executioner, and this miserable office shall pass away from my hands" (447). At the very moment when Ishmael leaves Abiram to his fate, he tries to convince Abiram (and himself) that he forgives Abiram his wrongs (448). Ishmael's guilt is effectively conveyed by the moaning winds and ghastly shrieks that pervade the heavens after the deed is done. The last words that Ishmael utters reveal his desire to act upon the moral laws of a Christian: "Abiram White, we all have need of mercy; from my soul do I forgive you! May God in Heaven have pity on your sins!" (452).

Despite these signs of disapproval, Cooper evidently recognizes that, within the context of the neutral ground, Ishmael's actions are inevitable and just. Because there is no civil law on the seemingly endless prairie, Ishmael's alternatives are to hang Abiram or to let him go. Bush's decision personally to enforce the lex talionis on the prairie is exactly the same as Captain Lawton's decision personally to enforce the lex talionis upon the Skinners. When we recall the grim justice of Lawton's whipping, it seems manifestly unfair to assume that Cooper disapproves of Bush's code of retaliatory justice, simply because Cooper disapproves of Bush's character. Nor should the emotional effect of Abiram's hanging be ignored. The grandeur and biblical simplicity of the scene lend to Ishmael's actions an aura of awesome sublimity that Natty Bumppo's feats of derring do never quite attain.

Cooper remains tellingly silent about the justice of Ishmael's decision. Only the epigraph to chapter XXXII provides any evidence, albeit indirect, of Cooper's attitude. Cooper chose to precede his description of the sentence and the hanging with a passage from *The Merchant of Venice*, IV, i. Bassanio, pleading with Portia for Antonio's life, urges her to take the law into her own hands in order to provide the merchant a just mercy: "And I beseech you, / Wrest once the law, to your authority: / To do a great right, do a little wrong." It is curious that, although Shakespeare's play exposes the wrongs of retaliation, the particular lines that Cooper selects provide a justification for Ishmael. If we assume that Cooper approves of Bassanio's plea, then Ishmael must be viewed as the judge who has wrested the law to his own authority and committed a little wrong (killed a craven murderer) in order to do the great right of serving justice. If Cooper, like Portia, disapproves of Bassanio's entreaty, the only conceivable parallel to Bassanio's speech is Abiram's contemptible plea that Ishmael forsake his law and pronounce forgiveness upon a murderer.

In sentencing Abiram, Bush believes that he is acting "according to the laws of God and man" (445). Whether right or wrong, Ishmael has finally recognized, as Natty Bumppo has not, that civil courts are necessary to enforce "the laws of God." The old trapper wrongly assumes that man's efforts are futile in the face of God's laws. Natty knows that "Mankind twist and turn the rules of the Lord, to suit their own wickedness" (295), but he also believes that "man's power is not equal to his will, . . . because the wisdom of the Lord hath set bounds to his evil workings" (297). The deeds of Abiram White prove that this second assumption is regrettably false. Nonetheless, because Natty believes in controlling providence, he is content to retreat from injustice and leave the Lord to take care of American lawlessness. Cooper emphasizes that Natty had had no intention of revealing Abiram's murder of Asa until Bush's court forced him to disclose the truth (437).

In assessing Bush's decision to hang Abiram, Cooper is torn between his Christian heritage and his keen awareness of practical necessity. Ishmael Bush's law may be primordial, but it brings social order to the neutral ground. Moreover, Cooper recognizes that, within the State of Nature, retaliatory killing is justifiable, unfortunate though that may be. Locke had argued that "every man in the State of Nature has a power to kill a murderer, both to deter others from doing the like injury . . . and also to secure men from the attempts of a criminal. . . . And upon this is grounded that great law of Nature, 'Whoso sheddeth man's blood by man shall his blood be shed.' "[24] In making this statement, Locke simply wished to determine the principles of justice in a natural state. Cooper, however, is not primarily concerned with providing a justification for retaliatory killing. Although Cooper seems in unspoken agreement with Locke's conclusion, Cooper's intent is to show that principles of natural justice, no matter how defensible with the natural state, must be superseded by the rule of Christian gentlemen and civil law. The terrifyingly primordial qualities of Bush's justice argue Cooper's point most forcibly.

In a novel that presents a grim picture of the peculiar combination of lawlessness and harsh legality which characterizes the first settlers, Natty Bumppo is forced to consider that Judge Temple might have been correct in his insistence upon civil statutes. When Natty first realizes that Bush is very like himself in character and background, the old trapper grudgingly entertains the idea that the civil law is necessary:

The law—'tis bad to have it, but I sometimes think it is worse to be entirely without it. Age and weakness has brought me to feel such weakness at times. Yes—yes, the law is needed when such as have not the gifts of strength and wisdom are to be taken care of. (31)

Although Natty carefully exempts men like himself from need of law, his statement little resembles the words of the Leatherstocking who, over the ashes of his burned hut, harangued against the deviltries of all civil law. If much of America resembles the prairie, and if Bush is the new representative borderer, Natty suspects that civil statutes may be essential.

[24] Locke, *Second Treatise on Civil Government*, pp. 22–23.

Cooper very explicitly shows us that Natty's mind is
so asocial that he cannot continue to view the problem of
social justice in a civil context. Later in the novel, Natty
reverts to his more characteristic faith, a primitive an-
archism in which each man is to govern himself in accord
with the moral law. Gesturing toward the prairie, he says
"This is a region, as you must all know, where a strong
arm is far better than the right, and where the white law
is as little known as needed. Therefore does everything
now depend on judgment and power" (253). This statement simply does not square with the events Natty observes. The entire novel proves that the strong arm is
considerably worse than the right, and that the white
law is desperately needed to provide a higher kind of
justice than retributory killing. Whereas Ishmael Bush
grows to understand the necessity of law, Natty Bumppo
relapses into his simplistic scorn for all civic statutes.

The ending of *The Prairie* leaves the land obtained by
the Louisiana Purchase still unsettled by man. The
Bushes' departure to the east is balanced by the death of
Natty Bumppo facing the west. Repulsed by the harsh-
ness of the prairie, Bush seems no longer willing to accept the harsh consequences of the lex talionis. At the
same time, however, he recognizes that, if he does not
practice retribution, he can no longer live on the prairie.
The death of Natty Bumppo deprives the new land of its
one inhabitant who was able both to guide his life by
Christian values and to survive. In Natty's epic statement, "when I am gone there will be an end of my race"
(475), one can trace Cooper's insistence that the qualities of Natty Bumppo are disappearing from American
life. After all of the characters die or vanish from the

prairie setting, the problem of bringing justice to the neutral ground remains unsolved.

Cooper, however, makes a valiant attempt to assure the reader that the passage of time will assure progress. Long after the departure of Natty and Ishmael, the power vacuum is filled, Cooper says, by white settlers who have absorbed the principles of Natty Bumppo, but brought them to national service. After witnessing the workings of the natural law of the prairie, both Middleton and Paul Hover return to society. As befits their separate social stations, Hover enters the state legislature and Middleton becomes a congressman.

Henry Nash Smith argues that Cooper created such frontiersmen in order to provide a suitable match for his heroines.[25] It is also possible that Cooper turned to such figures because they represented a theoretic solution to the dilemma of providing justice for the frontier. Whereas Natty Bumppo defected from social law, the Bushes, Kirbys, and Doolittles neither would nor should participate in the structures of civil power. Because the Judge Temples and Natty Bumppos were vanishing breeds, Cooper began to rely on types like Middleton and Hover to assume the responsibilities of government. The Middletons and Hovers, however, constitute a remarkably unsuccessful solution. Cooper always tells us that such figures bring the neutral ground to civil order, but never shows us the process. Middle class, well-meaning, industrious and reasonably intelligent, these figures are rarely convincing as characters and seem sadly misplaced as politicians. Nonetheless they become increasingly im-

[25] *Virgin Land*, pp. 71–76.

portant. In *The Oak Openings*, Cooper's last frontier
novel in date of composition (1848) and date of action
(1812), Cooper was to revivify Paul Hover, rename him
Ben Boden, and portray him as the heroic frontiersman.
Natty Bumppo had passed from American life before
1812, and we can only assume that, by 1848, Cooper was
in no mood to resuscitate him a second time.

THE COMPROMISE OF DEERSLAYER

The last two Leatherstocking Tales reveal that Cooper's
growing discontent with American civilization was complemented by a growing longing for the State of Nature.
In *The Pathfinder* Oswego and Lake Ontario provide
panoramic landscapes of the sublime in which Natty
Bumppo, Jasper, and even Charles Cap can detect the
workings of God. *The Deerslayer* reflects Cooper's desire
to dwell upon the Edenic years of Lake Otsego, a time
prior to the judge's settlement and long before the provincial mobocracy of *Home As Found*. All critics since
Lawrence have noted that Leatherstocking becomes less
of a recognizable American character and more of a
mythic ideal in the last two volumes. Moreover, *The
Deerslayer* describes a natural paradise that is nationally
representative. Cooper introduces his setting by telling
us that "he who succeeds in giving an accurate idea of
any portion of this wild region must necessarily give a
tolerably correct notion of the whole" (15). The fact that
The Deerslayer describes the beginnings of the corruption of an American Eden only enhances its attractions
for the reader.

Even in 1841, however, Cooper was by no means willing to totally idealize a prior State of Nature. The tender innocence of Deerslayer's first kill and the stunning descriptions of Lake Glimmerglass are finally not sufficient either to characterize Deerslayer as a saint and a knight, or to qualify Cooper's novel as an idyll. Vengeance may not be the natural law of Lake Glimmerglass, as it had been of the prairie, but the Hurons practice vengeance nonetheless. The virgin forest allows Deerslayer to worship divine laws, but it also allows Hutter and Hurry Harry a free hand for slaughter. If Deerslayer remains a saint, he is a saint who makes a decisive, necessary compromise with Christian principles. And finally, if we examine the action of the tale itself, rather than remember its descriptive passages, we find that Cooper is concerned to point out the hideous consequences of legalizing slaughter in a wilderness where man's aggressive tendencies certainly need no civil sanction.

The American Democrat, written only three years before *The Deerslayer*, had restated Cooper's conviction that civil laws must be "founded on the immutable principles of natural justice" and "formed on that consciousness of right, which God has bestowed in order that men may judge between good and evil."[26] Cooper surely believed that Judge Temple's laws were as close an approximation of natural and divine justice as man could devise. The conservation laws were designed to protect God's plenty from the vicious, even if in actuality they did not always do so. The bounty law that rules Lake Glimmer-

---

[26] *The American Democrat*, p. 75.

glass, however, violates any definition of moral or divine
law. It is a statute calculated to advance lawlessness and
expose the weak to the vengeance of the strong.

The entire narrative of *The Deerslayer* rests upon two
laws enacted by the colonial authorities. The French army
in Canada has passed a law paying bounty for the scalps
of all Englishmen and Delawares. The English army
along the Hudson has passed a law paying bounty for
the scalps of all Frenchmen and Hurons. Bush's code of
vengeance demanded blood only in retaliation; the
bounty laws reward unprovoked murder. White laws
paying a bounty for scalps had been passingly mentioned
in *The Wept of Wish-ton-Wish*, *The Last of the Mohicans*, and *The Pathfinder*. In the last of the Leatherstocking Tales, however, the scalp law becomes the
motivating force of all the action. The white Christians
have sunk to legalizing Indian codes of vengeance.

The plot of *The Deerslayer* is a simple succession of
legalized scalping raids that increase in brutality until
Tom Hutter, himself in pursuit of scalps, is scalped alive
in his own dwelling:

Judith moved forward, with a sudden impulse, and removed
a canvas cap that was forced so low on [Hutter's] head as to
conceal his face, and, indeed, all but his shoulders. The instant
this obstacle was taken away, the quivering and raw flesh, the
bared veins and muscles, and all the other disgusting signs of
mortality, as they are revealed by tearing away the skin,
showed he had been scalped, though still living. (382–383)

Judith's removal of the cap is Cooper's climactic disclosure of the consequences of bounty law—a tearing
away of the veil. Pitiable though the sight of Hutter may
be, Cooper is so outraged by Hutter's greed for bounty

that he coldly justifies Hutter's death as "evidence of the decrees of a retributive Providence," one of those "moments of vivid consciousness, when the stern justice of God stands forth in colors so prominent, as to defy any attempts to veil them from the sight" (385).

The punishment that overtakes Hutter seems to equalize vengeances and to satisfy blood lust. The reader is led to hope that so vivid a demonstration of the effects of the scalp law will convince frontiersmen of the necessity of restraint. Instead Cooper effectively ends his novel with the retaliatory slaughter of the Huron scalpers by the English army. The white troops, who supposedly bring Christian order to the wilderness, coldbloodedly bayonet the savages, their wives, and their wounded (573–574). It is not accidental that Deerslayer, returning from his furlough, is saddened by the blackness and gloom that seem to have descended over Lake Glimmerglass (440).[27]

The effect of such a law upon the borderer is Cooper's major concern. As in so many of the frontier novels, Cooper focuses on the moment when the settlers have first entered the wilderness. With the single exception of Deerslayer, Eden has not impressed its moral laws upon the frontiersmen. Tom Hutter and Hurry Harry are debased variants of earlier, representative frontiersmen

---

[27] Cooper's exposure of the consequences of the scalp law is neither unhistorical nor exaggerated. Parkman records that in 1764 the English governor of Pennsylvania proclaimed a high bounty for scalps. A white soldier named David Owens, who had been living among the Shawanoes, subsequently murdered and scalped four Shawanoe warriors, his own Indian wife, and his two halfbreed children (*The Conspiracy of Pontiac* [New York, 1962], pp. 405–406).

such as Ishmael Bush and Billy Kirby. Like Bush, Hutter
is a greedy individualist and a fugitive from the law he
defies. Unlike Bush, however, Hutter is openly scornful
of human life. Hurry Harry shares Kirby's good-natured
stupidity and massive strength, but Kirby had never
been a killer, nor had he shunned his social responsibilities as Harry does. In the figures of Hutter and Hurry
Harry, Cooper's frontiersmen emerge for the first time
as open racists whose contempt for the Indian is a means
of rationalizing avarice, while flattering their desires to
feel superior. The castle and the ark which the two men
have built on Lake Glimmerglass are the footholds of
civilization, but they are used to conceal stolen wealth
and facilitate murder. Hutter and March treat the neutral
ground purely as a source of wealth.

The Deerslayer is the only frontier novel in which the
frontiersman becomes an Indian, while the Indian resembles an honorable white. Rather than scalping their
white captives, the Hurons honorably ransom them for
chessmen. The Mingos venerate Hetty Hutter; Hurry
and Tom condescend toward her. When the Hurons declare war, they give forewarning through a bundle of
bound pine knots. Hurry shoots indifferently and without warning. Harry and Hutter are the first to seek
scalps; their method is to skulk after women and children during the night. In no previous tale has Cooper
portrayed whites organizing a scalping expedition, invading Indian camps, or shooting an Indian maiden.

Deerslayer's judgment upon the hunters and trappers
of the frontier is characteristically blunt: "Take 'em as a
body, Judith, 'arth don't hold a set of men more given to
theirselves, and less given to God and the law" (456).

The irony is that Natty, who will be first a hunter and then a trapper, is absolutely wrong—if he is referring to civil not moral law. In the opening scene, Deerslayer and Hurry Harry engage in a seemingly inappropriate debate concerning the "legality" of scalp law. The Deerslayer must learn that he has entered a world in which a Hurry Harry can justify murder by complacent reference to civil statute: "Just hearken to reason, if you please, Deerslayer, and tell me if the Colony can make an onlawful law? Isn't an onlawful law more ag'in natur' than scalpin' a savage? A law can be no more onlawful, than truth can be a lie" (49).

Under such circumstances, Cooper's principled hero is compelled to rebel against the laws of the civilization which needs his virtues. Natty replies to Harry that "When the Colony's laws, or even the King's laws, run ag'in the laws of God, they get to be onlawful, and ought not to be obeyed. I hold to a white man's respecting white laws, so long as they do not cross the track of a law comin' from a higher authority" (49).[28] Because Hurry Harry proves unable to understand that a civil law must be based upon a moral law, the conflict between the two frontiersmen hardens and widens in significance. Natty's refusal to scalp in violation of divine law is pitted against Hurry's insistence on a civil legality. The issue of the novel, therefore, is whether the youthful and as yet uninitiated Deerslayer can maintain his moral conscience,

[28] Natty's injunction is the one passage in Cooper's writings in which the author seems explicitly to sanction civil disobedience. Significantly, however, civil disobedience is condoned by a character who does not necessarily represent Cooper's opinion, and it is applied only to a law that antedates the American Constitution.

his conception of divine law, when almost all around him have succumbed to legalized brutality.

Natty, of course, never yields to scalping; he clings to his Moravian principles of Christian action as long as possible. He does so, however, only by remaining passive, imprisoned, and ineffectual until he returns from his furlough. Cooper emphasizes that Deerslayer is physically a stripling in comparison to Hurry Harry, who can outwrestle Indians by the handful and throttle the Deerslayer (26). Pistols explode in Deerslayer's hand (237). At times he even wanders without purpose or bearings (112–113). When the Deerslayer is not held captive by the Hurons, he is usually fleeing from them. By honorably insisting on fulfilling all terms of his furlough, Natty precipitates the final slaughter of the Hurons. Cooper admires the rectitude of his hero's principles, but acknowledges the price Natty pays for his moral virtue.

Cooper underscores Natty's helplessness through his treatment of Hetty Hutter. Like Natty, Hetty makes repeated but futile pleas for peace both to the savages and to the whites.[29] Hetty's literal belief in the biblical law of forgiving one's enemies, her hope that she can convince others of the truth of Christian mercy, only serve to earn her the name of "the Feeble Mind." On occasion, Cooper implies that Hetty is mad because she insists upon Christian principles. Like Parson Adams, Hetty possesses

[29] Hetty is named after the biblical Esther (190), whose dramatic appeal to King Ahasuerus that he cease persecuting the Jews resulted in the release of her people. In similar fashion, Hetty appeals to Rivenoak for the lives of Hurry Harry and Hutter. Her plea, however, is pathetically ineffectual.

a Christian naiveté that rebukes the civilization around her. In the neutral ground, however, her Christian naiveté is so utterly foreign as to seem a kind of insanity.

Crazed and pitiable though Hetty is, Cooper forces the comparison between her and the Deerslayer upon his reader. At the outset of the tale, the two characters share the same innocence, the same dread of killing, and the same helplessness in face of slaughter. Both are natural children of God, possessing an oddly identical heritage; Hetty's character illustrates her upbringing, "the wildness of Indian traditions and Indian opinions, . . . mingling with the Christian lore received in childhood" (396). Cooper emphasizes that Hetty and Natty are the physical inferiors and moral superiors of Judith and Hurry.

The white heroines of Cooper's frontier have consistently been products and spokesmen for civilization, but Hetty Hutter, asked to leave Glimmerglass, responds atypically:

I would rather stay here, where, if I wasn't born, I've passed my life. I don't like the settlements—they are full of wickedness and heart-burnings, while God dwells unoffended in these hills! I love the trees, and the mountains, and the lake, and the springs; all that his bounty has given us, and it would grieve me sorely, Judith, to be forced to quit them. (407–408)

In this passage, Hetty's voice is indistinguishable from the Leatherstocking's. When Deerslayer returns to meet his appointed time for torture, Hetty is the one who conducts him. Cooper refers to "the childish simplicity of character that the hunter so often betrayed—a simplicity so striking, that it frequently appeared to place him nearly on a level with the fatuity of poor Hetty" (416).

Cooper's elaborate comparison points up the futility of Christian principles in a world of vengeance. Hetty also provides a standard by which the initiation of Deerslayer is evaluated. Her practice of and adherence to Christian forgiveness remains unchanged. As a consequence, her death in the scalping wars tolls the inevitable end of the guileless principles for which she stood. By contrast, Deerslayer retains Hetty's belief that Christian mercy is divine law, but becomes a retaliatory killer in order to survive. R. W. B. Lewis accounts for the emerging differences between Natty and Hetty in a way that allows Natty to remain a wholly Adamic figure: "Hetty has an innocence which is, in fact, a self-delusive helplessness, a half-witted conviction of universal goodness, which exposes her to every physical and moral danger and finally kills her. It is partly by contemplation of that hapless girl, by conversations with Hetty and about her, that Hawkeye arrives at a more durable kind of innocence and at the insight that it must be bounded by an observation of ethical differences."[30]

Cooper himself, however, does not let Natty's "ethical differences" remain unchallenged. By the end of the novel, Deerslayer engages in retaliatory killing and preventative violence. After he has brained a Huron chief with a tomahawk, Deerslayer confronts Hetty's accusation of moral failure:

Why did you kill the Huron, Deerslayer? . . . Don't you know your commandments, which say 'thou shalt not kill!' . . . I saw it, and was sorry it happened, Deerslayer; for I hoped you wouldn't have returned blow for blow, but good for evil. (529–530)

[30] *The American Adam*, p. 105.

Deerslayer's self-defense, an awkward but frank compromise between expediency and principle, measures the changes wrought by an innocent's first warpath:

It's true, my good Hetty, 'tis gospel truth, and I'll not deny what has come to pass. But, you must remember, gal, that many things are lawful in war, which would be onlawful in peace. . . . Ah, Hetty, that may do among the missionaries, but 'twould make an onsartain life in the woods. . . . 'Twould have been a'gin natur' not to raise a hand in such a trial, and 'twould have done discredit to my training and gifts. (530)

Hawkeye's self-justification has the tone of an uneasy growth into wisdom. He knows that he has condoned a compromise of divine mandates in which he continues to believe. He also recognizes, however, that only such a compromise is practicable. Although Hetty wins the moral argument, it is Deerslayer who survives. By the conclusion of the novel, he confidently advances his new adaptation of Christian law: "I raised my hand ag'in 'em on account of what they were *striving* to do, rather than what they did. This is nat'ral law, 'to do, lest you should be done by'" (538).

Before Natty had killed his first Huron, he had been horrified by Hurry's advice, "Do as you're done by, Deerslayer" (91). Despite the widely different natures of the two borderers, Hawkeye has arrived at a moral law which in its practical consequences differs little from the creed of Hurry Skurry. Natty's is a law of necessary prevention; Hurry Harry's is a rationale for wanton cruelty. Yet the differences between their stated creeds are differences of motive and principle only; their effect is the same. For differing reasons, Natty and Hurry will both fire before they are fired upon. Significantly, it is Natty who pulls the first trigger in the climactic battle (569). Because self-ish men violate divine law, unselfish men must also violate it, if they wish to live in the wilderness.

Natty understands the delicacy of his compromise. Throughout the novel, he is evidently troubled by his recognition that, although he must never forsake Christian principles, he will rarely, if ever, be able to act upon them. He tells Hurry Harry that turning the other cheek is a white trait that white men can exercise only occasionally: "Revenge is an Injin gift, and forgiveness a white man's. That's all. Overlook all you *can* is what's meant; and not *revenge* all you can" (91). Although Natty treasures his Moravian upbringing, his idea of a "just man" is one who "uses the reason that God has given him, and he uses it with a feelin' of his being ordered to look at, and to consider things as they *are*, and not as he *wants* them to be" (218). By the end of his first warpath, Deerslayer has found his "callin'," only to discover that his "callin' " entails a troubling compromise; Hawkeye shall be a manly warrior who has "no relish for blood" (588).

Whenever Natty kills, he commits a sin by absolute standards, but morally he does not fall, because his values remain unaltered. Perhaps it is in this sense that the Pathfinder is said to be "a sort of type of what Adam might have been supposed to be before the fall, though certainly not without sin."[31] Evidently, the just man is one who retains moral purity despite killings and worldly wisdom.[32] Natty can remain an ethical hero only because

[31] *The Pathfinder*, p. 143.

[32] Or, in Chase's words, "The ideal American image is of a man who is a killer but *nevertheless* has natural piety" (*The American Novel and its Tradition*, p. 63).

the necessities of the neutral ground have driven him to such a compromise. In *The Last of the Mohicans*, after David Gamut has damned revenge and preached Christian forgiveness, Natty ruefully acknowledges, "There is a principle in that . . . different from the law of the woods; and yet it is fair and noble to reflect upon. . . . It is what I would wish to practice myself, as one without a cross of blood, though it is not easy to deal with an Indian as you would with a fellow Christian" (347).

In *The Deerslayer* Natty Bumppo kills with great reluctance and with evident turmoil. The scout of *The Last of the Mohicans* kills with ruthless efficiency, exultation, and minimal regard for principle. Twice Natty itches to shoot Magua in cold blood but is restrained (48, 144). He is proud that he has left a body to rot unburied over every square mile between Lake George and the Hudson (171–172). Nor does Natty mourn over Mingo corpses: "the honest, but implacable scout, made the circuit of the dead, into whose senseless bosoms he thrust his long knife, with as much coolness as though they had been so many brute carcasses" (145). This change in Natty's character is partially explained by the fact that *The Last of the Mohicans* belongs to the earlier tales in which Leatherstocking is less idealized. Part of the change is also accountable to the exigencies of the time and setting. Around Lake George, a neutral ground between French and British forces, only the ruthless survive; the brutalities of the massacre at Fort William Henry are accepted by everyone except the author and the reader. Nonetheless we should also realize that the hardening of Natty's character is due to the fact that he matures upon the frontier. As Natty grows more accustomed to the violence that accompanies his compromise, Cooper's true feelings about the State of Nature become clearer. When the State of Nature is fully superseded by the State of Civilization and the rule of law, such compromises should no longer be necessary.

By the end of *The Deerslayer*, Cooper's unstated judgment upon civilization emerges very clearly. The Leatherstocking Tales conclude, not with the founding of an advancing westward civilization, but with its extinction. After the settlers and their laws have come and gone, nature reclaims her own. The ark, the castle, the bleached bones of Hurons and Hutters, all decay in silence, while the cold still surface of Glimmerglass remains unchanged and the cycles of natural law indifferently repeat themselves. The cruelty and greed of the frontiresmen have led them to enact vindictive laws which have only brought about their destruction. In a comment prophetic of Judge Temple's arrival in Otsego, Deerslayer indicates the wisdom he has gained from his first brush with frontiersmen and soldiers: "This very spot would be all creation to me, could this war be fairly over, once; and the settlers kept at a distance" (590).

The closing sentence of the Leatherstocking Tales plunges Cooper's frontier into a gloom lightened only by the occasional glimpses of a Deerslayer or a Hetty Hutter:

We live in a world of transgressions and selfishness, and no pictures that represent us otherwise can be true; though, happily for human nature, gleamings of that pure spirit in whose likeness man has been fashioned, are to be seen, relieving its deformities, and mitigating, if not excusing its crimes. (597)

The Deerslayer is not so much "Cooper's idyll" or "a forest myth" as it is a ghastly bloodbath lightened by glimpses of powerless virtue. By entering Eden, man corrupts it.

The Deerslayer ends the series because it has in effect killed the hero whose life it is initiating. The dark ending, together with Natty's inability to counteract the effects of an evil civil law, form a tacit admission that Natty was, after all, only a gleam of "pure spirit." It is not accidental that one hundred fifty pages of *The Deerslayer* (chapters XXII–XXXI) are devoted almost exclusively to Natty Bumppo's preparations for death. The future of the frontier, perhaps of America as well, quite clearly belongs to Hurry Skurry March.[33]

The liberty from the law and the individualism for which Natty stood were feasible only if everyone in a frontier society could retain Natty's purity and moral conscience. The entire series has contradicted that possibility. In every frontier novel, the underlying conflict between Christian law and the law of revenge results in the triumph of bloodshed. Ironically, Cooper's great hero can do little to solve the problem of frontier lawlessness. Natty's greatness depends on his solitary independence,

[33] Marius Bewley, speaking of the national significance of these two frontiersmen, concludes that "Hurry is an indication of how things *will* be, Deerslayer of how they *might* have been" (*The Eccentric Design*, p. 96). George Dekker suggests that Hurry Skurry is Cooper's comment on log cabin democracy, William Henry Harrison and the Whig victory of 1840 (*James Fenimore Cooper*, pp. 159, 176–177). Whatever specific figure Cooper may have had in mind, Hurry Harry surely embodies Cooper's unspoken judgment upon the march of civilization.

but his independence renders him ineffectual in solving social problems. Although Natty opens paths for the forces he most detests, he retreats from social injustice and refuses to make social decisions. He possesses an "unerring sense of justice"[34] that is dependent solely upon a rifle and individual moral laws. By repudiating marriage, property and the civil law, Leatherstocking scorns the social ties that would render his virtues effective. Belonging to no race, rootless and solitary, Bumppo has no place in American life. Roy Harvey Pearce argues that "Natty's story was a kind of tragic story—the story of a hero of mythic proportions being cut down by a better kind of life than he could ever know or comprehend."[35] Incontestable though this conclusion is, we should add that Natty's tragedy belongs as much to the nation as to himself.

If Leatherstocking provides no practicable solution to the dilemma of a law for the frontier, the alternatives Cooper examines seemed no better. The absence of all law results in a massacre at Fort William Henry or the unchecked depradations of a Billy Kirby. Individual codes of moral law prove equally unsatisfactory. Stubborn adherence to the principle of revenge, Indian or white, starts a progressive chain of death and destruction which leaves little behind. Those who attempt literally to practice Christian morality must be protected by ruthless force; if unprotected, their Christianity leads to madness or death. Yet, when fallen man attempts to establish a code of civil law, that code seems likely, as in

[34] *The Pathfinder*, p. 143.
[35] "The Leatherstocking Tales Re-Examined," *SAQ*, XXXXVI (1947), 535.

The Deerslayer, to be a legal sanction of murder and self-interest. Even if a Judge Temple has the power to enforce beneficial laws, magistrates will use the framework of the law for their own ends.

The Leatherstocking Tales provide no solution to the problem of formulating a law for the frontier. The five novels circle around the complexities of the problem, redefining the issues for each successive tale, resting in a temporary solution, but moving on to contradict that solution in another volume. Cooper's mind had grasped the totality of the problem to the extent that he would not assent to an oversimplified solution. He saw the barbarity of the lex talionis and also its grim justice. Although he would desire Christian action, he was only too aware of its powerlessness to confront the conditions of the frontier. The failure of men to live within the moral law makes just civil laws all the more necessary, yet those laws impinge on the natural rights of the hunter in a State of Nature. When civil laws are enacted, Cooper lauds their possibilities for protection, but suspects the probability of their abuse. Natty Bumppo stands as Cooper's symbol of the just man in a State of Nature, yet his compromise is an individual creed that demands extraordinary self-discipline—an example that few could follow.

"THE OAK OPENINGS"

The conclusion of *The Deerslayer* does not provide a satisfactory terminus for a novelist who has committed himself to portraying the superior virtues of white civilization. In his last Indian romance, Cooper attempted to

resolve the seemingly insoluble questions of frontier
justice that had been posed by the Leatherstocking Tales.
The asocial hero is replaced by a middle-class white frontiersman. The triumph of white civilization is not only
praised in abstract generalities but shown in physical descriptions. The Indian's desire for revenge is washed
away by his conversion to Christian forgiveness. Because
the Indian bows to the supremacy of civilization, white
frontiersmen are no longer faced with the necessity of
retributive killing. As a result, the white claim to a morally superior culture is easily if not convincingly justified.
Thus, in this novel of 1848, Indian deference to white
civilization and white religion finally confirms the tenets
of Manifest Destiny.

The Oak Openings uses the conventions of frontier
romance for the purpose of a religious tract. By didactic statement and by fictional example, Cooper is
attempting to convince his reader of the benign influence
of divine providence in leading the individual soul to
biblical truth and the American nation to civilized prosperity. The preface declares his changed intention: "we
firmly believe that the finger of Providence is pointing
the way to all races, and colors, and nations, along the
path that is to lead the east and the west alike, to the
great goal of human wants. Demons infest that path, and
numerous and unhappy are the wanderings of millions
who stray from its course. . . . Nevertheless, the main
course is onward; and the day, in the sense of time, is
not distant, when the whole earth is to be filled with the
knowledge of the Lord" (vi).

Like *The Wept of Wish-ton-Wish, The Oak Openings*
gains importance among Cooper's works by virtue of its

historical position. The last of the frontier romances to be written was the latest in time of setting. In 1803 the fringe of western civilization had been the barren desert of the prairie, but in 1812 Cooper finds the frontier to be a temple of fertility. The open sunny meadows of Michigan are filled with foliage, springs, and deer. God's plenty has been bestowed, however, on condition of man's piety. Accordingly, the hero of the frontier is a middle-class white, Ben Boden, who has steadfastly refused to kill in violation of his pacifist morality. His vocation, the gathering of honey, is his reward for virtue, as well as a further indication of God's plenitude. Ben Boden serves as the model borderer who, unlike Natty Bumppo, remains an historical possibility for settled American society.

Old structural components of the Indian romance have, however, not been discarded. Ben Boden, Gershom Waring, and the two Waring maidens have established footholds of civilization on the fringe of settlement, footholds that are suddenly threatened by roving Indian tribes and by the successive downfalls of the forts at Mackinaw, Chicago, and Detroit. Using the War of 1812 as a cloak for violence, the Indians destroy the white settlements and drive Boden and the Warings to seek refuge in flight eastward. Thus, courtship and marriage, escape and pursuit, the attack on the white stronghold— all these familiar motifs, last rehearsed in *The Deerslayer*, are dutifully repeated, but redefined for the purposes of a new piety.

The problem of formulating a civil law for the neutral ground has suddenly become of no significance. Questions pertaining to colonial authorities, bounty law, and the War of 1812 are present as elements of the plot, but are pointedly ignored. The only issue of lasting consequence in the world of *The Oak Openings* is the individual's conversion to religious truth.[36] Gershom Waring must learn to rely on God's providence and forsake alcohol; his dwelling, called Whiskey Center, is conceived as a threat to ethical settlement. Whereas Waring's Yankee impiety is linked to his recourse to liquor, Ben Boden's natural piety has led him both to gather honey and to build the true center of American frontier civilization, Château au Miel.

In order to resolve the problems of Indian savagery and white vengeance, Cooper is driven to argue that the Indian can be totally and permanently converted to Christian principles—as Conanchet and Wyandotté could not. Scalping Peter, a magnificent symbol of Indian hatred against the entire white race, is smitten by the power of Christian forgiveness as he witnesses the Christlike death of Parson Amen at the hands of vengeful Indians. Significantly, Peter's conversion is not a change of conviction, but an actual descent of the Holy Spirit which has

[36] In 1849 Cooper was to publish *The Sea Lions*, his last and perhaps his finest sea tale. The splendor of sail and storm, revolutionary naval warfare, qualities of seamanship, and the hierarchy of naval authorities—all the concerns of previous sea fictions have become secondary trappings. The issue of *The Sea Lions*, like that of *The Oak Openings*, is the conversion of the unredeemed. Exposure to antarctic wastes converts Roswell Gardiner to religious orthodoxy. Written in sequence, the two novels are the creations of a man to whom earthly questions seemed no longer of ultimate importance. At the end of his career, Cooper may have intended to conclude his achievements in the forest and sea romance by recasting their materials through his strengthened religious vision.

brought the figure of the Indian within the fold of Christian salvation (419–420).

The avenger of the Indian race suddenly becomes the upholder of the white. The Old Man has become the New (456). Most importantly, as the Indian acknowledges Christian truth, he begins sincerely to justify his own extinction, together with the conquest of western lands by white civilization:

Bourdon; you are a pale-face, and I am an Injin. You are strong, and I am weak. This is because the Son of the Great Spirit has talked with your people, and has not talked with mine. I now see why the pale-faces overrun the earth and take the hunting-grounds. They know most, and have been told to come here, and to tell what they know to the poor ignorant Injins. I hope my people will listen. What the Son of the Great Spirit says must be true. (427)

Converting the Indian has washed away his claim to rightful possession of the land.

The last chapter of *The Oak Openings* attempts to allay Cooper's lifelong fears that Christian civilization had corrupted itself in the process of western settlement. Cooper works his journey to Michigan during June of 1848 into the last chapter of his novel and presents his ending as historical fact as well as conclusion to a fiction. He pictures the western frontier as bursting with promise. Fertile farms and efficient systems of transportation are everywhere. Fenced wheat fields surround neat villages. Cooper devotes a page to an ecstatic description of a thresher, calling the machine "a gigantic invention, well adapted to meet the necessities of a gigantic country" (495). The fertility, beauty, and growth of the oak openings have confirmed the dream of *Notions of the Americans.*

Ben Boden, who had sought solitude, has returned to the oak openings and become a revered state senator, much like Paul Hover before him. Cooper calls his bee hunter, now General Boden, "much improved in mind" and "a sincere Christian" (496). Scalping Peter reappears as a courteous gentleman, dressed in black, happily acclimated to western progress: "The Spirit of the Most High God had been shed freely upon his moral being, and in lieu of the revengeful and vindictive savage, he now lived a subdued, benevolent Christian!" (489).

Cooper declares his didactic purpose without equivocation. The career of Ben Boden is meant to illustrate "the power of man when left free to make his own exertions; while that of the Scalping Peter indicated the power of God" (496). Thus, in Cooper's last frontier novel, "the power of God" descends upon the wilderness only when necessary. The principle of American individuality, when exercised by the virtuous, operates unimpeded. When individuality is practiced by the Indian, however, God converts him. In short, the principles of liberty and divine intervention complement one another to create a prosperous Christian land.

Two doubts beset the reader who has completed *The Oak Openings.* The narrative of the novel had ended in 1812 with the expected and typical retreat of the white frontiersmen from the wilderness. The last chapter pictures Cooper's agrarian dream as an accomplished fact, yet Cooper has conveniently ignored all the trials of settlement during the thirty-six intervening years. More importantly, the complementary workings of a divine intervention and human liberty seem a facile solution to the dilemmas of governing the neutral ground. Because Cooper's previous novels had delved deeply and honestly into the complexities of frontier justice, both the pat resolution and the smug otherworldliness of *The Oak Openings* become all the more unacceptable. As Cooper's coda for the Indian Romance, *The Oak Openings* fails to earn fictional credibility.

6. The Gentry and Legal Change

> If the earth be the gift of nature to the
> living their title can extend to the earth
> in its natural State only. The *improve-*
> *ments* made by the dead form a charge
> against the living who take the benefit of
> them. This charge can no otherwise be
> satisfyed than by executing the will of
> the dead accompanying the improve-
> ments. . . . All that is indispensable in
> adjusting the account between the dead
> and the living is to see that the debits
> against the latter do not exceed the ad-
> vances made by the former.
>
> JAMES MADISON,
> letter to Jefferson, February 4, 1790

IN COOPER'S later novels, many of the evils that had seemed to threaten his ideal American republic were to subside to minimal importance. Concentration of power in the hands of the executive, growth of rootless commercial interests, threat of secession, slavery, foreign conquest—all of these familiar evils drop away and the danger predicted by *The American Democrat* becomes Cooper's ultimate concern. In the works of the 1840s, the problem of republican justice narrows almost exclusively to the threat of the demagogue who controls a deluded or selfish populace. The demagogue persistently reappears in one of three forms: the vulgar Yankee encouraging the people to strip the landed gentleman of his property, the editor creating false public opinion through the press, or the cunning lawyer citing democratic principles for self-advancement. In all three instances Cooper conceives of the demagogue as a man who mouths libertarian sentiments in order to subvert constitutional liberties. Conversely, he continues to consider the landed gentry as the disinterested upholders of liberty. Although the demagogue accuses the gentry of being aristocrats, Cooper insists that the demagogue is the true aristocrat, because he seeks covertly to obtain special political privilege at the expense of individual minority rights.

In each of his guises, the demagogue manifests the single intrinsic flaw which endangers the republic. If the American's individuality is in fact only greed or credulity, how can the demagogue be curbed without altering the libertarian polity upon which American greatness is based? Thus Cooper faced a decision of whether or not to advocate whatever changes in his ideal republican polity might be necessary to restrain the demagogue and save the republic. Throughout the 1840s, Cooper and his fictional spokesmen debate the advantages of restricting the suffrage, curtailing individual political rights, and resorting to governmental force. Until 1850, however, none of these antirepublican measures is ever supported —even implicitly. Although Cooper became increasingly anxious to conserve the social values of the old republic, he long remained unwilling to advocate aristocratic political privileges which might have brought back the ancient virtues.

Criticism of the Littlepage novels, Cooper's most ambitious work of the 1840s, reveals how easily and persistently Cooper's political principles have been distorted. Whereas Cooper sees himself as the conservor of con-

stitutional liberty, many of his readers see him only as a
growing conservative. Grossman notes that, although
Cooper had approved of the "revolutionary position" in
1830, he was against it during the Anti-Rent controversy
fifteen years later.[1] D. M. Ellis states that "these anti-rent
novels are another sign of Cooper's growing alienation
from American democracy, which he could not understand as a continuing process."[2] Richard Chase, A. N.
Kaul, and Granville Hicks all assert that the Littlepage
novels defend the rule of an "aristocracy" in American
life.[3] Hicks raises willful misunderstanding to new
heights when he declares that the Littlepage novels are
"the work of a confirmed reactionary" and that "perhaps
. . . it was a suppressed desire to be an aristocrat in the
political sense of the word that made [Cooper] so outspoken in his claim to social eminence."[4]

Before one reaches hasty conclusions about Cooper
becoming antirevolutionary, one should compare the
methods and objectives of European revolutionaries in
1830 with those of Hudson valley tenants in 1845. Before
Cooper is accused of favoring an "aristocracy," one
should attend to Cooper's definition of terms. And before
one asserts that Cooper has become a reactionary, one
must determine whether there are any specific changes

[1] *James Fenimore Cooper*, p. 200.

[2] D. M. Ellis, "The Coopers and New York State Landholding
Systems," in *James Fenimore Cooper: A Reappraisal*, *NYH*, XXXV
(1954), 418.

[3] Richard Chase, *The American Novel and its Tradition*, pp.
47–48; A. N. Kaul, *The American Vision* (New Haven, 1963), p. 93.

[4] Granville Hicks, "Landlord Cooper and the Anti-Renters,"
Antioch Review, V (1945), 106, 108.

in his republican political faith. To assess the consistency of Cooper's political ideals demands a more careful regard for the text of the Littlepage novels, especially *The Redskins*, than these novels have yet received.

The Littlepage Manuscripts defend a landed gentry but sharply criticize an aristocracy. The Mordaunts and the Littlepages possess neither noble title nor special political privileges; they are families that rise to prominence through their own merits. Cooper emphasizes that, although Corny Littlepage married above his class, Mordaunt and Hugh Littlepage, his descendants, marry decent, principled maidens who are far below them in social standing. The patriotic credentials of the Littlepage family during the Revolution are firmly established. The only true aristocrat in the entire series, the British Major Bulstrode, is sharply satirized for his snobberies and sense of privilege.[5]

All of the Littlepage narrators argue that such "aristocratic" distinctions as canopied pews have no place in the house of God. Mordaunt Littlepage is as sharply critical of aristocracy as he is fearful for the future of the new republic:

This is the great error of democracy, which fancies truth is to be proved by counting noses; while aristocracy commits the antagonist blunder of believing that excellence is inherited from male to male, and that too in the order of primogeniture! It is not easy to say where one is to look for truth in this life.[6]

[5] "In the character of Bulstrode, . . . the social order of privilege and power that Cooper had criticized so strongly in his European tales is banished from the series" (Ringe, *James Fenimore Cooper*, p. 118).

[6] *The Chainbearer*, p. 23.

In an editor's footnote, Cooper argues that the title "esquire," presently retained by ambitious lawyers, should be abolished because, after 1787, it implies special political rights that are unrepublican.[7] Uncle Ro and Hugh Littlepage, spokesmen for the gentry in 1845, rest their faith upon the equality of constitutional law and consider Anti-Renters, editors, and lawyers to be demagogic aristocrats. Most importantly, not one of the Littlepage narrators ever advocates any change in the constitutional, republican form of government. Ringe argues that Cooper's gentry grow more democratic as time passes; certainly they do not grow less democratic.[8] Even Uncle Ro Littlepage, who is the angriest conservative in Cooper's later tales, specifically lauds the fact that in America the landed gentry are accorded no political privileges.[9]

Although Cooper's political ideals have in no way changed, the standards by which Cooper attempts to determine their fulfillment have, by 1845, narrowed considerably. In *The American Democrat* and *Home As Found*, respect for the civil laws guaranteeing personal property was becoming, as we have seen, the test of the American republic. The utmost practicable freedom for the individual remained a cherished ideal, but by 1838 Cooper was finding it necessary to insist that "no civilized society can long exist, with an active power in its bosom that is stronger than the law."[10] In his view, the American citizen was becoming increasingly unable to

[7] *The Chainbearer*, p. 289.

[8] D. A. Ringe, "Cooper's Littlepage Novels: Change and Stability in American Society," *AL*, XXXII (1960), 284.

[9] *The Redskins*, p. 461.

[10] *The American Democrat*, p. 200.

perceive that, in a republic, individual liberties are guaranteed only by obedience to the law. Like Deerslayer, Cooper always believed that no civil legislature could possess authority over the laws of Christian morality. Yet, during the 1840s, Cooper's tendency to equate divine law with civil laws of property grew markedly:

Communities possess a power to omit certain interests from their rules of protection, if they see fit, certainly; but it is the power of *might*, and not that of *right*. They have no legitimate jurisdiction over the code of christian morals.—These they are bound to sustain, if they profess to be christian nations, having no authority to innovate on them. As respects property, so sacred is it held by the christian law, that we are commanded not to *covet* even, that of another, much less, to *steal* it.[11]

In very similar fashion, Mordaunt, Hugh and Ro Littlepage argue that the Tenth Commandment is upheld by the constitutional clause guaranteeing sanctity of contract.

The form of Cooper's fiction undergoes a change that corresponds to the narrowing and deepening of his social concerns. Cooper's sense of the process of history had always been acute, yet his chosen form of the romance had forced him to describe the history of a settlement through a narrative that usually transpired in less than a week. As a result Cooper had obtruded past history upon his narrative or had added historical material in preface and epilogue. During the 1840s, however, Cooper's major works are no longer separate romances but

[11] *Letters and Journals*, IV, 303–304. The passage is from a letter of 1842 to the *Evening Post*, in which Cooper approves Dickens' proposal for an international copyright law.

interconnected volumes of family chronicles that record the development of a settlement through generations of history. Cooper was well aware that the validity of purchasing a land patent, or a landlord's generosity in establishing a leasehold for new settlers, is more convincingly defended by chronicling the workings of history, than by calling forth the "beau idéal" of romance. We may also presume that Cooper's new form reflects a desire to insist upon the continuity of history and the demands of the past, two concepts which many of his countrymen seemed to have forgotten.

In the Wallingford and Littlepage novels, Cooper was attempting to give historical authenticity to fictions that affirmed the unchangeable, divine origin of civil laws of property. The immediacy and verisimilitude he sought could best be gained by disguising his own presence as novelist and projecting his opinions through a narrator who retells his life history. The choice of first person narration proved an effective means for Cooper to express his own criticisms, while claiming that their splenetic tone belongs solely to his narrator. In 1844 the aging Miles Wallingford sits down to pen, in two volumes, the story of his youth and marriage. Three generations of Littlepages leave manuscripts of family chronicles. For all seven volumes Cooper professes to serve only as the "editor" of history.[12]

The figure of Miles Wallingford provides the best in-

[12] Cooper had experimented with first person narration in *Autobiography of a Pocket Handkerchief* and *Ned Myers*, two occasional pieces which shortly precede the Wallingford novels. *The Monikins* (1835), ostensibly a dream vision, had been Cooper's first attempt to use a first-person narrator.

troduction to the Littlepage novels and to the Cooper of the 1840s. Miles shares Cooper's love of plain dealing. In Miles's voice, however, Cooper's most outspoken dislikes emerge as amusing crotchets: Wall Street, Yankee editors, land speculators, gossips from Salem, party politics. Like Cooper, Miles has abandoned his youthful Federalism; he caricatures Federalists and Republicans as Anglophiles and Francophiles. Cooper's arguments against impressment and reduction of the navy, Cooper's scorn for the unprincipled and the hypocritical, and Cooper's contempt for public opinion are all expressed through Miles's voice. Despite all Miles's adventures, the chief concern of his life has been his constant struggle to maintain the virtues of his landed estate, Clawbonny, against the insidious combination of land speculator, lawyer, and mortgage.

Miles's sharpest criticisms of the state of the republic never extend to advocating any change either in its polity or in its specific laws. Unlike Cooper, Miles is a landholder of a Hudson Valley estate, and therefore has an even more admiring view of a social aristocracy than Cooper does. Miles openly states that "manliness of character is far more likely to be the concomitant of aristocratic birth, than of democratic, I am afraid," and triumphantly concludes "that it takes an aristocrat to make a true democrat."[13] By such statements Miles means only that the well-born, wealthy, and landed gentry are more manly because of their strength of independent judgment. Significantly, whenever Miles insists that his nation must turn back to the old virtues of the republic, he

[13] *Miles Wallingford*, p. 213.

becomes a reactionary for the sake of liberty: "The signs of the times . . . have an ominous aspect as regards real liberty. . . . God alone knows for what we are reserved; but one thing is certain—there must be a serious movement backward, or the nation is lost."[14]

Miles's recollections of Clawbonny's history are intended in part as a warning to contemporary landholders. One of the "signs of the times" most distressing to Miles is the Anti-Rent agitation that in 1844 is gathering around his estate. He refers to Anti-Renters as "knots of men" who "set themselves up as special representatives of the whole community, and interpret the laws in their own favor, as if they were the first principles of the entire republic" (433). Commenting upon the import of the Anti-Rent conflict, Miles says "a crisis is at hand; and we are about to see the laws triumphant, or acts of aggression that will far outdo all that has hitherto rested on the American name" (433).

Miles' view of Anti-Rent[15] is indistinguishable from Cooper's: Anti-Rent is the gravest threat to the republic in its sixty-year history because, for the first time, the fundamental principles of republicanism are being flouted by groups that organize lawlessness. In a letter of January 1, 1847, Cooper declared "As to anti-rentism, in my judgment it is to be the test of the institutions. If men find that by making political combinations they can wipe out their indebtedness, adieu to everything like liberty or government. There will be but one alternative, and

[14] *Miles Wallingford*, p. 433.
[15] Appendix B provides a summary of the history of the Anti-Rent movement.

that will be the bayonet."[16] Such a statement shows us that Cooper conceives of Anti-Rent as a threat to liberty; Cooper's greatest fear is the despotism of martial law.

The Anti-Rent Wars in no way affected Cooper personally. Judge Cooper had sold all the lands of his patent to incoming settlers and Otsego County was at considerable remove from the locus of conflict along the Hudson. Nevertheless Anti-Rent aligned all the forces Cooper most detested against all the values he had always held most dear. In Cooper's beloved New York, the power and position of the landholding gentry were visibly endangered by the influx of tenants from New England. Cooper's penchant for enlarging experience led him to a perfectly consistent generalization: the hierarchy of the liberal gentlemen presiding over an agrarian society was being inverted by the rabble beneath. Republican theory was being distorted into a weapon employed against the class that formed the capital of the republican pillar.

The methods by which Anti-Rent tenants exerted pressure not only violated Cooper's standards for honorable civil conduct; they rendered the due processes of political change and law enforcement impossible for nearly a decade. As Anti-Rent gathered strength, the tarring and feathering of sheriffs attempting to serve legal process become common. For the sake of redressing tenant grievances, Anti-Renters condoned disregard for statute and civic order. Thus the Anti-Rent movement reduced considerable areas of New York to a state of

[16] *Letters and Journals*, V, 184.

insurrection precisely at a time when Cooper's own insistence upon the strict enforcement of constitutional law had grown markedly.

The warnings Cooper had issued against cant, demagoguery, press, and party were all confirmed by the methods employed by Anti-Renters. The continual use of Indian disguise was an affront to Cooper's demand for plain-dealing honesty. Touring Anti-Rent orators, such as Thomas A. Devyr, perpetually resorted to demagoguery and egalitarian cant. Civil laws of property and sanctity of contract truly were threatened by such groups as George Henry Evans' National Reformers, who demanded the breakup of long-deeded estates and whose slogan was "Vote Yourself a Farm."[17] Horace Greeley and other Anti-Rent editors were by no means averse to playing upon Anti-Rent sentiment for personal political advantage. When Anti-Rent Associations dangled their voting power before the Whigs and Democrats in the Albany legislature, Cooper correctly forecast a pattern of intimidation and official sycophancy that only confirmed his fears about the influence of parties and of pressure groups upon the republic.

Because Cooper believed that Anti-Rent was "the test of the institutions," he designed a massive three-volume work to assess it. Typically, he intended his trilogy to provide an analysis of changing American social conditions through the microcosm of Littlepage experiences. What Templeton had represented for the America of 1793 and 1838, the Littlepages would represent for the America of the 1750s, the 1780s and the present. In Janu-

[17] D. M. Ellis, *Landlords and Farmers in the Hudson-Mohawk Region* (Ithaca, 1946), pp. 252–253.

ary of 1845 Cooper outlined his plan to Bentley, his British publisher:

"The Family of Littlepage" will form three complete Tales, each perfectly distinct from the other as regards leading characters, love story etc., but, in this wise connected. I divide the subjects into the "Colony," "Revolution" and "Republic," carrying the same family, the same localities, and same *things* generally through the three different books, but exhibiting the changes produced by time, etc. In the Colony, for instance, the Littlepage of that day, first visits an estate of wild land, during the operations of the year 1758, the year that succeeded the scenes of the Mohicans, and it is there that the most stirring events of the book occur. In the "Revolution" this land is first settled, and the principles are developed, on which this settlement takes place, showing a book, in some respects resembling the Pioneers, though varied by localities and incidents.—In the "Republic" we shall have the present aspect of things, with an exhibition of the Anti-Rent commotion that now exists among us, and which certainly threatens the destruction of our system.—You know I write what I think, in these matters, and I shall not spare "The Republic" in all in which it is faulty and weak, as faulty and weak it has been to a grievous extent in these matters.[18]

The proposed subtitles indicate an intent to represent the three stages of American social and political history. Cooper's letter reveals two interrelated purposes. The series was to record the gradual erosion of American society to its present verge of destruction. By presenting the true history of the New York land patents, the Littlepage novels were to provide a necessary corrective to Anti-Rent.

The slow deterioration of a stable order is convincingly portrayed by two complementary tendencies that remain

[18] *Letters and Journals*, V, 7.

constant throughout the series. While the Littlepage gentry become less and less central to the agrarian communities they have established, the threat to their supremacy grows ever greater. Corny Littlepage is a sharply individualized and deeply sympathetic man, without whom Mooseridge and Ravensnest could never have been settled. By 1784 his son Mordaunt is resented as an absentee landlord; Mordaunt reestablishes his power, but relies strongly on other characters, Frank Malbone and Andries Coejemans, to carry out his wishes. Hugh and Uncle Ro Littlepage have no personal influence on their estate whatsoever. Returning after years in Europe, they remain peripheral, shadowy figures who are defined almost exclusively by their political attitudes.

As the landed gentry evolve through the three stages of American life, they become increasingly less winning. Their decline in personal influence is accompanied by the increasing shrillness of their political judgments. Cooper emphasizes, however, that the principles of the gentry have not changed. Corny, Mordaunt, Hugh, and Ro Littlepage all stand firmly for sanctity of contract, the rule of equal law, the social benefit of large landholders and the political freedom to establish one's superiority. For Cooper their increasingly negative views and dwindling achievements are clearly to be attributed to the successively more powerful threats to their way of life. In 1758 the only danger to Mooseridge and Ravensnest is a colonial war that passes quickly and is not caused by class prejudices. By 1784 the threats are still manageable, but Thousandacres and Newcome are motivated by subversive resentments against law and landlord, which Corny had never had to combat. When Hugh and Ro

Littlepage return to their leasehold estate in 1845, they find themselves threatened by physical violence, political chicanery, and the calumny of the press. The gentry and their unchanging republican principles have become the victims of social change.

"SATANSTOE"

Cooper's "Tale of the Colony" pictures a simple, idyllic society, which later generations will betray. Corny Littlepage is as fond of established traditions, Anglo-Dutch gentry, and stone ancestral homesteads as his creator. In New York, Westchester, and Albany, a hierarchy of social classes allows the colonial world to maintain individual liberties and civil order without any evidence of the confining rigors of civil law. Lawlessness is curbed, not by statute, but by the respect of all individuals for the greater privileges and responsibilities of the ruling gentry. Cooper's world is one in which children, slaves, tradesmen, and gentlefolk all turn out with deferential curiosity to witness the passing of the armorial coach of the great Albany patroon. In return, the great landholders practice noblesse oblige to all their dependents. The Schuylers and Van Rensselaers, and in lesser degree, the Littlepages and Mordaunts, not only advocate but administer the "apothegms of David, and the wisdom of Solomon" (495) for the betterment of a society in which their extensive landholdings are unquestioned save by an occasional, respectful Indian.

In the long discussions by the fireside at Satanstoe, the animosity between New Yorker and New Englander is only a never-failing source of laughter and conversation.

Corny realizes that the grasping hypocrisy of Yankee levelers is utterly opposed to the slow honesty of the Anglo-Dutch. He even considers the two races to embody the contrasting faces of the colonial, but the New Englander poses no threat to Littlepage supremacy. Jason Newcome's gaucheries are evident to all and there is but one of him. The antagonism that touches Corny's life is not the distrust between New York and Connecticut, but the contempt of the Englishman for the provincial. As an aging writer of manuscripts, Corny is somewhat of a sentimental Tory, but the youthful self he recreates is narrowly suspicious of all scarlet coats.

Cooper's colonial idyll is a world in which all is given and reliable. Every individual who has power is a patrician known and related to his fellow gentry; all tradesmen and tenants are loyally attached to one of these interrelated families. Because there are no fundamental differences of principle in Corny's world, the constraints of civil justice are unnecessary. Only a settled, homogeneous society could tolerate customs like the Pinkster Festival and the Dutch Frolic, or could be merely amused at the rough pranks of Guert Ten Eyck.

Cooper dwells fondly upon the settled comforts of colonial life in New York, but his love of old hierarchical customs should not be confused with any approval of Tory politics. Corny Littlepage, writing before the Revolution, distrusts the agitation against Parliament, but Cooper is quick to reveal, in *The Chainbearer*, that his hero later became Whig, contributed significantly to American military victories, and was eventually elected to the first Congress. Lest Corny's Toryish views of 1748 be confused with Cooper's views, the editor of *The*

Chainbearer tells us that he does not share all of Corny's opinions.[19] Above all, we must recall that for Cooper the great charm of the colonial society of *Satanstoe* is its childish innocence, a form of naive good will which all New Yorkers share, and which must and should be replaced by the sterner realities of republican manhood. Because Cooper recognized that "the enjoyment of the past is like the pleasure of the fool who dreams of the wine he drank yesterday,"[20] he was always reluctant to romanticize the past without important qualification.

Satanstoe moves backward in its stages of civilization while it moves forward chronologically. The reader is taken from the graces of a settled, coastal society, to the cruder village of Albany, and finally back to the wilderness itself. Simultaneously, however, the reader senses that, after obtaining a glimpse of a colonial society that ended in 1776, he is propelled forward to a frontier which represents the future, not only of the Littlepages, but of America itself. The wilderness beyond Albany displays all the violence and bloodshed which Cooper always attributed to the State of Nature. In *Satanstoe,* however, unlike the Leatherstocking Tales, the neutral ground has become closed. The forest setting is no longer a neutral territory where representative social forces contend for power. Instead, land is considered to be owned property suitable for individual development. In the Littlepage Manuscripts only demagogues and Yankees treat the forest as neutral ground.

In the second half of *Satanstoe*, Cooper begins to build his case against Anti-Rent. Neighboring patents north-

[19] *The Chainbearer,* p. vii.
[20] *The Bravo,* p. 22.

east of Albany are purchased by the Littlepages and the Mordaunts. The Indian title is extinguished by a binding though unjust contract, and the colonial deeds are signed. By emphasizing these two contracts, Cooper establishes the cornerstone of his forthcoming argument—the inviolable right of the landlord to specify any terms of leasehold on legally deeded property. Cooper also insists that the landholding gentry do not immediately profit from their patents, but grant generous terms of leasehold in order to insure profit for their descendants.

The ferocities of the wilderness argue that the restraints of property law and agrarian civilization are essential. The barbarism of the retreat from Ticonderoga, the besieging of the blockhouse at Ravensnest, and the unsightly aspects of the fledgling community cause Corny, Herman, and Anneke to retreat from the "sad events" (489) of the wilderness as quickly as possible. Cooper effectively reworks a scene from his Indian romances in order to further sympathy for the risks which landlords assume. After the purchase of the tract at Mooseridge, Corny travels through his forest to a tree-arched grove that is described as the Temple of God and the natural instructor of the moral law. Mr. Traverse and his chainbearers, the men who bring property law to the wilderness, sit within the forest cathedral, resting after their measurings of land. Upon closer examination, Corny finds that God's Temple has proved customarily uninstructive; all three men are scalped. The victims, however, are no longer merely settlers, but the surveyors for an agrarian estate that provides social order. The slaughter of the chainbearers is not God's punishment upon the concept of property—as Natty Bumppo would have seen it—but the first of a series of acts in which human savagery impedes the gentry's efforts to civilize the wilderness.

Satanstoe ends in boundless promise. After Ravensnest is defended and Major Bulstrode returns to England, the future belongs to Corny Littlepage and Anneke Mordaunt. Their marriage would fulfill the dream of any landholding patrician. At age twenty-two, Cornelius Littlepage becomes sole heir to one town house and four country houses: Satanstoe in Westchester, Lilacbush on the lower Hudson, Mooseridge in the wilderness (for future development and sale), and Ravensnest in the wilderness (for leasehold only). Corny is understandably hopeful that, by his efforts, the youthful crudities of Ravensnest may evolve into a higher stage of settlement. He remarks that Ravensnest resembles "the hobbledehoy condition in ourselves, when we have lost the graces of childhood, without having attained the finished forms of men" (435).

"THE CHAINBEARER"

In 1784 Mordaunt Littlepage, sole son of Corny and Anneke and bearer of both their names, returns to the long-neglected patents at Ravensnest and Mooseridge. *The Chainbearer*, Mordaunt's account of the experience of return, is ostensibly similar to *The Pioneers*— as Cooper intended. Mordaunt Littlepage, like Judge Temple, is a well-bred patentee who superintends a growing settlement in upper New York shortly after the Revolution. Comparison of the two books reveals significant changes in Cooper's conception of American social con-

ditions without any change in Cooper's political and social ideals. Mordaunt Littlepage reaffirms Judge Temple's
attitudes and principles in a harsh, threatening tone, because the opposition to the landholding gentry seems
infinitely greater. Thousandacres and Jason Newcome
dwarf Billy Kirby and Hiram Doolittle. Whereas Temple
had stood over the action of *The Pioneers* as a judge,
Mordaunt Littlepage has only the power of attorney in
acting for his absentee father.

In substance Mordaunt's principles are indistinguishable from Judge Temple's. Both believe in the worth of
the gentleman and the social benefit of large landed proprietors. Predictably, Mordaunt appeals to unchangeable,
yet unspecified, divine laws as his ultimate standard
(138). His insistence that existing laws be firmly and
equally applied to all citizens (104) recalls the judge's
decision to condemn the Leatherstocking despite Natty's
personal services. Like Judge Temple, Mordaunt believes
that strict enforcement of statutes is especially necessary on the frontier, where property is continually threatened. He too is convinced that all the benefits of Christian
civilization derive from one source:

Now, all the knowledge, and all the arts of life that the white
man enjoys and turns to his profit, come from the rights of
property. . . . Without these rights of property, no people
could be civilized; for no people would do their utmost, unless
each man were permitted to be master of what he can acquire,
subject to the great and common laws that are necessary to
regulate such matters. . . . When the rights of property are
first established, they must be established fairly, on some
admitted rule; after which they are to remain inviolable—
that is to say, sacred. (123–124)

For Mordaunt Littlepage as for Judge Temple, civil laws conserving property are conceived as a protection for the individual rights of all settlers, and thus as a benefit to the entire community. Mordaunt insists that disinterested justice is to the benefit of the poor, not the rich (104). His greatest fear is that defiance of the law will lead to a despotism that will spell the end of liberty (428).

Indistinguishable in political principles, Mordaunt and Judge Temple differ only in their political attitudes. Although Mordaunt has been as active a revolutionary patriot as Judge Temple, he is openly skeptical about the future of the republic, whereas Judge Temple had been merely silent. Mordaunt fears the tyranny of the majority and compares a mass herding of pigeons to the mass herding of people in a republic (219). Unlike Temple, whose merits were socially beneficial because he was a judge, Mordaunt Littlepage fears that disinterested justice is least likely in a republic. The courts, he believes, will be continually susceptible to popular political influence (219–220).

Mordaunt's skepticism, added to the greater dangers threatening his property, lead him to support measures of law enforcement far more severe than those of Judge Temple. Mordaunt is convinced that whipping posts are the best means of dealing with lawless frontiersmen (271) and later urges that the felling of one tree on another's property be declared a felony (287). His unwinning severities, however, do not necessarily indicate a sweeping change in Cooper's attitudes. Because Leatherstocking came willingly to court and Templeton's citizenry respected their judge, Temple anticipated no need for harsh measures. Cooper himself, however, had always been critical of the leniency of republican justice. Even in *Notions of the Americans*, Cooper had declared his forebodings: "The great fault in the exercise of the criminal law, in most, if not all, of the States of America, is a false humanity. . . . Punishment, in order to be impressive, should be prompt and infallible. The indiscreet use of the prerogative of mercy is one of the great errors of American criminal policy."[21]

In order unequivocally to substantiate the principles of the landed gentleman, Cooper changes the nature of his isolate hero. Andries Coejemans, like Stephen Stimson of *The Sea Lions* (1849), recalls Leatherstocking. Blunt but upright, shrewd and practical, Coejemans is the celibate who keeps one step ahead of civilization and reverences the God he finds in nature. Illiterate to the verge of greatness, but trusting to his definition of Christian law, Andries demonstrates his wondrous competence in the wilderness. Like Harvey Birch, Coejemans venerates Washington; he too has fought for the colonies during the Revolution, lost his family, and departed in silence to the west. Inevitably, Andries' huts are fifteen miles from the nearest hamlet.

By 1845, however, Cooper has transformed the values of his hero without altering the qualities. Andries is a chainbearer whose job is to determine the exact property rights of the society that follows him. Thus Natty's personal virtues are devoted to the upholding of civil laws of property. An employee of Mordaunt Littlepage, Andries longs to serve the gentry and believes that his

[21] *Notions of the Americans*, II, 251–252.

chains are a social duty that gives him moral freedom. Significantly, Cooper informs us that Chainbearer is a member of a fallen line of Dutch gentry.

During three separate disputes, Andries sides with Mordaunt Littlepage against the squatter who, like Natty Bumppo, claims the right of prior possession. Chainbearer, a fictional descendant of the Leatherstocking, has fully endorsed the principles of Judge Temple. Evidently, the principles of the isolate hero has proven to be so easily and frequently distorted into a sanction for license that Cooper felt his hero must be forgotten or fundamentally changed.

The Littlepages' liberality as sellers, lessors, and developers of their lands is strongly challenged by two figures of unforgettable magnitude. Aaron Thousandacres and Jason Newcome clearly symbolize the differing methods that many Americans were using in order to attack the position of the gentry. Cooper forces his reader to compare the two men by accenting the qualities they share. Both are egalitarian Yankees invading a stable social order. While Aaron Thousandacres operates a timber mill at Mooseridge, Jason Newcome works a mill site at Ravensnest. As lawyer, estate agent, and factotum, Jason is a composite of Dickon Jones and Hiram Doolittle, just as Aaron Thousandacres is a composite of Billy Kirby and the squatter theories of the Leatherstocking. In *The Chainbearer*, however, all these threatening figures are greatly magnified in force and newly leagued against the gentry. Jason and Thousandacres, land agent and squatter, conspire to deprive the Littlepages of their land and timber.

Aaron Thousandacres is an amalgamation of all the

overtly lawless tendencies Cooper has always detested. Kirby's occupation, Natty's theories of land possession, and Bush's character are combined into one figure whose power for lawlessness has grown in Cooper's mind until Thousandacres has become a grotesque. The massive stature and slow indomitability of Ishmael Bush have been exaggerated to the point where Thousandacres, born in the far reaches of Vermont, seems neither civilized nor controllable. Aaron has squatted on seventeen different patents, spawned twelve living children, and cut and sold every tree on every acre[22] he could reach.

Thousandacres shares a simplistic assumption, common to many of Cooper's Americans, that the civil law is a threat to liberty. Thousandacres is so obsessed with law and landlord that he cannot complete a speech without declaiming his contempt for attorneys, deeds, courts, or statutes. Aaron's justification for timber thievery is an extended pastiche of garbled phrases that echo concepts dear to Cooper. Natural rights, equality, individual need, the doctrine of use, divine law, the plenitude of nature—Aaron twists them all into an honest, fierce, but uncomprehending rationale for cutting and selling timber on land which another owns (330–341). The Bible is cited as proof that God intended man to take everything he can seize. When Aaron discovers that Mordaunt fought for the liberty of the colonies, he is momentarily

[22] Cooper's facility for names sometimes suggests Dickens. Names selected for representatives of the lowborn, go-ahead forces of American life are especially apt: Hiram Doolittle, Steadfast Dodge, Aristabulus Bragg, Hurry Harry March, Joel Strides, Aaron Thousandacres, Jason Newcome, Opportunity Newcome, Sam Tongue. Of all these characters, only one appears in a novel that precedes 1838.

mollified, until he is able to redefine liberty as license: "Now, I call it liberty to let every man have as much land as he has need on, and no more, keepin' the rest for them that's in the same sitiation. If he [Mordaunt] and his father be true fri'nds of liberty, let 'em prove it like men, by giving up all claims to more land than they want. That's what I call liberty! Let every man have as much land as he's need on; that's my religion, and it's liberty, too" (386).

The angry debates between Coejemans and Thousandacres reveal how the conflict between Natty and the judge has deepened in hostility without changing in terms or in outcome. The polite arguments of Natty and Judge Temple have become blunt accusations. Thousandacres proves to be as unable to refute Coejeman's defense of property laws as Natty had been unable to outargue the judge. The debate in *The Chainbearer*, however, is quite uneven and only occasionally comic. If we compare Thousandacres to Ishmael Bush and to Natty, we see how Cooper attributed squatter's arguments to increasingly less sympathetic characters as he grew older. Conversely, Cooper's anxiety to convince his reader of the truth of the judge's viewpoint has led him to select as its spokesman a character whose ordinary social standing and practical virtues are more clearly apparent. Chainbearer, unlike Mordaunt Littlepage or Judge Temple, can in no way be accused of defending self-interest.

The climactic scene of *The Chainbearer* reworks a memorable scene from *The Prairie*. Aaron Thousandacres calls for his patriarchal chair and holds a court of judgment. Unlike Ishmael, Aaron is prosecuting no crimes but his own. Whereas Bush had stubbornly adhered to a

principle of equal retaliation, Thousandacres follows no
code whatsoever. In an ominously comic scene, Aaron
charges that Mordaunt Littlepage is guilty of being a
lawyer and an aristocrat. Although these charges are
untrue as well as absurd, Mordaunt is promptly found
guilty and imprisoned on his own land. When Chainbearer challenges the authority of Thousandacres' court,
Aaron orders that Chainbearer be imprisoned without
specifying a charge. Enraged by the unanswerable arguments of Coejemans before the bar of justice, Aaron's
family shoots the Chainbearer in order to silence him.

Aaron's predecessors in the Leatherstocking Tales had
been both the cause which made the law necessary and
the greatest threat to its continuance. Despite his gigantic stature, however, Thousandacres is quelled with surprising ease. His travesty of a court is broken up by the
arrival of magistrate and posse and, in the scuffle, Aaron
is cut down by a conveniently unidentified bullet. If
statutes are strictly enforced, open defiance of land titles
and legal authorities is comparatively easy to suppress.

Cooper shows us that, by 1784, liberty and property
are more endangered by Jason Newcome than by Aaron
Thousandacres. Jason shares all of Aaron's qualities save
stupidity and openness, and all of Hiram Doolittle's
qualities except an underlying respect for the gentry.
Newcome is the representative new man because he cites
natural rights, individual freedom, and the equality of
man under law as arguments to gain the legal power
with which these concepts can be subverted. By flattering the majority, Jason attempts to abolish the class distinctions that make the landed gentleman possible. Like
all of Cooper's demagogues, Jason confuses social equal-

ity with political equality. He preaches that each man has a natural right to whatever amount of his neighbor's property will make the two equal in wealth as in law.

A revolution has occurred between the close of *Satanstoe* and the opening of *The Chainbearer*. The establishment of a republic polity turns Jason Newcome from an amusing oddity into an insidious force. When Mordaunt Littlepage arrives at Ravensnest in 1784, he sees a crude community like Templeton arising before his eyes. There at the outset is Jason Newcome, engaged in calling a town meeting for the purpose of choosing a denomination for the new church. Without deviating from the democratic principle of majority rule, Jason convinces seventy-three of the seventy-eight voters to establish the Congregational Church, although only twenty-six voters favor it. His technique is to eliminate the less popular sects by forcing a majority to vote them out of contention—one after the other. By misusing majority rule, Jason has established minority rule, and by cunning talk of individual liberty, he has abrogated minority rights guaranteed by the constitution. Lest the reader be merely amused, Cooper continually interrupts Jason's demagoguery to assert that the scene discloses the fatal flaw of the American republic.

Unlike Thousandacres, who defied civil law, Jason's demagoguery is more likely to succeed because his appearance of law-honesty renders him practically immune from punishment. When the civil law arrives to bring Thousandacres to justice, Jason Newcome, "justice of the peace" (434), rides at the head of the posse that arrests his former partner. Only the presence of a Mordaunt Littlepage, together with the power his property gives him, quell the danger of Jason Newcome. Thoroughly understanding his adversary, Littlepage simply removes Jason from his position as land agent, and replaces him with a member of the impoverished Dutch gentry, Frank Malbone.

Because Mordaunt has not sold the mill site of Ravensnest, Jason obtains neither the property nor the cash necessary to his ambitions. The republican political power that Jason seizes is checked only by the financial and social power of the Littlepages. It is not surprising, therefore, that Mordaunt grants Jason Newcome a new leasehold on excessively generous terms. In 1784 Mordaunt does not need legally to proceed against Jason; he can still afford to forget. Nonetheless, it remains clear to all of the Littlepages that their civil power depends upon their property, and that the tide of political power is turning against them.

Cooper's handling of Jason Newcome raises a problem common to his characterization of all the go-ahead sharpsters in his novels. His attempt to trace the origins of his "new men" remains unsatisfactory. Despite the historical immigrations from the east, it is not sufficient for Cooper to blame demagoguery on the leveling tendencies of New England Puritanism. Nor are we convinced when demagogues simply spring into existence like proletarian devils in the midst of the gentry's garden. By blaming New England, or by refusing to treat the problem, Cooper understandably slights the possibility that the traits of his subversive characters can be traced to certain social consequences of the national political faith. Jason Newcome perfectly illustrates some of

Tocqueville's conclusions concerning the effect of democratic beliefs: tyranny of the majority, leveling, excessive individuality, use of public opinion as a weapon, and a tendency to consider money as the sole criterion for determining social and moral distinctions.

"THE REDSKINS"

Because of its egregious faults as a novel, *The Redskins* has generally been denounced or ignored; it has never been examined in detail. The fictional weaknesses of the book all too easily cause readers to distrust, or even despise, Cooper's case against Anti-Rent. In analyzing *The Redskins*, one must clearly separate the merits of Cooper's argument from its demerits, the historical truth of his account of Anti-Rent from its historical errors, and the artistic blunders of Cooper's tale from the principles it seeks to support.

The Redskins was clearly the book for which the Littlepage trilogy was written. The gradual emergence of social lawlessness and the eclipse of the gentry were to end in violent, domestic conflict. In *Satanstoe* the blood shed to establish Ravensnest had seemed to Corny to be a necessary sacrifice for a community that was to evolve settled, gracious forms of living. By 1784, however, jealous, alegal settlers had already darkened Corny's expectations. Ravensnest was in the first stage of settlement without exhibiting either the stability or the social conviviality that Templeton had then attained. In *Home As Found* Cooper had implied that Templeton, then in the second stage of settlement, would evolve into the third, when "men and things come within the control of more general and regular laws."[23] By 1846 Ravensnest should long since have reached the third stage of settlement, but the returning Littlepages discover, much to their dismay, that the third stage will never arrive.[24]

On the Littlepage patents all has changed. The lands which comprised Mooseridge have been entirely sold, passing to new settlers utterly beyond Littlepage control. Hugh and Ro, who closely resemble Edward and John Effingham, must disguise themselves in returning to Ravensnest, lest they be tarred and feathered by their own tenants. The qualities of Jason Newcome, formerly confined to one symbolic figure, have spread to a number of lesser tenants: Josh Brigham, Tom Miller, Hubbard, and Shabbakuk Tubbs. Jason's descendants carry on a more active assault against the gentry than he had ever dared. Opportunity Newcome ogles Hugh Littlepage while she praises Anti-Rent. Seneca Newcome, unlike his grandfather, has become an accredited lawyer, but shows his concern for law by attempting to burn the Littlepage homestead while safely disguised in calico. The Yankee lawyer is now an arsonist.

[23] *Home As Found*, p. 189.
[24] Cooper's 1845 letter to Bentley proves that Cooper at no time planned a four-volume work consisting of one novel for each generation of Littlepages. To be sure, Cooper skips an entire generation in the Littlepage genealogy by stating that Malbone Littlepage, Hugh's father, died at an early age, and by incorporating Uncle Ro into *The Redskins*. It is possible that the series was planned as a trilogy with a gap of one generation because Cooper felt he had already depicted the second stage of settlement in *Home As Found*. One conclusion is sure: the third generation of Littlepages was not slighted because of Cooper's haste to publish *The Redskins*.

By 1846 a significant realignment of social forces has taken place. Formerly, the Littlepages maintained friendship with many families of the landholding gentry and were opposed only by hostile Indians and the few disreputable whites who were alien to their ways. In *The Redskins*, however, the Littlepages are opposed by their own tenants and isolated from their fellow gentry. Their only predictable support comes from the well-bred in their own employ, such as Reverend Warren, impoverished Episcopal minister of Ravensnest, and John Dunning, the cynical land agent. Defense for the gentry now devolves chiefly upon the Indians, whose presence at Ravensnest is historically absurd, but who twice disperse threatening mobs of Anti-Renters. Throughout *The Redskins*, Indian honesty and adherence to tribal law is contrasted to the defiance of law by Anti-Rent "Injins." The savage's new respect for civil laws of property has led the Indian to ally himself with the gentry and their faithful blacks against the gentry's own tenants. The Indian finally serves as a standard of principled fidelity against which whites are judged.

Conversely, the Anti-Renters now resemble the savage. Like Mordaunt sixty years previously, the two returning Littlepages are greeted by a public gathering before the Ravensnest church, a gathering in which public behavior reveals communal change. Whereas Jason Newcome had been scheming to establish the Congregational Church, the citizens are now being urged to deny the Littlepage title to Ravensnest, to refuse payment of rent, to resist arrest, and to prepare to seize the land themselves. While the Anti-Rent lecturer delivers his jeremiad against landlord, law, and feudalism, the "Injin" tenants "dance about the church, flourishing their rifles and knives, . . . whooping and screaming" (289).

By bringing the Anti-Renter into the church pulpit, Cooper equates perversion of the divine law with attack on leasehold. Through six pages of unforgettable rant, the Anti-Rent lecturer twists true republican principles into a justification for robbery. He defines equality as equalization of property and urges that defiance of existing statutes is the best means of achieving it (279). Abolition of "feudal" rent will assure the continuation of national progress (277). The "Injins" are informed that liberty entails abolishing all restraints upon the actions of "the people" (277). A further corollary is that majority rule demands the curtailment of minority rights (278). While attempting to subvert the validity of all property deeds, the Anti-Rent preacher reaches a climax of self-contradiction: "I contind that the tenants has this precise, lawful possession, at this blessed moment, only the law won't let em enj'y it. It's all owing to that accursed law, that the tenant can't set up a title ag'in his landlord. You see by this one fact, fellow-citizens, that they are a privileged class, and ought to be brought down to the level of gin'ral humanity" (276).

The longer one studies the speeches and actions of Devyr, Boughton, Evans, and Brisbane, the more one realizes that Cooper's characterization of Anti-Rent thinking and Anti-Rent methods is by no means unjust.[25] Attacks on inequality of property, denial of the validity of civil law, and disregard for minority rights were com-

[25] Henry Christman, *Tin Horns and Calico* (New York, 1945), passim. Christman, of course, cites these speeches for the purpose of justifying the Anti-Rent position in every detail.

mon techniques of Anti-Rent rhetoric. Cooper is surely justified in denouncing demagoguery, arson, tarring and feathering, and armed violence as weapons of Anti-Rent persuasion. His charge that both parties in the state legislature were anxious to propitiate Anti-Rent voting power is clearly substantiated by political developments in Albany between 1840 and 1846. As Cooper claimed, Anti-Renters had made "feudal leasehold" the scapegoat for all their woes, some of which—soil depletion and inefficient farming—were their own responsibilities.[26] Cooper's conviction that Anti-Renters were motivated by money rather than principle is confirmed by the fact that the years in which Anti-Rent violence was at its height, 1844 to 1845, were also the years of lowest wheat prices between 1837 and 1867.[27]

Cooper recognized that, in terms of existing civil laws, the landlords were fully justified. The Anti-Rent argument that many of the landholders' deeds were illegitimate was patently false. An act of the state constitution of 1777 specifically validated all land grants made by the crown. No landlord title was ever successfully challenged during the Anti-Rent agitation. Cooper was also correct in asserting that the tenant had no legal rights to the land beyond those specified in his written lease; all other "rights" were concessions made by liberality of the landlord and could be legally revoked at any time. In regard to the fundamental constitutional question, Cooper's reasoning was equally valid. Whenever Anti-Renters in *The Redskins* refer to their rallying cry, "the spirit of the institutions," the Littlepages counter with article I, sec-

[26] Ellis, *Landlords and Farmers*, pp. 218, 227.
[27] Ellis, *Landlords and Farmers*, p. 229.

tion X, clause I of the Constitution, which states that
"No state shall . . . pass any . . . law impairing the obligation of contracts." Repeatedly, Cooper asks how "the
spirit of democracy" can be opposed to the Constitution
that has created democracy. Historically, Cooper's legal
arguments were always upheld. Although quarter sales
and perpetual leases were declared illegal for future contracts, the courts never overturned the provisions of
existing leases. The Anti-Renters won their struggle, not
because they were vindicated in law, but because tenant
violence and popular sentiment rendered it politic for
landlords to sell.

Cooper argues convincingly that neither the landlord
leases, nor his defense of them, was based on "feudal" or
"aristocratic" reasoning. Cooper is correct in asserting
that no tenant was ever forced to assume a lease, and that
the option of purchase or leasing was always available to
an immigrant. He is also correct in arguing that even the
durable leases could be surrendered at any time provided
the quarter sale was paid.[28] Because of this option, Cooper
concludes that "as for feudality, so long as the power to
alienate exists at all in the tenant, he does not hold by a
feudal tenure" (45). Cooper repeatedly insists that the
landlord is not an aristocrat because he has no political
privileges. Throughout the Littlepage Manuscripts, Cooper approves of the abolition of entail and primogeniture
by the state in 1777, the banning of feudal tenures in
1787, and the passing of nearly universal manhood suffrage in 1821.

The weaknesses of Cooper's argument, however, are

[28] Christman, *Tin Horns and Calico*, p. 6.

more evident than its merits. Cooper may prove that the gentry's leaseholds are not antirepublican, but he cannot prove that they are not unjust. By satirizing all references to "the spirit of the institutions," Cooper refuses to consider whether a durable lease, quarter sale provisions and day's works were feudal in practical effect, though not in law. He is unwilling to acknowledge that a durable lease bound the tenant to the soil because the quarter sale made it impracticable for him to alienate. It is incontestable that the leasehold system perpetuated poverty, encouraged soil depletion, and created hardship for present tenants. Cooper flatly asserts, however, that "the longer a lease is, other things being equal, the better it is for the tenant" (47). Moreover, Cooper is historically inaccurate in stating that the original tenants preferred leasehold to freehold.[29] His attacks on Anti-Rent political pressure ignore the effective lobbying of landlords in Albany from 1841 to 1844.

The most objectionable aspect of Cooper's attack on Anti-Rent is his refusal to consider the merits of legal changes that would reform tenant grievances. The moderate, legal compromises advocated by Governor Seward in 1840 and by Samuel Tilden in 1845 only roused Cooper's scorn. Without offering legal proof, Cooper contended that three of Tilden's proposals—to commute a leasehold into a freehold upon the landlord's death, to place an income tax on rents, and to outlaw subsequent quarter sales—were all unconstitutional. In the preface to *The Redskins*, Cooper announces that he is prepared to defend leasehold because it is a legal institution even

[29] Ellis, *Landlords and Farmers*, p. 10.

though it might be feudal: "It is pretended that the durable leases are feudal in their nature. We do not conceive this to be true; but, admitting it to be so, it would only prove that feudality, to this extent, is a part of the institutions of the state" (ix). Whether the law serves man or not, man must serve the law.

Thus, throughout *The Redskins*, Cooper rejects the legal changes that might have resolved the conflict without abridging sanctity of contract. If Cooper was fully convinced that leasehold was a desirable social institution, his refusal to consider legal ways of abolishing it would be understandable. The oddity is that Cooper clearly recognizes, underneath all the hectoring of the Littlepages, that leasehold is a debilitating system. He admits that "it would be a great improvement in the condition of the tenants all over the state, could they change their tenures into freeholds" (137); Mordaunt Littlepage recognizes the same economic fact in *The Chainbearer*. And yet, when Uncle Ro Littlepage passes judgment upon officials who condemn the methods of Anti-Rentism, yet believe that leasehold is a hardship which should be legally changed, Uncle Ro dismisses their reasonings as "twaddle" (458).

Cooper's social ideals provide the explanation for this curious contradiction. Behind Cooper's contempt for Tilden's proposals lies his fear that, if the leasehold system is broken up by legal, republican change, the gentleman landholder, the capital of society, will fall with it. If the continuing power of the gentry is dependent upon the leasehold system, Cooper is willing to defend leasehold as a legal institution despite its injustices: "Admitting that there were false principles of social life,

embodied in the relation of landlord and tenant, as it
exists among us, *it would be a far greater evil to attempt
a reform under such a combination, than to endure the
original wrong*" (527).

Cooper's laudable desire to defend minority liberties
and sanctity of contract have led him into a number of
untenable conclusions. He argues that the impoverished
tenants of 1845, unable to alienate because of the quarter
sale, should be bound by the legal contracts made between their ancestors and Cornelius Littlepage in the
1760s.[30] In order to defend the legal rights of the gentry,
Cooper defends the leasehold system, thus forgetting
that a tenant farming under a lease is not the same as the
independent yeoman who, in *Notions of the Americans*,
had been the source of his national faith. Because of Cooper's anxiety to contain Anti-Rent, Cooper condones the
violence of the Indians against the "Injins," yet he
continues to criticize the "Injins," because they resort to
extralegal violence.

The artistic blunders of *The Redskins* obscure the
merits of Cooper's argument, while they point up its
faults. Hugh and Ro Littlepage do not illustrate the merits they attribute to their own class. Their strident tones,
repetitious lecturing, and incessant self-justification render them the voices least likely to gain the reader's trust.
Grossman notes that "we resist Hugh not because he may

[30] "For Cooper, the tenants' choice is decisive not only for the
profitable rent-free years but for all time. Their descendants must
pay rent forever, because the ancestors found it cheaper to begin
that way, and in fact could afford no other. There is something
chilling but admirable in the forthrightness of Cooper's secular
Calvinism that men do not achieve but are predestined to property
and poverty" (Grossman, *James Fenimore Cooper*, p. 207).

not be right but because he can be so tiresomely righteous."[31] Because the Littlepages have determined to vindicate the ways of the Littlepages, Cooper serves as an
unfortunate illustration of one of his most perceptive
insights: "there is no more certain way of arriving at any
particular notion, than by undertaking to defend it; and
amongst the most obstinate of our opinions, may be
classed those which are derived from discussion in which
we affect to search for truth, while in reality we are only
fortifying prejudice."[32]

Partiality and tone do not wholly explain the failure of
Hugh and Ro to earn the reader's trust. Their diatribes
against Anti-Rent are inserted into the meager narrative
with little discernible cause. Three times the Littlepages
assert that Anti-Rent forebodes national catastrophe,
yet all the meetings, disguises, and raids around Ravensnest result only in the burning of one barn. When the
Anti-Rent rabble finally advances on Ravensnest, disguised and armed, seeking to tar and feather Hugh Littlepage, if not to seize his lands, the social revolution toward
which the series has been pointing seems imminent.
Cooper assures us that the "Injins" feel no fear of the
law, because it is administered by the people (498). Despite all their confidence in impunity from the law, however, the tenants meekly fall back upon the appearance
of one sheriff. At the end of *The Redskins*, the reader can
only conclude that he has listened to a landlord's para-
noia rather than objective social observations. Talk of
national revolution ends in restoration of the status quo.

The incongruity between Littlepage fears and the tame-

[31] *James Fenimore Cooper*, p. 213.
[32] *The Pathfinder*, p. 230.

ness of the plot reflects a deeper conflict within Cooper himself. Not only is Cooper well aware that the historical events of 1846 do not yet warrant Littlepage pessimisms; he very evidently does not entirely credit his own dark predictions. Even in *The Redskins*, Cooper claims that four-fifths of America's citizenry are sensible yeomen who will repudiate Anti-Rent (418). After insisting that all local magistrates are corrupted by demagoguery (419), Cooper resolves the climactic conflict of his book by introducing an honest county sheriff. Cooper's desire to believe in the virtues of the republican citizen was not easily discarded.

Rather than serving as the climax to a trilogy, *The Redskins* trails off into historical indecision. Discussing the outcome of the Anti-Rent struggle, Cooper states only that "the result is unknown" (527). Although order is fully restored at Ravensnest, the Littlepages, like the Effinghams before them, are contemplating expatriation. Whereas the Effinghams were fleeing American provinciality, the Littlepages are now fleeing the tyranny of the majority. Hugh Littlepage moves to Washington in hope of obtaining from the federal government the disinterested justice that Albany has denied all landlords (529). Cooper says of Hugh, "should Washington fail him, he has the refuge of Florence open, where he can reside among the other victims of oppression, with the advantage of being admired as a refugee from republican tyranny" (536).[33]

---

[33] In the year in which *The Redskins* was published, Cooper's longing to expatriate, which had remained dormant since 1838, flared up once more. A letter to Paulding written in May 1846 states: "If I were fifteen years younger, I would certainly go

The unresolved ending is a glaring example of the deeper miscalculation that ruins *The Redskins* and the unity of the trilogy. As a social history of America, the Littlepage Manuscripts conclude with a volume that narrows into the polemics of a local struggle. The Anti-Rent War aroused Cooper's deepest fears for the survival of the American republic, but its immediate manifestations were not serious enough to warrant Cooper's pessimism. In a letter Cooper declared that *The Redskins* was written hastily in an attempt to warn Albany and the voters of 1846 against the dangers of Anti-Rent.[34] By restricting himself to contemporary history, Cooper was compelled to end his national trilogy with inconclusive fears.

The Redskins is Cooper's most conspicuous failure because it brings a work of great potential to an inconsistent and unsuccessful end. Prior to 1845 no American author had ever attempted so ambitious a project in fiction. A century later Faulkner was to create a greater trilogy using the same materials.[35] Nevertheless, the

---

abroad, and never return. I can say with Woolsey, 'If I had served my God with half the zeal I've served my *country*' it would have been better for me" (*Letters and Journals*, V, 131–132).

[34] *Letters and Journals*, V, 148.

[35] Although it is unlikely that Faulkner knew the Littlepage Manuscripts, the similarity in form and content between the Snopes and Littlepage trilogies is remarkable. The Snopeses combine the sly ambitions of the Newcomes with the violent illegalities of Thousandacres. Unlike Cooper, Faulkner had no interest in arguing for the supremacy of a patrician class. Therefore the Snopeses, unlike the Newcomes, are allowed to work their way into regional power. Cooper's desire to preach political moralities blinded him to the fact that his gentry held few possibilities for interesting fiction. By permitting Flem Snopes to reveal himself through his own actions, Faulkner's work acquires greater dramatic power. We fear Flem Snopes because he succeeds.

achievement of Cooper's first two volumes, especially of *The Chainbearer*, is evidence that Cooper's powers did not decline with age. *The Redskins* may reduce the Little-page Manuscripts to a mass of fragments, but its composition was an artistic failure from which Cooper greatly profited. Less than one year after completing his trilogy, when Cooper returned to the problem of portraying national disaster in fiction, he carefully avoided the flaws that had proved so damaging to *The Redskins*.

Passages from *Notions of the Americans* reveal how dark Cooper's assessment of the state of American life had become by 1846. In 1824 Cadwallader and the Bachelor had observed the workings of government in a frontier town of upper New York.[36] The election of community officials in the town meeting proceeds with dispatch and good humor. The town's citizens display "an admirable respect for the laws and institutions of their country" along with "perfect good sense and practical usefulness."[37] The voters are landholding farmers whose sole interest is communal benefit; there are no Down East immigrants. Surveying the hierarchy of governing bodies from town meeting, to board of supervisors, to country representatives, to the state legislature, Cooper commends the simple efficiency and broad justice of the system. The popular will rules without abridgment of minority rights. The passage closes with a tribute to the effects of universal manhood suffrage and an attack on the representation of property in government.

Elsewhere in *Notions of the Americans*, Cooper had

[36] *Notions of the Americans,* I, 257–271.
[37] *Notions of the Americans,* I, 259.

gloried in the fact that "the little States of Connecticut and Rhode Island contain, beyond a doubt, the two most democratic communities in the civilized world."[38] Speaking favorably of the submission to public will in the two states, Cooper had asserted that the fruit of this so-called "excessive democracy" is that Connecticut has elected three governors from the same patrician family.[39] Cooper had evidently been convinced that the New England democrat would vote the gentry into power: "Here is proof that the sovereign people can be as stable in their will, as the will of any other sovereign."[40] Such a generality was a hope which Cooper cast in the language of certainty. Jason Newcome, who manipulates the popular will to oust patrician families, was to come from the state of Connecticut.

Cooper's view of the New York frontier in the Littlepage Manuscripts bears no resemblance to these passages. Respect for law has become defiance of law, good sense has become prejudice, and devotion to the community has become devotion to self. The popular will threatens minority rights and the gentry are being forced from power. More significant than the change in Cooper's assessment of American facts, however, is the continuity in Cooper's definition of republican principles. The political merits that Cooper claimed for New York in 1828 remain the standards by which Cooper judges the New York of 1846 and finds it wanting. The only exception is

[38] *Notions of the Americans*, I, 162.

[39] Cooper is referring to the Wolcott family of Litchfield. Oliver Wolcott, Jr., a Republican, was governor of Connecticut from 1817 to 1827.

[40] *Notions of the Americans*, I, 163.

the change from Cooper's praise of freehold in 1828 to his defense of leasehold in 1846.

The regrettable failure of the Littlepage Manuscripts is not any change in Cooper's political principles, but the fact that vast changes in American social and political values were compelling Cooper to reach further backward in time in order to find a form of republican society that suited his unchanging principles. To maintain the power of the gentry, Cooper was forced to support leasehold and to assert that the contracts by which leasehold was legalized should be accepted as timelessly valid. By 1846 Cooper's desire to perpetuate a social hierarchy within a republican polity had led him, not to deny the right of legal change, but to ignore its merits.

7. Fanciful Kingdoms:
The End of the Republic

> Though I trust the friends of the proposed
> Constitution will never concur with its
> enemies in questioning that fundamen-
> tal principle of republican government,
> which admits the right of the people
> to abolish the established Constitution
> whenever they find it inconsistent with
> their happiness; yet it is not to be in-
> ferred from this principle that the repre-
> sentatives of the people, whenever a
> momentary inclination happens to lay
> hold of a majority of their constituents,
> incompatible with the provisions in the
> existing Constitution, would, on that ac-
> count, be justified in a violation of those
> provisions.
>
> ALEXANDER HAMILTON,
> *The Federalist*, No. 78

THROUGHOUT Cooper's later years, whenever he considered the threat to federal rather than local justice, he
found a single problem arising in different forms. In New
York the demagogue endangered constitutional liberty
and minority rights by attacking the property titles of
the gentry. In Washington the demagogue endangered
constitutional liberty and minority rights by dint of legislative usurpation and constitutional amendments. After
Cooper's return from Europe, the threat to federal justice
seemed increasingly important to him. Although the dan-

gers were the same in kind, they were different in degree. Cooper felt that congressional demagogues were directly threatening to overturn the Constitution, whereas Anti-Renters, lawyers, and editors were only violating its provisions. Although both groups struck at the constitutional tree, the Anti-Renter cut at the branches, whereas congressional demagogues strove to uproot the trunk.

The Monikins (1835) and *The Crater* (1847) reflect Cooper's attempt to evolve forms of fiction that could treat such national political problems more directly and forcefully than either the adventure romance or the novel of manners. In both of these works, Cooper turns a seemingly apolitical sea journey into an allegory of the state of the republic. John Goldencalf and Noah Poke happen upon Swiftian kingdoms named Leaphigh and Leaplow, which embody Cooper's equally satirical views of England and America in 1835. In *The Crater*, Mark Woolston builds a republican utopia on a South Sea island; Mark's experiences, Cooper says, form "a timely warning" to "those who now live in this republic."[1] These two fictions, written near the beginning and the end of the last period of Cooper's career, record the utter destruction of the republican dream Cooper had advanced in *Notions of the Americans.*

In a superficially light-hearted tone, *The Monikins* probes at the very flaws in American political practices which Mark Woolston's republic would be designed to counteract. Cooper's fears of the effect of party politics upon political integrity and constitutional law recur throughout his descriptions of Leaplow's capitol. By

---

[1] Preface to *The Crater*, pp. ix–x.

1835 Leaplow's republican government has become the property of two parties, the Horizontals and the Verticals, who manipulate the decisions of lottery boxes that determine who shall win the game of "Rotation in office" (252). The spectrum of effective political action is confined to two perpendicular lines—the Horizontal and the Vertical. Although there are no definable differences in principle between the lines, they are utterly opposed to one another. Success in politics demands that the monkey-men literally toe a party line and execute certain maneuvres: gyrations, summersaults, and sleight of hand. Progress is measured by movement along any party line toward the central intersection, but advancement is usually dependent upon seniority, because quality of mind represents a threat to party discipline. He who is not on the Horizontal or Vertical line is in political limbo. The greatest monkey, "the patriotic patriot" (259), is he who summersaults from one party line to the other without being detected.

Perhaps the most significant detail in Cooper's apt, unforgettable figure is that the entire spectrum is endlessly rotating. Most obviously, the rotation suggests that American politics is a wheel of fortune repeating itself indifferently and without progress. Cooper, however, had a more specific intent. The rotation of the wheel perpetually shifts the two party lines away from the one fixed and constant truth in American politics, "the constitutional meridian" (263).

Not content to convey his warnings solely by the metaphor of wheel and line, Cooper takes his travelers and his reader into Congress in order to reveal how Horizontals and Verticals violate the constitutional meridian.

The Verticals (Whigs) propose a resolution that "the color which has hitherto been deemed to be black, is really white" (381). Their resolution violates article IV, clause VI of the Leaplow Constitution ("the Great National Allegory") which states that "The Great National Council shall, in no case whatever, pass any law, or resolution, declaring white to be black" (382). When the newly elected Goldencalf raises the proper constitutional objection, his cry for strict construction is shouted down. No member of the council has ever read the constitution; to cite its provisions would be a dangerous precedent. Faced by the automatic, unthinking opposition of the Horizontals, the Verticals agree to a compromise resolution stating "that the color which has hitherto been deemed to be black, is really *lead-color*" (390).

Party proves as damaging to individual integrity as to constitutional law. Three of the travelers are immediately enlisted by opposing parties as vote-getting candidates of great potential among fellow immigrants. Noah Poke, one of Cooper's blunt sea tars, is swept into the council, follows a Godlike (party leader in the senate, probably Daniel Webster), and is corrupted by money and power. The cabin boy, Bob Smut, exercises his arrogance and stupidity as a senator, whereas the principled Goldencalf is so amazed by council chicanery that he remains helpless. In the monikin account of Genesis, Satan is renamed John Jaw. Jaw's sin was not pride but demagoguery, and his hold upon party discipline through popular resolutions enabled him to gather enough followers to cause the fall of monkeys.

Despite the acidity of Cooper's satire, *The Monikins* is not a debunking of republican government. Cooper's continuing national faith emerges from the argumentative discussions between John Goldencalf and Brigadier Downright (335–351). Goldencalf, an Englishman of immense wealth, subscribes enthusiastically to the Social Stake theory of government (82–83). He believes that those who have the most property have the greatest stake in society, and therefore are the best suited to rule. Goldencalf's trust in the restriction of the suffrage and the representation of property are directly challenged by Brigadier Downright, Cooper's honest, disillusioned republican. To Downright and to Cooper, the Social Stake theory of government ends in a commercial aristocracy; Social Stake corresponds exactly to Cooper's view of the designs of the American Whig party.

The errors of Goldencalf's Social Stake theory do not preclude his making telling political criticisms which the brigadier cannot refute. Goldencalf is convinced that the power of the vote, given to the poor, will strip the rich of their possessions. The brigadier counters that, if the vote is not given to the poor, the rich will pass laws enabling the rich to become richer. Although a protective and therefore restrictive government is the ideal of both men, they disagree concerning the means of achieving it. When Downright argues that the people cannot vote to betray their own interests, Goldencalf replies that a propertied aristocracy is the best judge of national welfare. Their differences can end only in the ultimate assertion and the ultimate denial. Goldencalf states that "when all vote, all may wish to abuse their trust to their own advantage, and a political chaos will be the consequence" (350). The scene fades away as Brigadier Downright, stroking his chin, quietly replies "Such a result is impossible!" (350).

Although conditions in Leaplow render Goldencalf's predictions plausible, Cooper never approves them. Brigadier Downright speaks both for Cooper's long-standing political ideals and for the plain-dealing honesty of character Cooper had always commended. Downright is willing to acknowledge that all men are monkeys, or that all monkeys are men, yet he still maintains that universal manhood suffrage is workable as well as praiseworthy. In his eyes, a representative democracy remains the best polity despite the selfishness and greed he observes at Leaplow.

Goldencalf gradually undergoes changes of political conviction that bring him closer to Downright's republican views. Goldencalf discovers that the English system of Social Stake rewards corruption. He then learns that American politics are becoming discouragingly like English politics. The workings of the National Council reveal that party politics has become the republican demagogue's form of Social Stake (424–425). Rather than denouncing Leaplow, Goldencalf repudiates Social Stake altogether. At one point, Goldencalf even advances Cooper's favorite political metaphor. The popular base of the Leaplow tripod gives its government greater stability than the three unsupported legs of king, Lords, and Commons (372–373).

In 1835 Cooper maintains a hesitant faith in Leaplow's future. The Eclipse of Principle by Pecuniary Interest[2] darkens the entire land, but the eclipse lasts only nine years. Although the novel concludes with the devouring of Brigadier Downright, Judge Judas People's Friend has

[2] Probably a reference to Whig attempts to defend the United States Bank.

been disgraced and stripped of power. Goldencalf concludes his tale with a list of cynical political maxims
gleaned from his experiences, yet none is more damaging than "of all the 'ocracies (aristocracy and democracy
included), hypocrisy is the most flourishing" (450).

"THE CRATER" AND THE CONSTITUTION

I

In Cooper's mind the effect of party demagoguery
upon the political integrity of a legislator pointed directly
toward the chink in the defenses of the republican polity
—the changeability of constitutional law. Within the
farcial, removed kingdom of Leaplow, the problem could
be controlled by the satirist's pen. In the United States
of America, however, the possibility that demagogues
could use the machinery of party to subvert constitutional law was not a fiction. To Cooper, who had devoted
his career to a defense of America and its Constitution,
the problem was quickly aggravated into its most acute
form: could not the demagogue use the Constitution in
order to pull it down and thereby destroy the very foundation of the republic?

In *The Crater* Cooper constructs an ideal republican
polity that seems to possess all the virtues of the American republic, without any of the flaws that render party
demagoguery so menacing. Even this republic, however,
becomes a prey to the faults Cooper had so brilliantly
satirized through the kingdom of Leaplow. *The Monikins*
maintained a playful tone because the problem of demagoguery did not seem capable of causing a governmental

overthrow. At the end of *The Crater*, however, Cooper invokes divine chastisement upon his country by obliterating Woolston's corrupted republic. The eruption of the volcano that buries the Crater civilization beneath the sea is announced to be the forerunner of the day in which a vengeful God will obliterate the entire earth (494).

Such an appallingly violent and seemingly arbitrary ending indicates that by 1847 Cooper's national pessimism had become literally nihilistic. Cooper's obliteration of the Crater republic can only be viewed as the outgrowth of years of brooding about the inability of a republic to resist the powers of demagoguery. If Cooper had been willing to advocate unconstitutional repression, the attempt of demagogues to take advantage of the changeability of constitutional law could easily have been contained. Cooper, however, had always honored the right of constitutional amendment. Ironically, it was this constitutional right, he felt, that was being twisted into a means of voting the Constitution out of existence. Not until 1847 was Cooper willing openly to acknowledge that the problem was insoluble. To follow the development of Cooper's national forebodings between 1833 and 1847 is to recognize that the volcano that was to explode was within James Fenimore Cooper. If we would understand the cataclysm with which *The Crater* concludes, we must attend to the complexities of the political dilemmas that Cooper faced.

After 1833 Cooper was certain that the danger to the supremacy of constitutional law was the success of the legislative branch in disrupting the republic's balance of powers. On three separate occasions,[3] Cooper was convinced that Congress had willfully overreached its constitutional authority. In 1834, certain that he was retiring as the literary defender of republican values, Cooper felt impelled to forewarn his countrymen:

If this Union shall ever be destroyed by an error or faults of an internal origin, it will not be by executive, but by legislative usurpation. The former is easily enough restrained, while the latter, cloaked under the appearance of legality and representation, is but too apt to carry the public sentiment with it.[4]

In 1834 Cooper also specified the insidious means by which the legislature could disrupt the salutary balance of powers: "far more danger is to be apprehended from the legislature, through innovations on the principles of the Constitution under the forms of law, than from either of the two other branches of government."[5]

A Letter to His Countrymen is only the first of many works to attack legislative usurpation and the congressional demagogue.[6] The reasoning with which Cooper supports later warnings is both full and consistent. Not only does the legislator conceive and enact the law; he also creates the public opinion that shall support it. The

[3] The Senate's censure of Jackson's removal of funds from the Bank, the withholding of Jackson's salary by Congress, and the congressional defiance of Jackson's treaty for French reparations. See the "A.B.C. Letters" in *Letters and Journals*, III, 61–139.

[4] *A Letter to His Countrymen*, pp. 87–88.

[5] *A Letter to His Countrymen*, p. 68.

[6] See the following passages: "A.B.C. Letters" in *Letters and Journals*, III, 61–210; *Sketches of Switzerland*, part I, vol. I, pp. 208–212; *The American Democrat*, pp. 154–159, 196–200; *The Oak Openings*, pp. 479–480.

sheer number of legislators in Congress allows the individual to avoid responsibility by dividing it among his fellows. The root of the danger, however, is that Congress possesses the maximum of authority but can exercise it with a minimum of risk. Cooper repeatedly applies one aphorism to the United States Congress: "where the greatest power resides, there are we to look for its greatest abuse."[7]

Faced with the threat of legislative demagoguery, Cooper searched, often desperately, for the means by which it could be controlled. His initial impulse, as we have seen, was to fall back upon strict construction and vehemently insist that the Constitution be rigidly respected as the fixed body of civil law. At other times Cooper relied heavily upon the tenth amendment.[8] Increased use of the executive veto and impeachment of members of Congress were measures he openly advocated.[9] Nor was Cooper unaware that *Marbury v. Madison* had established the power of judicial review over the constitutionality of congressional legislation. Hugh Littlepage was preparing to appeal to the Supreme Court against the unconstitutionality of Anti-Rent measures.[10] Cooper himself declared "no appeal can lie from the acts of Congress, except on the ground of unconstitutionality."[11]

At the same time, however, Cooper was depressed by the inadequacy of all these means of restraint. He recognized that article V of the Constitution gave to Congress

[7] *Letters and Journals*, III, 132.
[8] *A Letter to His Countrymen*, p. 78; *The American Democrat*, pp. 85–88; *Letters and Journals*, III, 170.
[9] *Letters and Journals*, III, 130–139.
[10] *The Redskins*, p. 536.
[11] *The American Democrat*, p. 93.

the power of altering constitutional law by amendment. In Cooper's view, the tenth amendment stripped the executive of at least as much power as the Congress. Before his eyes, Congress was openly scoffing at Jackson's use of the veto. To threaten impeachment was very well until one confronted the fact that the Senate acted as its own court. At that point Cooper stated, "admitting that a legislator may be impeached, the majority that committed the abuse would neither impeach nor condemn itself."[12] The effective use of the power of judicial review seemed so unlikely to Cooper that he rarely mentioned it as a viable alternative.

The irony of Cooper's fear of constitutional change is that he strongly believed in the right of constitutional amendment. Hoping that public opinion and legislative demagogues would leave the Constitution intact, Cooper nonetheless declared, even in 1838, "it is a requisite of liberty, that the body of a nation should retain the power to modify its institutions, as circumstances shall require."[13] Throughout his career, Cooper insisted that the only provision of the Constitution that was legally unchangeable was the right of each state to equal representation in the Senate. Every other element of the American polity, he grimly recognized, could be constitutionally amended at any time.[14]

In 1828 Cooper had advocated change with a quiet if naive trust: "When the interests of the majority are in favour of a change, there is something very like wisdom

[12] *Letters and Journals*, III, 132.

[13] *The American Democrat*, p. 111.

[14] *Gleanings in Europe: France*, pp. 327–330, fn. 2; *Sketches of Switzerland*, part I, vol. I, p. 55; *The American Democrat*, p. 86.

in permitting it."[15] Two years later, in the *Letter to General Lafayette*, Cooper crowed over the adaptability of the constitution and the stability of the popular will:

The American people can re-elect Mr. Jackson to the presidency next autumn, if they please; and before the autumn that will succeed, they can *constitutionally* destroy his office altogether. They have senators, and representatives, and judges, to carry on the machinery of government; but all these delegated powers are held at the command of the nation, in its character of the assembled interests. The result is the most tranquil community I have yet visited.[16]

Within a very few years Cooper was to cease glorifying change and to begin doubting the popular will, but he was never to repudiate the right of the constituency or its legislators to modify their own polity.

Civil disobedience was a recourse that Cooper would not condone. It is true that, through the isolate heroes of his romances, Cooper had expressed his own longings to disobey a civil law that conflicted with a divine law. Contemplating the sober responsibilities of citizenship in a political treatise, however, Cooper became an outspoken foe of civil disobedience. He was firmly convinced that, in a republic, respect for the law was the citizen's sole assurance of freedom:

Obedience to the laws, and a sacred regard to the rights of others, are imperative publick duties of the citizen. As he is a "law-maker," he should not be a "law-breaker," for he ought to be conscious that every departure from the established ordinances of society is an infraction of his rights. His power can only be maintained by the supremacy of the laws.[17]

[15] *Notions of the Americans*, I, 235.
[16] *Letter to General Lafayette*, p. 40.
[17] *The American Democrat*, p. 142.

Only when public opinion is manipulated until individual rights are legally threatened does Cooper even consider the fitness of defying a law: "It is, therefore, a publick duty of the citizen to guard against all excesses of popular power, whether inflicted by mere opinion, or under the forms of law."[18] Under these extreme circumstances, however, Cooper remains careful to avoid an explicit sanction of civil disobedience; to "guard against" excesses of power "under the forms of law" is not openly to defy them.

Faith in the republican polity forced Cooper to allow full freedom of action to those forces in American life that he most detested. We have seen how Cooper accepted universal manhood suffrage and denounced the representation of property despite his evident desire that the propertied gentry might retain political power. In 1838 Cooper was still declaring, "All that democracies legitimately attempt is to prevent the advantages which accompany social station from accumulating rights that do not properly belong to the condition, which is effected by pronouncing that it shall have no factitious political aids."[19]

Cooper's fears that the power of the press could create and manipulate a false public opinion were unbounded, yet his own war against Whig editors was restricted solely to an effort to "bring the press, again, under the subjection of the law."[20] Significantly, Cooper did not advocate censorship of the press. Instead he sued it for libel under existing laws, while simultaneously stating,

[18] *The American Democrat*, p. 143.
[19] *The American Democrat*, pp. 135–136.
[20] *Letters and Journals*, III, 382.

"without the liberty of the press, there can be no popular liberty in a nation."[21]

The logical corollary to Cooper's refusal to curtail the liberty of the press, the franchise, or the power of constitutional amendment, was his refusal to overstep the existing limits of constitutional law in punishing the abuses of demogoguery:

The inference that I could wish to draw . . . is the absolute necessity of construing the Constitution of the United States on its own principles; of rigidly respecting the spirit as well as the letter of its provisions; and of never attempting to avert any evil which may arise under the practice of the government, in any other manner than that which is pointed out by the instrument itself. On no other terms can this Union be perpetuated.[22]

Admirable though such a position is, it incurs a great danger. If one can only restrain threats against the republic by invoking the Constitution, the demagogue who uses the Constitution to subvert it cannot be effectively punished. Precisely this difficulty was to cause the downfall of Mark Woolston's government.

Thus, by the mid-1830s, Cooper's political thought had frozen into a state of passive apprehension. While fearing the combination of demagogue, party, and legislature, he would not advocate curbing these subtle and inherent abuses by curtailing constitutional liberties. Nor would Cooper condone civil disobedience if it meant defying laws which, no matter how wrongly conceived, had been duly enacted. Therefore his sole recourse was to hope that the democratic constituency retained suffi-

[21] *The American Democrat*, p. 178.
[22] *A Letter to His Countrymen*, p. 69

cient integrity and intelligence to repudiate the demagogue, avoid the dangers of party, and use the vote
against self-seeking legislators. In 1834 Cooper acknowledged that legislative usurpation had but one remedy:
"The constituency is its own protector, or our pretension
to real liberty would be idle."[23]

Cooper could only issue shrill warnings while await-
ing the outcome. His predictions of the national future
were to remain unsure because his evaluations of the all-
important constituency fluctuated wildly. His *Sketches
of Switzerland*, for example, frequently shifts from
travel memories to contemporary politics. In an attempt
to reassure himself about the American voter, Cooper
penned the following passage:

As to what are called popular excesses and violence, they are
commonly the results of systems which deprive masses of the
power to act in any other manner than by an appeal to their
force. Bodies of men may be misled, certainly, and even justice when administered violently becomes dangerous; but in
all such cases it will be found that a sentiment of right lies
at the bottom of even the mistaken impulses of the majority.[24]

Twenty pages later, however, the "sentiment of right" is
forgotten. Rage against the congressional censure of
Jackson ends in a grudging reference to the "radical defect in the most radical feature of the government, viz.
an incompetency in the constituency to discharge the
duties which this very constituency has imposed on
itself."[25]

As Cooper matured he perceived ever more clearly

[23] *A Letter to His Countrymen*, p. 69.
[24] *Sketches of Switzerland*, part I, vol I, p. 178.
[25] *Sketches of Switzerland*, part I, vol. I, p. 211.

that the constituency was finally the only defense against legislative demagoguery. Simultaneously, however, he became increasingly certain that the constituency was incompetent to bear the responsibilities demanded of it by republican government. In Cooper's novels his representative Americans grow more selfish or deluded while his gentry grow less powerful. From these premises, Cooper logically concluded that the change in the character of the constituency would result in a change of republican government. In the words written after 1833, therefore, one can trace the gradual emergence of images of national revolution and national holocaust that were to culminate in *The Crater*.

The touring Bachelor of *Notions of the Americans* had been amazed at the civil order displayed during the contested presidential election of 1824.[26] Cadwallader had dismissed the possibility of congressional tyranny by declaring "we have happily got the country into that onward movement, that there is little or no occasion for legislative impulses."[27] In 1828 the only revolutionary danger for America had been the remote possibility that the executive might wish to make himself a monarch.[28] *A Letter to His Countrymen* was Cooper's first warning against legislative usurpation, but in 1834 Cooper remained sufficiently confident of the manageability of Congress that he was willing to lay aside the pen.[29] One

[26] *Notions of the Americans*, II, 164–184.

[27] *Notions of the Americans*, II, 25.

[28] *Notions of the Americans*, II, 222–223.

[29] At the end of *A Letter to His Countrymen*, Cooper had declared, "Were it a matter of more than feeling, I trust I should be among the last to desert my post. But the democracy of this country is in every sense strong enough to protect itself" (99).

year later, *The Monikins* predicted a temporary national eclipse, but the cause of darkness was Pecuniary Interest and not the violations of Leaplow's Constitution.

Three years witnessed a significant change. In *The American Democrat* Cooper suspects that mobs, led by demagogues, may so oversway the legal ordinances of the *Constitution* that national well-wishers may be forced to unite with antidemocrats to repress the threat of the people.[30] He openly states "Whenever the government of the United States shall break up, it will probably be in consequence of a false direction having been given to publick opinion."[31] A letter to Greenough, also written in 1838, reveals fears of revolution:

In short, my good friend, this is a country with no principles, but party, no God, but money, and this, too, with very little sentiment, taste, breeding, or knowledge. So much has it altered for the worse, within a dozen years, that I seriously distrust a design to push things to extremes with a view to produce a change of government, through the reaction. Nothing is more common, than to meet with avowed monarchists. Depend on it, things can not last, in their present state, in this country, and that ere ten years there will be a great change, one way or the other.[32]

Thus, as Cooper looked about him in 1838, he believed that the nation had become so rabidly egalitarian that monarchy was a possible reaction, yet his underlying republicanism made him equally unwilling to view monarchy as anything but a terrible threat.

Three Mile Point served to fan the flame of national

[30] *The American Democrat*, p. 200.
[31] *The American Democrat*, p. 207.
[32] *Letters and Journals*, III, 331.

foreboding. In 1840 Cooper interrupted his romance about Columbus to define "the strongest national trait that exists among us at this moment" as "a disposition to extend the control of society beyond the limits set by the institutions and the laws, under the taking and plausible appellation of Public Opinion."[33] Although public opinion was still considered a "plausible" cause for legislation, public opinion was nonetheless ruining the nation. Thus, during the same year, Cooper wrote to his son Paul, "Depend on it, my son, we live in bad times, and times that threaten a thousand serious consequences, through the growing corruption of the nation. If public virtue be truly necessary to a republic, we cannot truly be one, but, unknown to ourselves, must be something else. The fact is, governments often profess to be one thing and practice another, and we are not what we profess to be."[34]

The Monikins had been cast in the form of a Swiftian fantasy because Cooper had been only half serious in his criticisms. By 1843, however, eight years after publication of his *"comico-serio, romantico-ironico-tale,"*[35] Cooper somberly declared, "I believe Monikins will be found to contain a tolerably plain prediction of the present state of this country, moral and pecuniary, with a very clear indication of the cause."[36] When the Anti-Rent agitation was added to the accumulation of past grievances, Cooper saw the local violence as a symbol of national disaster. Although the Littlepage trilogy did not

[33] *Mercedes of Castille*, p. 97.
[34] *Letters and Journals*, IV, 106.
[35] *Letters and Journals*, II, 258.
[36] *Letters and Journals*, IV, 344.

wholly succeed in conveying the betrayal of American republicanism, Cooper hit upon the metaphor through which *The Crater* would vividly express his political forebodings. In *The Redskins*, Cooper referred to Anti-Rent as a "volcano, which is raging and gathering strength beneath the whole community, menacing destruction to the nation itself."[37]

Beginning with *Home As Found*, the demagogues in Cooper's fiction mount an increasingly aggressive attack on his landed gentlemen, an attack whose success Cooper is long unwilling to admit. In 1838 the citizens of Templeton had merely passed resolutions and circulated rumors in an attempt to substitute public opinion for law. When the Effinghams had counterattacked, Dodge and Bragg were rendered ineffective and withdrew to the west. Seven years later the citizens of Ravensnest reopened the attack on the gentry, but supplemented gossip and resolution with open defiance of legal statutes. At the conclusion of *The Redskins*, the outcome of the citizens' attacks was left in doubt, but in this novel it was the Littlepages, not the Newcomes, who withdrew. When in 1847 Cooper wrote *The Crater*, he was at last willing to portray the consequences of political subversion. As a result, *The Crater* recognizes the inevitable fact, which the Littlepage trilogy had seemed so unconvincingly to hide: neither the landed gentleman nor his constitutional law can withstand the machinations of the demagogue. In *The Crater* Cooper does not hesitate to specify the means by which the gentry is overturned. While the gentry respects constitutional limitations of

---

[37] *The Redskins*, p. 407.

its power, demagogues amend the constitution to pull the gentry down.

II

Mark Woolston's colony is a utopia because its civil laws illustrate Cooper's unchanging conviction that the just civil law will correspond to the divine law. As settlers arrive to populate the expanded reef, the Deistic divine laws Mark has observed in the heavens (151–156) become the groundwork of the community's civil government. Through Mark Woolston, Cooper constructs a utopia in which republican institutions maintain a social hierarchy. As original inhabitant, chief landowner, and educated gentleman, Mark assumes the governorship of the crater colony and rules in conjunction with a Council of Three who, like himself, were duly and unanimously elected for their merit as well as influence (240).[38]

The debate concerning the classification of Mark's government, whether his utopia is an autocratic oligarchy designed to resist change[39] or a Jeffersonian democracy,[40]

[38] Cooper's creation of a Council of Three with nearly unlimited powers recalls the Council of Three that had ruled Venice in *The Bravo*. *The Crater* does not, however, praise the same kind of aristocratic oligarchy that Cooper once had damned. Unlike the polity of Venice, Mark Woolston's council is elected by the people, a constitution is drawn up, equality of political rights is rigidly respected, and aristocratic distinctions are discouraged. In *The Bravo*, the senators had served their own advantage; in *The Crater*, the council serves the common weal.

[39] John C. McCloskey, "Cooper's Political Views in *The Crater*," *Modern Philology*, LIII (1955), 113–116; Thomas Philbrick, "Introduction" to *The Crater* (Cambridge, Mass., 1962), pp. xv–xvi.

[40] D. A. Ringe, "Cooper's *The Crater* and the Moral Basis of Society," *Papers of the Michigan Academy of Science, Arts and Letters*, XLIV (1959), 376.

is largely a semantic issue that reveals as much about the contender as it does about Cooper. The important question is the degree to which Mark's utopia is consistent with Cooper's previous definitions of an ideal polity. In nearly every detail Mark's colony embodies Cooper's political ideals as well as qualities of the idealized settlement units of the frontier novels. Desiring to establish a utopia of small independent farmers, Mark and the council grant each settler a deed to 150 acres of land. Thereafter, however, no restrictions may be placed on the dealings of individual landholders.[41] The community has no taxes. Property rights, inequality of wealth, and inequality of worth are rigidly respected. Governor Woolston builds two stone homesteads on extensive tracts of land, yet acts as a benevolent patriarch by financing the construction of kilns, quarries, mills, and reservoirs for communal benefit. Mark's liberal values and untitled family origin are consistent with Cooper's portraits of the landed gentry from Judge Temple of *The Pioneers* through the Littlepages. Although the council agrees that Mark is legally and morally entitled to retain ownership of all the lands and ships of the colony (355), Mark releases nearly all of his vast properties to the state. His outright refusal to be considered the "suzerain" (355) of the community reveals Cooper's determination to show that the words "feudal" or "aristocratic" could not be charged against his hero. Mark's action also indicates a rather naive faith characteristic of Cooper's gentry; Mark

[41] When Cooper constructs his utopian republic in 1847, its economic base is the yeoman freeholder, not a tenant farming under a lease.

believes he has no cause to doubt that his settlers will continue their grateful deference.

The great governing principle of Mark's community fuses the two concepts that Cooper had always considered the sine qua non of republicanism—protection of individual rights and maximization of liberty:

So long as a man toiled for himself and those nearest and dearest to him, society had a security for his doing much that would be wanting where the proceeds of the entire community were to be shared in common;[42] and, on the knowledge of this simple and obvious truth did our young legislator found his theory of government. Protect all in their rights equally, but, that done, let every man pursue his road to happiness in his own way; conceding no more of his natural rights than were necessary to the great ends of peace, security, and law. (351)

Thus Cooper's utopia attempts to combine the virtues of a minimum of law and a leader who is a landed gentleman. Mark is a governor who "had no relish for power for power's sake, but only wielded it for the general good" (351). Refusing to take commercial or political advantage of his settlers, "Governor Woolston acted in the most liberal spirit to all around him" (384). Like Cooper, Mark feels that the problem as well as "the great desideratum" of government is "the ascertaining, as near as human infirmity will allow, the precise point at which concession to government ought to terminate, and that of uncontrolled individual freedom commence" (351).

[42] Thomas Philbrick has shown that Cooper's repeated criticisms of communal economics in *The Crater* are designed as a refutation both of Fourierism and of Horace Greeley ("Introduction" to *The Crater*, pp. xix–xxiv).

One may well question whether "the precise point" at which Cooper limits individual freedom has remained entirely unchanged. Mark's republic pursues some policies that are quite foreign to the republican utopia of *Notions of the Americans*. Immigrants to the Crater colony are carefully screened and school books are censored. Only two lawyers apply for citizenship, but they are refused because the council fears immediate danger to the Crater Constitution. All the offices and branches of government are in the Colony House, which is entirely owned by the governor. Mark is thoroughly opposed to any established church (415), yet relieved that the sole minister is an upright Episcopalian. Mr. Warrington is appointed the judge of the colony because he is a gentleman farmer without legal training (353–354). Cooper's suspicions of lawyers have led him to believe that judicial experience is likely to impair true judgment.

Because immigration quotas, school censorship, and a single church community are instituted with communal approval, such measures are not, in Cooper's eyes, antirepublican. Avoidance of regular elections, however, seems a serious inroad upon Cooper's conception of republican government. The governor and his council were all elected by democratic ballot, but they were elected for life with no provision for future elections (240). In *Notions of the Americans* Cooper had approved of regular elections; in 1847 he disapproves of them.

Cooper would not have denied the change. In his defense, however, he surely would have appealed to an argument made in all his political writings since 1828. The definition of a republican polity is that the citizenry elect representatives to govern them and thereby deter-

mine by what laws—democratic, aristocratic, or feudal—
they shall be governed. It is crucial that, in setting up a
polity designed to restrain demagoguery, Cooper chooses
to create a community whose citizenry as a whole decides to curtail elections. Neither Cooper nor Mark Woolston will limit manhood suffrage, represent property,
grant special privilege, or revoke the right of constitutional amendment.

There are two logical explanations for Cooper's desire
to curtail the power of the ballot. In 1847 Cooper's definition of utopia did not allow political parties the breeding ground of elections through which they would gain
strength. *The Monikins* plainly demonstrates that congressional demagoguery, rotation in office, and loose
construction are in great measure traceable to the pressures of frequent elections. We may also assume that
Cooper wished to encourage his reader's assumption that
the gentry was secure against overthrow. Whatever the
reasons, Cooper was reticent about them. All he will say
of the decision to establish political tenure is that "This
last provision was made to prevent the worst part, and
the most corrupting influence of politics, viz., the elections, from getting too much sway over the public
mind" (353).

The dangers to Cooper's utopia approach from without and within. Declaring that "the serpent of old was
about to visit this Eden of modern times" (420), Cooper
introduces a bloodthirsty native chieftain named Waaly,
who proceeds to attack the colony in open warfare. This
exterior threat, however, is rather easily expunged by
the governor's schooner and militia. The true serpent
arrives unobtrusively in the form of a trinity of evil

forces: four dissenting ministers, one lawyer, and one newspaper editor. Behind all three is the figure of the demagogue, the man with whom Cooper's political philosophy can not cope, because he profits by the institutions in which Cooper believes.

While Mark Woolston continues to insist upon man's right to individual liberty, his government is overthrown beneath him. Even the absence of regular elections cannot secure the republic from revolution. The tactics by which antirepublican revolution succeeds are the tactics Cooper had feared since 1834. Mark's assailants use the newspaper to propose a convention for the purpose of altering the Crater constitution (472). Citing the constitutional clause permitting amendment as their legal justification (473), the demagoguges amend the constitution out of existence.

Cooper's demagogues know that the gentry will meet defiance with a strong arm, but are helpless against subversion. Accordingly, their method of conquest is always a subtle playing upon popular credulity through democratic processes. In *The Crater* the process is an exact repetition of Jason Newcome's machinations in *The Chainbearer*. Adhering to the principle of majority rule, the demagogues of Craterdom call a series of town meetings in which a majority of the voters, though a minority of the populace, vote to elect representatives to the convention. At the convention, the constitution and the council are dissolved by vote of the majority, the landed gentleman is stripped of his governorship, and the demagogues reign (474). In drawing this pattern of passive virtue and active roguery, Cooper is pointing out that a republican polity cannot preserve traditional good unless the principled and honest will bother to vote. By asserting that a majority of the people still favored the old government (474), however, Cooper is, perhaps unknowingly, reaffirming his faith in the soundness of the constituency.

The crucial point is that the revolution which overturns Cooper's utopia has been effected by strictly legal means: "the minority now actually ruled in Craterdom, by carrying out fully the principle of the sway of the majority" (480).[43] After the new lawyer is appointed the new judge (475), the court of Craterdom deprives Mark Woolston of his estate on the crater by deciding against him in court. A statute is passed declaring private ownership of property on Vulcan's Peak illegal (486). Mark is thus denied all his property rights by the same due process of law that causes his Eden to fall to communal ownership. Cooper tersely states that "[Mark's] right did not preserve him from the ruthless plunder of the demagogue" (476).

Cooper has projected his own political convictions and dilemmas into the character of Mark Woolston without alteration. Although the governor commands all the military, social, and financial powers of the colony, and although he knows at all times exactly what is transpiring, his scruples concerning constitutional limits of power render him helpless in combating his own overthrow. Like Cooper, Mark refuses to advocate censorship of the

[43] Ringe misleads when he says that "The government is overthrown through a series of illegal manoeuvres" ("*The Crater* and the Moral Basis of Society," p. 378). The danger is intrinsic as well as extrinsic; Mark's government cannot protect itself against legal demagoguery.

press; instead, he attempts to quell the *Crater Truth
Teller* by refuting its demagoguery through his own editorials. By resorting to the written word as his defense,
Mark only proves that his underlying trust in the active
support of his constituency is a pathetic delusion.

Like Cooper, Mark Woolston claims that "the laws of
God were nothing but the great principles which ought
to govern human conduct" (469), and that the constitution is "the expression of those just and general principles
which should control human society, and as such should
prevail over majorities" (470). Also, like Cooper, he insists upon the full protection of minority rights (355).
When the editor of the *Truth Teller* blusters of how
"a majority of any community had a right to do as it
pleased" (469), Mark forthrightly counters with a conviction that *The American Democrat* had declared quite
unsurely: "even in the most democratical communities,
all that majorities could legally effect was to decide certain minor questions which, being necessarily referred to
some tribunal for decision, was of preference referred
to them" (470). Both Governor Woolston and author
Cooper uphold majority rule, yet they try to claim that
a majority decision can only decide inconsequential issues. Self-declared leaders of "the people" know, however, that they wield sufficient political power to decide
whatever consequential issues they please.

Incisive but unheeded in debate, Mark's principles
render him incapable of effective counteraction. His
scrupulous commitment to the legalities of his republican
polity force him to submit to his displacement. Although
Mark believes that the demagogues have far overstepped

their constitutional authority, his respect for the power of amendment prevents him from disbanding the constitutional convention. Neither author nor hero is willing to subvert the principle of majority rule for the purpose of replacing the rule of an irresponsible minority by the rule of a responsible one.[44]

While the demagogues gather, Cooper states "the governor did not deny that men had their natural rights, at the very moment he insisted that these rights were just as much a portion of the minority as of the majority" (471). In a tone of understated irony, we are informed "Nor did the governor run into extremes in his attempts to restrain the false reasoning and exaggerations of the demagogue and his deluded or selfish followers" (471). When the revolution has become irrversible, Mark is momentarily smitten by the "thought of knocking the whole thing in the head, by the strong arm" (476). Characteristically, Mark rejects the solution of force almost immediately; he "submitted to the changes, through a love of peace" (476). Cooper seems to commend Mark for strength of principle in resisting the temptation of unconstitutional repression, yet he also acknowledges the price which the Crater republic pays for Mark's political integrity.

Cooper's admission that the rule of right could not survive the onslaught of demagoguery led inevitably to the reexamination of a fundamental assumption of his

[44] "A minority may be right, certainly, but a minority, under this form of government, that wishes to substitute its peculiar views for the fundamental law, is attempting to subvert the institutions" (*Letters and Journals*, III, 103).

political creed. In works such as *Notions of the Americans*, the European novels, and *The American Democrat*, Cooper had always contended that, whatever its faults, a republican or democratic polity had a benign effect upon its people. When even the best of governments is shown to fall, however, Cooper is forced to a new admission: "It makes very little difference how men are ruled; they will be cheated; for, failing of rogues at head-quarters to perform that office for them, they are quite certain to set to work to devise some means of cheating themselves" (473).

The sudden cataclysm with which *The Crater* concludes seems at first glance to be an arbitrary, irresponsible manipulation of the plot that detracts from the novel's credibility. The eruption is so explosive and unapologetic, however, that one cannot regard it merely as an agent of poetic justice. In leveling the fallen paradise that was his land, Cooper is expressing his anger at the impossibility of solving the dilemmas underlying his twenty years of political speculation. The revolution in the crater colony is Cooper's final admission that a republican polity could neither perpetuate an agrarian hierarchy nor control the demagogue. Against his will, Cooper has admitted that a republic cannot sustain both minority rights and majority rule. Most ironically of all, *The Crater* confirms an argument Cooper had formerly attributed to European aristocrats and American Whigs: if political power is separated from property, political power will eventually deprive property of its constitutional rights. Rather than condemning Cooper's ending because it is arbitrary, one should commend it as an honest refusal to gloss over the insoluble.

III

The novel in which Cooper admits the failure of the republic is one of his artistic triumphs. Cooper seems deliberately to have avoided the literary blunders that had ruined *The Redskins,* his most recent attempt to portray national disaster. Rather than tieing *The Crater* to events of contemporary history, Mark's settling of undiscovered lands allows Cooper freely to shape his own political forebodings in fiction. Whereas Ravensnest had been locally owned property, Mark's symbolic island endows *The Crater* with timeless national significance. Three novels describing the growth and decline of a settlement have been compressed into one. The impact of national betrayal, dissipated through five hundred pages of *The Redskins,* is tersely recounted in *The Crater's* last chapters.

Cooper's long struggle toward a form of fiction capable of dealing with large questions of American political destiny culminates in *The Crater.* Mark's self-contained Pacific island proves a far more manageable microcosm for presenting utopian conceptions of society than either a blockhouse or a sprawling frontier community. *The Crater* describes the processes of communal growth and communal disintegration without relying upon irrelevant escape and pursuit sequences. Narrative suspense and love interest have become of minimal importance; *The Crater* is a sea tale with few nautical adventures and a frontier narrative with little racial violence. By refusing to confine the action of his novel to a time span of three or four days, Cooper frees himself from flimsy plotting and attains a wider perspective from which the entire history of the symbolic settlement can be unfolded. Mark's island remains the American neutral ground because it is an unformed land upon which men can exercise their virtues and vices. Unlike the wilderness or no-man's-lands of previous novels, however, the neutral ground of *The Crater* rewards virtue with fertility and punishes vice with obliteration.

The eruption of the crater is Cooper's recognition that only inhuman powers are sufficient to control the demagogue. Cooper will not directly state that the destruction of Mark's republican paradise is providential, yet the inference is unavoidable. The epigraph to chapter XXIX, in which Mark's government is overthrown, reads "Vox Populi, Vox Dei." Although in context the epigraph seems a bitter recognition of political fact, it ultimately proves to be false. At the end of *The Crater* the voice of God punishes the voice of the people. A letter, written shortly after *The Crater* was completed, reveals the intent of Cooper's cataclysmic ending: "Divine Providence reigns over even majorities, and the 'vox dei' may interpose, after all, to save us from its miserable counterfeit, the 'vox populi.' "[45] By 1847 God's wrath has become Cooper's sole recourse against demagoguery.

In the twentieth century, Cooper's fears that legislative usurpation and congressional demagoguery could subvert the Constitution through the power of amendment may appear unhistorical, if not alarmist. Surveying the decade preceding 1860, we usually assume that slavery and sectional economics, rather than constitutional problems, were the decisive causes of civil war. Perhaps we

[45] *Letters and Journals*, V, 394.

should recall that Buchanan, Douglas and Calhoun, Charles Sumner and Abraham Lincoln, were all very concerned to denounce differing kinds of "usurpation" to justify their several policies. We might even recall that, in our time, executive usurpation of congressional war making powers, and demagoguery in both the legislative and executive branches, have hardly been dead issues. At the very least, we must recognize that, in the context of pre-Civil War America, *The Crater* was by no means the expression of one aging man's crankish, irrelevant fears. Both the founding fathers and many of Cooper's contemporaries conceived of the dangers to the republic exactly as Cooper did.

Throughout the writings of Adams, Jefferson, Hamilton, and Madison, the greatest fear for republican justice is usurpation of power by one of the separate branches of government. Jefferson's fears of executive encroachment are widely known, but he was no less suspicious of the lawmaking powers of Congress. In letters to Madison, Jefferson acknowledges that his insistence on a Bill of Rights stems from his fear of legislative usurpation.[46] Madison's *Federalist* No. 48, which Cooper had surely read while preparing *Notions of the Americans*, is solely devoted to warning the New York citizenry that "the danger from legislative usurpations" is a greater threat

[46] Letters of December 20, 1787, and March 15, 1789. In the second of these letters, Jefferson acknowledges that "The executive, in our government, is not the sole, it is scarcely the principal object of my jealousy. The tyranny of the legislatures is the most formidable dread at present, and will be for many years. That of the executive will come in its turn; but it will be at a remote period." In *Notes on Virginia*, Jefferson expresses fears that the legislative branch is legally empowered to alter the Virginia Constitution.

to the proposed Constitution than dangers of executive tyranny.[47] John Adams' letters to Roger Sherman and his *A Defense of the Constitutions of Government* are filled with dire warnings against legislative usurpation. Adams is sure that the greatest danger to the American republic is the comparatively unchecked power of a popularly elected legislature which will devolve into an oligarchy ruled by demagogues: "It is, moreover, possible that more than two thirds of the nation, the senate and house, may in times of calamity, distress, misfortune, and ill success of the measures of government, from the momentary passion and enthusiasm, demand a law which will wholly subvert the constitution."[48] In *The Federalist* No. 78, Hamilton argues that courts of justice are the only "bulwarks of a limited Constitution against legislative encroachments." Like Cooper, Hamilton honors "the right of the people to alter or abolish the established Constitution," yet tries to contend that congressional legislators cannot amend the Constitution without popular approval.[49]

In the Jacksonian period, fear of "usurpation" grew even stronger. Increasing federal powers were considered an encroachment upon States' Rights, while Nullification was considered by its opponents to be an encroachment upon constitutional powers granted to the federation. Congressional Whigs branded Jackson's use of veto and appointment powers as executive usurpation. Perry Miller summarizes the constitutional thought of the pe-

[47] Madison, *The Federalist* No. 48 (New York, 1966), p. 147.

[48] Letter to Roger Sherman in *The Political Writings of John Adams*, ed. G. A. Peek, Jr. (New York, 1954), p. 170.

[49] Hamilton, *The Federalist* No. 78, pp. 230–231.

riod from 1828 to 1860 as a time in which, for all political thinkers, "the bogeyman was 'usurpation,'" and the greatest political danger was a loosening of constitutional restrictions upon power.[50]

By 1847 Cooper's long struggle to find a permanent solution to these pressing problems of past and contemporary political thought had ended in admitted failure. Because Cooper was finally prepared to acknowledge that he could find no legal solution to the threat of congressional demagoguery, he also admitted that America could no longer be exempted from the cyclical implications of natural law. In Cooper's previous romances, natural laws of rise and decay had operated unceasingly, despite contrasting assertions that America's future was one of linear progress toward a glorious fulfillment. Not until writing *The Crater* was Cooper willing to subject the destiny of America to the remorseless cyclical law to which he had long since consigned the old world. By adapting the cyclical scheme of *The Course of Empire*[51] to the development of Mark's republic, Cooper linked the fall of republican values with the grandest and most universal staging he could select. In the execution of his novel, he pursued Cole's melancholy implications with uncompromising honesty to their dark and destructive end.

[50] *The Life of the Mind*, pp. 221–222.

[51] I am indebted to the following studies of Cooper's relation to Cole and the Hudson River School: James F. Beard, "Cooper and His Artistic Contemporaries," in *James Fenimore Cooper: A Re-Appraisal*, NYH, LII (1954), 480–495; H. M. Jones, "Prose and Pictures: James Fenimore Cooper," *Tulane Studies in English*, III (1952), 133–154; D. A Ringe, "James Fenimore Cooper and Thomas Cole: An Analogous Technique, *AL* XXX (1958), 26–36.

Obliteration of the republic on so vast a canvas brought Cooper to end his tale in weary anger. The last paragraph of *The Crater* addresses the demagogues from the vantage point of eternity:

Let those who would substitute the voice of the created for that of the Creator; who shout "the people, the people," instead of hymning the praises of their God; who vainly imagine that the masses are sufficient for all things, remember their insignificance, and tremble. They are but mites amid millions of other mites, that the goodness of Providence has produced for its own wise ends; their boasted countries, with their vaunted climates and productions, have temporary possessions of but small portions of a globe that floats, a point, in space, following the course pointed out by an invisible finger, and which will one day be suddenly struck out of its orbit, as it was originally put there by the hand that made it. (494)

Such a farewell is vengeful nihilism of a depth that suggests *The Mysterious Stranger*. Cooper's bitterness, however, is the price he paid for his great moment of tragic admission. In the figure of Mark Woolston, everything in which Cooper believed fell through legislative usurpation to the demagogue. After nearly thirty years of service as the literary spokesman for American republicism, Cooper acknowledged that the republic could not be saved. Whatever he might choose to write in the four years yet remaining to him could only provide an afterword to a career that had already ended.

8. Way of the Reactionary

> Politics, under democracy, resolves itself
> into impossible alternatives. Whatever
> the label on the parties, or the war cries
> issuing from the demagogues who lead
> them, the practical choice is between the
> plutocracy on the one side and a rab-
> ble of preposterous impossibilists on
> the other. It is a pity that this is so. For
> what democracy needs most of all is a
> party that will separate the good that is
> in it theoretically from the evils that
> beset it practically, and then try to erect
> that good into a workable system. What
> it needs beyond everything is a party of
> liberty. It produces, true enough, oc-
> casional libertarians, just as despotism
> produces occasional regicides, but it treats
> them in the same drumhead way. It will
> never have a party of them until it in-
> vents and installs a genuine aristocracy,
> to breed them and secure them.
>
> H. L. MENCKEN, *Notes on Democracy*

THE FALL OF Mark Woolston's utopia left Cooper with
much to write against but precious little to write for. In
1847 Cooper had finally acknowledged the inability of
a republic legally to resist the threats of demagoguery
and false public opinion. By the late 1840s, Cooper had
also concluded that the dangers to his agrarian republic
had become greater in degree, though different in kind,
than the dangers of the 1830s. The Free Soil and Aboli-
tionist movements, women's rights, Fourierism and the

Fundamentalist revival, added to the spectacular illegalities of Anti-Rent, all seemed, in Cooper's eyes, to prove the inability of Americans to govern their lives rationally or with regard for proven traditions. A go-ahead lawyer in *The Ways of the Hour* approvingly notes that "pro-nigger, anti-gallows, eternal peace, women's rights, the people's power, and anything of that sort, sweeps like a tornado through the land" (217). Faced with these aberrations, Whig commercialism seemed the lesser evil.

In *The Crater* Cooper had in the main adhered to his republican values, even though he recognized that, by doing so, the influence of the gentry and the rule of their constitutional law would end. In the years after *The Crater*, Cooper begins to redefine the American republic as a restrictive polity in order that the supremacies of the gentry and of constitutional law be preserved. His positions on universal suffrage and the right of legal change alter markedly. More importantly, he begins to support measures that effectually grant the propertied gentry special political privilege. In order to preserve the old social virtues and the stability of constitutional law, Cooper thus became, in his very last years, both a reactionary and, by his own definition, an aristocrat.

Possible explanations for the change may be found both in Cooper's fiction and in New York history. Bitter, repressive feelings are the likely aftermath of completing such a book as *The Crater*. Cooper does not advocate reactionary, aristocratic principles until Mark's republic has been shown to fail. We should also recognize that Cooper's leanings toward aristocratic politics depend upon a further loss of faith in the power of judicial restraint. It is not accidental that Cooper's reactionary sentiments first emerge in a novel that attacks trial by jury. And surely the political disillusionment of Cooper's last works was spurred by state political developments. To Cooper, the passage of the New York Constitution in 1846 confirmed the downfall of American political integrity. In his last novel and his last piece of social criticism, Cooper was searching for measures which would forestall the passage of similar constitutions elsewhere.

Historically, the Constitution of 1846 had been prompted by pressure of popular resolutions that induced a majority of the state legislature to approve a convention for constitutional change. Thus, although the method of convening was strictly in accord with the stipulations of the Constitution of 1821, the impulse for change was popular rather than legislative in origin. The convention passed what was loosely termed "the people's constitution." Among its democratic reforms were the provisions that virtually outlawed future leasehold contracts by landlords. The only remaining restriction upon universal manhood suffrage, the trifling residence requirement left intact in 1821, was abolished. Tenure of office was reduced to one year for assemblymen and two years for state senators. Provisions were made in the constitution that greatly eased its amendment.[1]

Cooper struck out often and bitterly against "the people's constitution" that had turned so many of his political fears into law. *The Redskins* had been written hastily in hopes of warning the residents of New York against the proposed changes in leaseholds. The germ of

[1] E. P. Cheyney, "The Antirent Movement and the Constitution of 1846," in *History of the State of New York*, ed. A. C. Frick (New York, 1934), VI, 308–313.

the grand national betrayal of *The Crater* lies in the passage of the New York Constitution of 1846. Shortly after the demagogues of Craterdom have decreed their new constitution, Cooper inserts into his text a rebuke to "the electors of the State of New York," who have recently exhibited "moral cowardice" (476) by conceding to a clamorous but deluded minority of the voters. In *The Ways of the Hour*, specific onslaughts are leveled at rotation in office, unwarranted expansion of the franchise, the ease of constitutional amendment, and the injustices legally done to landlords.

Whereas *The Redskins* had dealt with Anti-Rent, and *The Crater* with the threat of revolution by amendment, *The Ways of the Hour* attacks the Constitution of 1846 from yet a third vantage point. Among the provisions of the new constitution were measures for democratic reform of the judiciary. Cases in law and equity were to be decided by the same courts. Each county would have its own judge. The truly significant measure, however, and the one that aroused Cooper's ire, was the provision that all New York judges, formerly appointed by the governor or the senate, were henceforth to be elected by the people.[2]

To make judicial offices elective was to subject the branch of legal restraint to all the corrupting influences of American politics. The judiciary, guardian of individual liberties, would be governed by the tyranny of public opinion. While preparing *Notions of the Americans*, Cooper had surely read Hamilton's warning: "That inflexible and uniform adherence to the rights of the

[2] Cheyney, "The Antirent Movement," pp. 315–316.

Constitution and of individuals, which we perceive to be indispensable in the courts of justice, can certainly not be expected from judges who hold their offices by a temporary commission."[3] During the seven years following publication of *Home As Found*, Cooper had successfully resorted to the courts as his own shield against the damaging falsities of public opinion created by the press. By 1845 he was certain that the judiciary was one of the few restraints upon legislative demagoguery and constitutional amendments. Significantly, the forces that caused Mark Woolston's utopia to fall did not include corruption within the judiciary; in fact, the demagogues only overthrew Eden because a strong judiciary was utterly and rather inexplicably absent.

When, therefore, Cooper considered the possibility that demagoguery might legally influence the workings of the judiciary through the power of the ballot, he was admitting that the last defense of republican liberty might have been overrun by enactment of state constitutional laws. If this were so, a turning toward reactionary, aristocratic principles would seem inevitable. At the outset of *The Ways of the Hour*, Thomas Dunscomb says of his country "if the patient is to be saved at all, it must be by means of the judiciary" (29). In order to determine whether his nation was or was not redeemable, Cooper wrote a five-hundred-page novel that assesses the American judiciary system through the events of one local trial. It is fitting that Cooper entitled this last novel *The Ways of the Hour* and published it in 1850. By attempting to reveal the ways of America through the conduct of an

[3] *The Federalist Papers* (New York, 1966), No. 78, p. 232.

extended court trial, Cooper gave conclusive evidence that questions of law and political justice had remained the crucial center of his thought and writings.

The focus of attack throughout *The Ways of the Hour* is the system of trial by jury. In an aristocracy Cooper felt that popular juries might serve as a bulwark against the abuses of privilege (v). A democratic polity, however, demanded a different assessment: to delegate the administration of criminal justice to the people was to give judicial powers to the very forces which a republican judiciary had been created to restrain (290). The possibility that a popular jury would possess the necessary, impartial regard for facts and law seemed to Cooper dangerously remote.

Cooper's feelings about the comparative merits of judge and jury parallel his attitude toward the executive and legislative branches of government. A judge holding tenure during good behavior is the executive power of the judiciary and the only source of a truly disinterested justice. In *The Ways of the Hour* an extended tribute is paid to the honest, hard-working qualities of the American judge, whose principled integrity is complemented by legal experience (280). The jury, however, became associated with the legislature—a popular body, irresponsible by sheer weight of numbers, whose powers and impunity Cooper wished to suppress.

When the 1846 Constitution created an elective judiciary in the state of New York, Cooper foresaw a form of judicial usurpation in which jurors would begin to make law while elective judges would become too timid to insist upon legal precedents. Trial by jury, combined with an elective judiciary, would reduce the process of legal decision to the level of the common mind. In Cooper's eyes, rotation of office had come to the bench, with the result that "the whole machinery of justice is left very much at the mercy of an outside public opinion" (287). To remain in office a judge must retain the approval of the people who comprise the juries; the jurors of a republic, however, habitually believe the public opinion of a fact rather than the fact itself. Consequently, one warning is repeated throughout *The Ways of the Hour*: "What I most complain of is the fact that the jurors are fast becoming judges" (18).

The Ways of the Hour examines one criminal case of extreme difficulties as the exemplum of judicial usurpation. Mary Monson, a rich young gentlewoman who has dwelt as a secretive outsider in a small town, is accused of murdering and robbing the elderly couple with whom she lives, and then burning their house. Significant evidence is practically nonexistent: two skeletons charred beyond recognition, a missing stocking which contains the victims' hoard of gold, Mary Monson's presence in the house at the time of the arson and murder. Facts are added that cloud all interpretations with ambiguity. A massive ploughshare is found beside the two skeletons, a mysterious German employed by the couple has disappeared, and Mary Monson will reveal nothing either of herself or of the facts pertaining to her case.

The ambiguities serve to arouse our curiosity while they allow the lawyers, the judge, and the jury a splendid opportunity to exhibit the faults inherent in trial by jury. Cooper was too much the realist not to recognize that, after the "reforms" of 1846, the source of judicial corruption must lie within the citizenry itself. Biberry, the last of Cooper's American villages, has retained none of the genial decencies that had characterized the Templetons of previous eras. Like Lewis's Gopher Prairie, Biberry is a compound of mediocrity, provincialism, gossip, and malice. Cooper wastes no time in physical descriptions of its fertility or beauty. By 1850 there seems to be no gentry left in the American village to offset the vulgarity of the lower classes. Consequently, the small town prejudices of Biberry's citizens operate unchecked. Seizing upon any untoward event as a source for exciting rumors, Biberry resents all foreigners and brands any distinction as evidence of snobbery. The citizens envy of Mary's gentility expresses itself as a contempt for her "aristocracy." Cooper's former assumptions about rural virtue and urban amorality have all been reversed. The genteel, principled figures hearken from New York or Europe, whereas the village breeds aggressive provincialism.

Cooper's last novel distinguishes between two kinds of American lawyers. Thomas Dunscomb is the Christian gentleman whom Cooper has finally united with the clear-headed attorney. Timms, a sharpster using the law for self-advancement, has risen professionally above his class origins, but resents the gentry he tries to emulate. Dunscomb's thinking is guided by principles of the common law; Timms knows that law will be established by popular juries whose opinions he must sway. Whereas Dunscomb comes to Biberry as the great lawyer from New York, Timms's practice has been confined to Biberry and the environs of Duke's County. A first irony is that Dunscomb hires Timms as associate counsel to defend Mary Monson. A second is that the unscrupulous associate is the more successful and effective lawyer. Cooper emphasizes that Dunscomb, representative of the old guard, is out of touch with the realities of contemporary legal practices.

Thomas Dunscomb is the last of a series of cantankerous, well-bred bachelors who voice the harshest feelings of Cooper's later years. His social credentials are expectedly impeccable: an old Episcopalian family, a large town house, and a country estate along the Hudson. Like Kent, Story, and Rufus Choate, legal giants of previous decades, Dunscomb fears demagoguery, attacks on private property and the noble weakness of the federal Constitution.[4] More importantly for our purposes, Dunscomb shares all of these fears with his creator.

Like Mark Woolston, Dunscomb has recognized the vulnerability of constitutional law. The opening chapter of *The Ways of the Hour* is largely concerned with Dunscomb's persistent refutation of the toast "The constitution of the United States; the palladium of our civil and religious liberties" (14). Later in the novel Dunscomb argues that the Constitution cannot guarantee liberty or property because of the provision for constitutional amendment (192). In his view, no healthful checks on popular power remain, not even in the judiciary:

The power of the masses is getting to be very formidable—more formidable in a way never contemplated by those who formed the institutions, than in any way that was foreseen. Among other things, they begin to hold the administration of justice in the hollow of their hands. (252)

In the first chapter, Dunscomb summarizes the political effect of trial by jury in a republic: "Nay, by George,

[4] Perry Miller, *The Life of the Mind*, pp. 223–230.

they [the jurors] are getting to be legislators, making the law as well as interpreting it. How often does it happen, now-a-days, that the court tell the jury that such is the law, and the jury comes in with a verdict that such is *not* the law? . . . No-no—the trial by jury is no more a palladium of our liberties, than the Constitution of the United States" (18–19).

The legal chicanery surrounding the trial of Mary Monson vindicates Dunscomb's gravest fears. As soon as Mary Monson is arrested, the country lawyers engage in methods of jury tampering that outrage Dunscomb, even though he realizes the necessity of employing them himself. While Dunscomb quietly turns his back and talks of the highest principles, Timms circulates false rumors and bribes the newspapers for columns favorable to Mary Monson. Public opinion for acquittal is aroused by false tales of Mary's hardships. The prosecution insinuates Mary's guilt because she has a Swiss maid, plays the harp, speaks foreign tongues, and will not display herself at the goal window before the greedy eyes of the good people of Biberry. The two most dependable techniques of Biberry law are "horse-shedding" and "pillowing," Timms' terms for the purchase of "talkers," who prejudice unsuspecting jurors through supposedly casual discussions in stable and bedroom.

Mary Monson's case involves lurid, bizarre details, but her trial, Cooper wisely insists, is utterly common. At the outset of the trial, the reader is told that "the circuit and oyer and terminer for Duke's presented nothing novel in its bench, its bar, its jurors, and we might add its witnesses" (281). The judge is capable and dutiful, the jury honest if common, and even the bar seems no more knavish than a realist would anticipate (281–284). By accentuating the ordinary respectability of all participants, Cooper renders the injustice of the court's proceedings more distressingly everyday.

After a careful and factual sorting out of all the inconclusive evidence, the court draws near to a judgment. The district attorney, who had made a canting speech about Mary's aristocratic ways, delivers a restrained and impartial summation to the jury (446–448). The judge's charge is warmly sympathetic to Mary as an individual; he contends, quite reasonably, that the circumstantial evidence against her is flimsy and debatable. Having led his reader to believe that Mary should and will be acquitted, Cooper quietly describes the adjournment of the jury to deliberate, and its subsequent recall. Unexpectedly, the jury passes a verdict of guilty; the judge has no recourse but to sentence Mary to hanging. Like Governor Woolston, Mary's judge is an impartial executive figure who is helpless against legal, popular errors.

By omitting the crucial scene of the jury's deliberation, Cooper rests his case against the jury on shock effect. The reader is left with stunning evidence of a jury's disregard for facts and reason. Searching to explain the jury's contempt for the judge's opinion, the reader recalls that Mary's judge has been elected under the new constitution and must therefore curry popular favor rather than lead it. We recall Timms's contemptuous observation: "You will remember that our judge is not only a bran-new one, but he drew the two years' term into the bargain. No, I think it will be wisest to let the law, and old principles, and the right, and *true* liberty, quite alone; and to bow the knee to things as they are" (228).

Of the process by which the jury reached its verdict Cooper tells us but two facts. The jury's decision was determined by pressure from one of its members, a crony of the prosecution lawyer whose mind has been prejudiced by rumors and newspaper accounts (457). A second factor was "a morbid satisfaction in the minds of several of the jurors, in running counter to the charge of the judge" (457). The theoretical virtues of trial by jury emerge as injustices in the courtroom. Mary is tried by public opinion rather than by law, and then is sentenced unjustly by a jury of her inferiors.

Since 1828 Cooper's assessment of the effect of public opinion on the administration of American justice has totally reversed. In *Notions of the Americans*, Cooper had praised the American judicial system because the judges obeyed the will of the people: "the judges are amenable to public opinion, the severest punishment and the tightest check in a free community."[5] Eight years later, Cooper was still convinced that the American judiciary system represented public opinion and did not usurp the law-making function:

The judiciaries are no practical exception to this rule [of responsible representation], for they perform no original acts of government, are purely interpreters of the law on principles which the other representatives may alter at will, and discharge their trust under such responsibilities as to render abuses very unlikely to occur. They, too, are practically representative, through the fact that the constituency has retained a power to set them aside, or to modify their organization, and their trusts, at pleasure.[6]

[5] *Notions of the Americans*, II, 160.
[6] *Sketches of Switzerland*, part I, vol. I, p. 208.

After 1846, however, Cooper ceased celebrating the power of the constituency to alter the structure of the judiciary. Judges had remained "amenable to public opinion," but public opinion had become the threat to laws of individual liberty rather than their guarantee.

Mary Monson's trial ends in her acquittal, not because the ways of American justice establish her innocence, but because the man she has been convicted of murdering appears in the courtroom. Because all of Dunscomb's fears about the state of the judiciary system are confirmed, Dunscomb must conclude that America, the patient, cannot be saved. Accordingly, Dunscomb believes that the ways of America have so betrayed the national promise that repressive measures are finally necessary. The fall of judicial integrity proves to be the final blow. By the end of the novel, Dunscomb emerges as a reactionary in sentiment if not in policy.

One by one, Dunscomb abandons the liberties which, for Cooper, had once comprised the greatness of the republic. Dunscomb tries to claim that the true republican denies the ultimate power of popular opinion; he identifies himself as "a democrat . . . as between forms of government; but I never was fool enough to think that the people can really rule, further than by occasional checks and rebukes" (249). Unlike Cadwallader or the author of *The American Democrat*, Dunscomb appears to deny to the citizenry the right to make the law through election of representatives. Dunscomb asserts that the masses should be given "all power that they can intelligently and usefully use; but not to the extent of permitting them to make the laws, to execute the laws, to interpret the laws" (86).

Dunscomb fervently believes that the most effective government is one in which the people choose permanent agents who then appoint responsible and able officials whose tenure would be limited only by good behavior (86). Under such a polity, governing officials would be appointive rather than elective, and the citizenry, once the agents were chosen, would lose all future control over their governors. Mark Woolston's government had avoided the danger of frequent elections, but the council members had been directly elected. Unlike all of Cooper's previous gentry, Dunscomb is prepared to curtail the suffrage; he proposes to "disfranchise any district in which the law could not be enforced by means of combinations of its people" (22–23).

When Dr. McBrain incredulously exclaims to Dunscomb "you surely would not place restrictions on the press!" (87), Dunscomb replies, "I would though, and very severe restrictions, as salutary checks on the immense power it wields" (88). After the arrest of Mary Monson, Timms asks Dunscomb his opinion of the power which the press exerts upon the law. Dunscomb's response concedes that true liberty demands curtailment of liberty of the press: "As respects proceedings in the courts, there never will be any true liberty in the country, until the newspapers are bound hand and foot" (140).

The Ways of the Hour quietly lists the undesirable traits of five immigrant groups in a tone suggestive of the Know-Nothing (103). Cooper's earlier works contain no justification of slavery that is so callous and blunt as Dunscomb's fiat, "African slavery is an important feature in God's Laws" (195). American reporters are described as "funguses" that "flourish on the dunghill of the common mind" (222). Dunscomb is certain that, in a republic, no legislator will ever have the courage to tell the electors they are not to be trusted (83).

The problem posed by *The Ways of the Hour* is not whether Dunscomb is a reactionary, but whether Cooper can be equated with him. Most critics have assumed that Dunscomb's opinions are Cooper's opinions, despite clear evidence that Cooper does not approve all of Dunscomb's prejudices.[7] Perry Miller's contention that Dunscomb is a portrait of James Kent is equally unlikely.[8] The longer one studies Cooper's relation to Dunscomb, the more

[7] After Dunscomb has denounced the proposal for codification of the common law, Cooper states "Dunscomb was an ultra himself, in opposition to a system that has a good deal of that which is useful, diluted by more that is not quite so good" (84). Dunscomb's grumblings against divorce laws, the "cup and saucer" law, and female follies in general are exaggerated for comic effect; these attitudes cannot be attributed to Cooper.

[8] *The Life of the Mind*, pp. 180, 249. Miller offers no evidence and no reasoning to support his contention. Although Cooper had known Kent personally during the days of the Bread and Cheese Club, there are very few references to Kent in Cooper's correspondence. Cooper's last letters mentioning Kent the man and Kent's *Commentaries* were written in 1842 and 1845 respectively. Kent had been dead for three years when *The Ways of the Hour* was written. Nowhere in the novel does Cooper suggest any parallel between Kent and Dunscomb. Dunscomb is a graduate of Columbia, a bachelor and a practicing lawyer; Kent was a graduate of Yale, married, and had been a New York State supreme court justice, as well as chancellor, professor, and commentator on the law. In *The Ways of the Hour*, Dunscomb twice refers to Kent's *Commentaries* (133, 172); he is obviously referring to the writings of another man.

The only conclusions one can draw are that Dunscomb echoes the legal attitudes of the great conservative jurists of previous decades, and that Cooper sometimes assigns Dunscomb auctorial authority.

difficult the problem becomes. In many particulars Dunscomb voices Cooper's assessment of present and future injustices, be they political, cultural, or judicial. Dunscomb's diatribes are expressed in a diction and tone, however, that Cooper as author seems anxious to avoid. One also wonders whether Cooper's approval of Dunscomb's opinions of American facts extends to Cooper's approving of Dunscomb's reactionary solutions. Dunscomb himself clearly desires a return to an appointive judiciary and an end to trial by jury. Cooper's preface, however, acknowledges that, given the many injustices of jury trials, "the difficulty is to find a substitute" (vii).

The Ways of the Hour concludes with changes of social power that are prophetic of the national future. The landed gentleman, Thomas Dunscomb, retires from the practice of law to his country estate, named Rattletrap. Aging and disaffected, Dunscomb has found the self-knowledge to admit "I am too old, in the first place, to like change" (299). Timms, Dunscomb's former assistant, has successfully used his law practice as a springboard to the state senate, where he is preparing for a career of congressional demagoguery (512). As the gentry vanish from American life, the vulgar who use the law assume power.

Early in the novel Timms had sidled up to Dunscomb, blown his nose with his fingers, and told his superior, with a sudden and disarming frankness, that Dunscomb represents an "old-fashioned aristocracy, about which nobody cares anything in this country. We have no such aristocrats, I allow, and consequently they don't signify a straw" (135). Timms may confuse the gentleman with the aristocrat, but he is correct about the degree of popular resentment. Cooper and Dunscomb have no alternative but to substitute the permanence of religious laws for their lost social faith. Cooper's last chapter describes the beauty of a colonial Anglican church still standing near Rattletrap, "one of those little temples reared by our fathers in the days of the monarchy, when, in truth, greater republican simplicity really reigned among us, in a thousand things, than reigns today" (498).

In *The Spy* or *Lionel Lincoln*, Cooper never would have contended that the colonial era was the time of "republican simplicity." Because republican values are now associated with colonial America, the little church is a religious anachronism that serves as a reminder of contemporary political decline: "What the church is now enduring the country itself most sadly wants—a lesson in humility; a distrust of self, a greater dependence on that wisdom which comes, not from the voices of the people, not from the ballot-boxes, not from the halls of senates, from heroes, god-likes, or stereotyped opinions, but from above, the throne of the Most High" (498). In his final years Cooper judged life by religious standards because his political faith seemed no longer practicable.

REPUBLICANISM REDEFINED

New York, Cooper's sixty-page introduction to an unfinished state history, is his last assessment of the American polity. Cooper's purpose is to present the recent compromise of 1850 as evidence that the greatest danger to the republic is not the furor over slavery. Believing that "the institution of domestic slavery cannot last," Cooper assures his reader that "the slave interest is now

making its final effort for supremacy, and men are deceived by the throes of a departing power."[9] The two
flaws that Cooper singles out as paramount threats to
the republic are complementary sides of one problem
that thirty years of political thought had been unable to
solve. Inevitably, a democratic republic abets the demagoguery that serves to corrupt it. Was the blame, however, to be fixed upon the demagogues themselves, or
upon the people who render them powerful?

Characteristically, Cooper begins by advancing the alternative he wishes to believe:

The people have yet to discover that the seeming throes of
liberty are nothing but the breath of their masters, the demagogues; and that at the very moment when they are made to
appear to have the greatest influence on public affairs, they
really exercise the least. Here, in our view, is the great danger
to the country—which is governed, in fact, not by its people,
as is pretended, but by factions that are themselves controlled
most absolutely by the machinations of the designing. (38)

The statement clearly implies that, once the people learn
to recognize the demagogues who delude them, they will
restore true liberty and return the gentry to power. Practically the last words that Cooper wrote to his countrymen are an explicit plea for a return to old political leadership: "Could Virginia be made to see her true interests,
. . . the glory of the Old Dominion would speedily revive,
and her fine population of gentlemen would shortly take
its place again where it so properly belongs, in the fore-
most ranks of the nation" (62).

Since 1830 the figures to whom Cooper has attributed
the traits of demagoguery have significantly changed.

[9] *New York* (New York, 1930), p. 19.

Cooper's first demagogue was the European aristocrat, his second the Whig congressman, and his third the Anti-Rent tenant who attacks personal property. His last demagogues, however, are the abolitionists of the early fifties, whom Cooper calls "dissolute politicians, who care only for the success of parties, and who make a stalking-horse of philanthropy" (34). Cooper, of course, views all of these figures as men who employ political cant in order to gain special political privilege. Nonetheless, the changes in the identity of the demagogue show an increasing distrust of Americans who profess high principles.

Three pages after damning the demagogue, Cooper redefines national danger from the other side of the medal:

However repugnant it may be to the pride of human nature, or the favorite doctrines of the day, there can be little question that the greatest sources of apprehension of future evil to the people of this country, are to be looked for in the abuses which have their origin in the infirmities and characteristics of human nature. In a word, the people have great cause to distrust themselves. (41–42)

By thus admitting that the populace and the demagogue are equally culpable and equally dangerous, Cooper deepens the likelihood of downfall. In *The Crater* demagogues had forced a revolution without the approval of a majority of the citizens. The qualities of the people of Biberry, by contrast, were the root of the injustices in Mary Monson's jury trial. Only in *New York*, however, does Cooper openly fuse his two most troubling fears.

Former defenses against the double-edged problem are explicitly abandoned. The weakness of executive and judiciary branches represents a sad loss to the balance of power. Frequency of elections is no longer a check upon entrenched abuses of privilege, but a means for demagogues to obtain privilege. Any promise of beneficial legislation is obviated by the assumption that "calm, disinterested, and judicious legislation is a thing not to be hoped for . . . and this for the very simple reason that men, acting in factions, are never calm, judicious, or disinterested" (58). After raising the specter of congressional usurpation, Cooper grimly declares that all provisions of the Constitution may be amended save the right of equal representation in the Senate (25–26).

Having denied the efficacy of all legal restraints upon demagoguery and public opinion, Cooper is faced with the choice of prophesying a subversive revolution, as he had done in *The Crater*, or of redefining republicanism as a restrictive polity. Much more forthrightly than in *The Ways of the Hour*, Cooper chooses the latter alternative. In *New York* Cooper assigns auctorial authority to Dunscomb's reactionary ideas:

There is no obligation, unless self-imposed, to admit any but a minority of her [America's] whites to the enjoyment of political power, aristocracy being, in truth, more closely assimilated to republicanism than democracy. Republicanism means the sovereignty of public *things*, instead of that of *persons*; or the representation of the *common* interests, in lieu of those of a monarch. There is no common principle of popular sway recognized in the Constitution. In the government of the several states monarchy is denounced, but democracy is nowhere proclaimed or insisted on. (21)

The passage clearly supports restricting the suffrage to a minority of the population. It also asserts that maintaining republican principles entails denying the political power of the citizenry. Cooper's statement implies that a minority of American whites should alone have the power to determine the common weal. Cooper thus contradicts his previous political writings by defining republicanism as a polity in which power is vested in the minority, rather than the majority. In effect such a policy demands special political privileges for the minority and is therefore, by Cooper's own definition, aristocratic. After twenty years of contrasting European political aristocracy to American republicanism, Cooper finally declares that aristocracy is "in truth, more closely assimilated to republicanism than democracy."

The irony of such a passage is that Cooper considers this redefined polity to be perfectly consistent with his former definitions of liberty, republicanism, and constitutional law. He is wholly sincere in declaring that his greatest fears remain the rule of the bayonet and the loss of individual liberty. Nonetheless, his desire to maintain consistency of values has led him to untenable contradictions. The defense of true liberty demands abridgment of individual liberties that have been legalized by federal and state constitutions. Republicanism is defended, not only against demagogues, but against the majority who possess political rights. In *The Crater* Mark Woolston had been unwilling to sacrifice republican principles for the sake of preserving the political leadership of the gentry. In *New York* Cooper sanctions aristocracy, political privilege, and, by implication, representation of property as measures necessary to perpetuate the rule of principled gentlemen. The saddest aspect of the change is

Cooper's attempt to convince his reader, and perhaps himself, that his political values have remained consistently republican.

Even in *New York* Cooper's love of country leads him to search for facts that could justify confidence in the national future. By 1851, however, Cooper is driven to rest his hopes upon aspects of American life which he had bitterly opposed in earlier years: the city, commerce, and the power of property.[10] Throughout *New York* Cooper asserts that, no matter how badly republican political laws may fail, society and commerce operate by independent physical and moral laws that will continue to provide order to national life (57–59). America's greatness, formerly dependent upon its political institutions, is now dependent upon its prosperity, territorial expansion and imperial culture.

The passage of *New York* that summarizes the destiny of America is Cooper's last reassertion of national faith:

Every man sees and feels that a state is rapidly advancing to maturity which must reduce the pretensions of even ancient Rome to supremacy, to a secondary place in the estimation of mankind. A century will unquestionably place the United States of America prominently at the head of civilized nations, unless the people throw away their advantages by their own mistakes—the only real danger they have to apprehend: and the mind clings to this hope with a buoyancy and fondness that are becoming profoundly national. We have a thou-

[10] "So obsessed had [Cooper] become with the need to defend Property that he now recognized commerce—Thurlow Weed's generous patron—as an acceptable ally in his fight against Fourierists, Anti-Renters, and violators of the Fugitive Slave Laws" (George Dekker, *James Fenimore Cooper*, p. 253).

sand weaknesses, and make many blunders, beyond a doubt, as a people; but where shall we turn to find a parallel to our progress, our energies, and increasing power? (37–38)

Cooper had always written his paeans to America in self-conscious prose of brash overstatement. Now, however, self-consciousness arises because Cooper is forcing himself to repeat assertions he no longer fully believes. His statement begins confidently, slips suddenly into doubt, recognizes its own desperation, and attempts a final recovery.

In March of 1849 Cooper was preparing the eleven-volume edition of his novels to be published by George Palmer Putnam. Textual revisions were made and new prefaces added in an attempt to evaluate and modernize. For the preface to *The Spy*, Cooper chose to rework the text of the previous preface written in Paris on April 4, 1831. After omitting the two opening paragraphs of the fourth preface, Cooper copied the remainder nearly verbatim until he came to the opening of the last paragraph:

A brighter prospect is beginning to dawn on the republic, which is about to assume that rank among the nations of the earth which nature has designed her to fill, and to which her institutions invariably tend.[11]

At this point Cooper made his one substantive correction. Striking out the entire paragraph of the 1831 preface, Cooper replaced it with a passage that ends as follows:

There is now no enemy to fear, but the one that resides within. By accustoming ourselves to regard even the people as erring beings, and by using the restraints that wisdom has

[11] Fourth preface to *The Spy* (Leipzig, 1842), p. x.

adduced from experience, there is much reason to hope that the same Providence which has so well aided us in our infancy, may continue to smile on our manhood.[12]

The assumptions of infallible institutions and republican virtue have given way to a deep distrust of the constituency.

Cooper's revision also indicates, however, that the unrelieved blackness of *The Ways of the Hour* cannot be accepted as a definitive sign of despair. Like *New York*, the last preface to *The Spy* looks toward the national future with a muted hope that providence may yet advance its favored people. The very fact that Cooper wrote *The Ways of the Hour* and *New York* indicates that his faith in the constituency could not be utterly extinguished. Every line Cooper penned testifies to his unshakeable trust that the people will believe and act upon the truth, if only the truth is declared to them.

CONCLUSION

In mid-career Cooper created an unintentional caricature of the development of his political thought. *The Monikins* opens with a lively sketch of Thomas Goldencalf, father of John and a cause of his son's vagaries concerning Social Stake. As a foundling of sixteen, Thomas Goldencalf had discoursed eloquently concerning "justice and the sacred rights of man" and "was heard shouting 'Wilkes and liberty' in the public streets" (16–17). At twenty-two he railed at taxation and the public debt, but was noncommittal concerning the ideals of government (21). Success

[12] Fifth preface to *The Spy*, Darley edition, p. xii.

and maturity convinced Thomas that "exclusive privileges and exclusive benefits" (40) were necessary to a
social order based upon "protection of property" (41).
During Goldencalf's manhood, "it was observed that all
his opinions grew less favorable to mankind in general"
(41), while he made increasingly frequent allusions to
the benefits of the gallows (41). At the end of his career
as a wealthy stockjobber, Goldencalf adopted the refrain
"Property, sir, is in danger, and property is the only true
basis of society" (49). The years preceding death were
a gloomy silence punctuated only by jeremiads that
contained "regiments and bayonets glittering in every
sentence" (52).

To envisage Cooper as a Goldencalf whose values are
agrarian rather than commercial is a tempting falsifica-
tion. Although the figure of Goldencalf illuminates the
progression of Cooper's political thought, it ignores the
conflict that forms the significance of Cooper's career.
Unlike Goldencalf, Cooper's attitudes were never uniform. He did not travel the familiar road from youthful
liberal to aged reactionary with complete conviction. The
progression of Cooper's feelings parallel Goldencalf's
feelings, but Cooper did not alter his political principles
until two years before his death. Unlike Goldencalf,
Cooper's political and social ideals were at odds from the
outset. In the 1820s Cooper believed as strongly in the
importance of property as he did in natural rights and
liberty. His devotion to republican rights of individual
liberty was always advanced on the expectation that the
gentry would be voted into power. Until publication of
New York, Cooper's insistence on punitive law and property rights was balanced by a refusal to grant special

privilege, to curtail universal manhood suffrage, or to deny the citizenry the right to political change. Cooper's deep-rooted faith in republican ideology and republican institutions remained inviolable until the publication of *The Ways of the Hour*. The testy vehemence of Cooper's criticism, and the violent ending of *The Crater*, are tributes to the persistence of his republican principles. If Cooper had blithely condoned exclusion and repression, his political attitudes would have been as ideologically simple as the attitudes of Thomas Goldencalf.

Goldencalf's political opinions, like those of most men, were only rationalizations for his self-interest. It cost Goldencalf nothing to turn so easily from Wilkes and liberty to property and bayonets. Wilkes was Goldencalf's excuse for accumulation, and property law was security for the power of his moneys. A similar change, however, cost Cooper everything. Repeated subversion of republican law drove Cooper to believe that a true republic could not withstand demagoguery. In a symbolic fiction of 1847, he felt compelled to acknowledge the probable destruction of the country for which he wrote. By advocating that the suffrage, press, and popular power be curbed, Cooper abandoned at his death the libertarian republic which his writings had undertaken to defend.

Cooper's insistence that a democratic republic perpetuate the rule of agrarian gentlemen proved an attempt to secure the impossible. Although the ways of the landed gentry finally emerged as the stronger value, Cooper cannot, like Goldencalf, be accused of self-interest. Superintending no landed estate, employing no tenants, and holding no office, Cooper's defense of law and property grew firmer while his wealth, popularity, and influence declined.

Although Cooper was in no sense an original political thinker, his convictions concerning the differences between democracy, aristocracy, and monarchy were fully tested through thirty years of thought and observation. Having committed himself to the political faith of a democratic republic, Cooper nonetheless approached problems of political justice within his unformed land in all their complexity. His refusal to oversimplify the immense problems of government carried him into obtrusive political sermonizing. Nonetheless, his writings are richer because, in his hands, the romance escapes to the frontier only to confront questions of moral and civil justice in their most immediate and compelling form. Cooper's novels are thus imbued with problems of American political and social justice, which are likely to remain crucial and unsolved.

Cooper retains stature despite literary imperfections so evident that they scarcely need rehearsing. He never found a form wholly adequate to portray his vision either of the glory or the downfall of his American dream. Nor, among all of Cooper's volumes, is there one that may be accounted among the greatest achievements of American literature. Filling out thirty-two novels to a prescribed length of five hundred pages had inevitable consequences: turgid prose, repetition, formlessness, cheap plotting, and lengthy stretches of empty words.

And yet Melville was right to insist that Cooper "possessed not the slightest weaknesses but those which are only noticeable as the almost infallible indices of pervad-

ing greatness."[13] Cooper's achievement should ultimately
be measured, not by post-Jamesian standards of novelistic
art, but by the significance and integrity of his career
as an American man of letters. To follow the development
of his works is to experience an honest and significant
conflict between political ideals and social preconcep-
tions neither of which the author was willing to abandon.
Cooper recognized that the responsibility for republican
leadership should devolve upon men of principle, culture,
and education. He also recognized that the egalitarian
implications of democratic ideology would gradually
deprive the republic of the men most qualified to guide
it. Believing in the justice of a republican polity, Cooper
feared that its helplessness before demagoguery would
spell the end of the individual liberties by which republicanism was defined.

Like Tocqueville, Cooper understood the tendency of
the American people to extend the meaning of equality
from equality of political right into equality of condition.
The anger that mars Cooper's later works is the artistic
price exacted by his desire to clarify the distinction. In
the heyday of Jacksonian democracy, Cooper insisted
that a republican polity must maintain full equality of
political rights without depriving society and government
of those citizens, superior in merit, principle, and influence, who were necessary to sustain disinterested republican justice. Cooper had the moral courage necessary to
argue publicly that a republic that cannot combine political equality with inequality of condition was doomed
to failure.

[13] Letter read at the Cooper Memorial Service, in *Memorial of
James Fenimore Cooper* (New York, 1852), p. 30.

Appendix A

THREE MILE POINT

Judge William Cooper owned certified legal title to a strip of land on the western shore of Lake Otsego called Three Mile Point. In the judge's will, there was a stipulation bequeathing Three Mile Point to his heirs to be held in common until 1850, when the youngest descendant bearing his name would inherit the property. In 1821 the point had been publicly sold as the property of the heirs of Judge Cooper, but redeemed by those heirs within a month. The public had used Three Mile Point as a picnic area by concession of the Cooper family during and after the judge's lifetime. Upon returning to Cooperstown in 1834, James Fenimore Cooper became the executor of his father's will.

Public use resulted in the destruction of one shelter built on Three Mile Point by the Cooper family, and in the inadvertent burning of its replacement. As restitution the townspeople replaced the burned shelter by another at their own expense. In July 1837 trees on the point that were associated with memories of the judge were damaged.

On July 22, 1837, Cooper circulated among the villagers a handbill warning against trespassing on the point. The villagers held a meeting at 7:00 P.M. that evening to protest Cooper's notice. At this meeting a set of resolutions was passed which included the following: that the undersigned would wholly disregard Cooper's notice, that, because Judge Cooper intended the citizens to use the point, the citizens had a right to use it, that J. F. Cooper was "odious," and that all of his books should be removed from the village library. These resolutions were not published in the newspapers as stipulated, but handed to Cooper himself.

Between August 2 and August 14, 1837, three Whig newspapers, *The Chenango Telegraph*, *Albany Evening Journal*, and *Otsego Republican*, all printed an account of the controversy which was personally abusive and false in its details. Cooper began legal proceedings against the editors of all three. On August 16 and 28, Cooper published full accounts of the entire controversy in *The Freeman's Journal*. By publishing the resolutions of the meeting in the town newspaper, Cooper stifled the quarrel within Cooperstown. By suing the three newspaper editors, however, he began his long legal war with the Whig press.

For the most reliable and detailed accounts of the controversy, see *Letters and Journals*, III, 271–353 and E. R. Outland, *The "Effingham" Libels on Cooper* (Madison, Wisc.: University of Wisconsin Studies in Language and Literature no. 28, 1929), 31–51.

Home As Found denies none of the above facts, nor does it add others. Cooper's fictional account is wholly reliable in factual outline. The only differences are omissions of materials that make the unjustified actions of the townsmen more understandable. Cooper does not mention in his novel that the point had been publicly sold and then redeemed. Nor is there mention made of the public erection of the fishing shelter. *Home As Found* acknowledges but deemphasizes the fact that the point had long been used by the townspeople with family consent.

Appendix B

OUTLINE OF THE ANTI-RENT WARS

Colonial land patents of the seventeenth and eighteenth centuries had deeded vast tracts of land along the Hudson to prominent colonists who often assumed the title "Lord of the Manor." Well into the nineteenth century, these estates had remained the property of descendants of the original grantee. Consequently, an area comprising Rensselaer, Columbia, Dutchess, Albany, Greene, and Delaware counties was controlled and largely owned by a few families who had retained the social power and position of an aristocracy, though without noble title. Among the most prominent of these partician landholders were the names of Rensselaer, Livingston, Schuyler, Philipse, De Peyster, and Verplanck, each of whom in the 1840s owned substantially in excess of 50,000 acres.

Much of the acreage of such patents was leased rather than sold to settlers, leaving many who farmed the land in the position of tenants. The tenants held land under various forms of leases—durable, two-live and three-live leases being the most common. Although rent was often waived for the first five to ten years of settlement, it was thereafter due annually in the form of a stipulated number of wheat bushels, chickens, or days of labor, sometimes commutable to cash. The proprietors usually reserved all rights to mines and mill sites. The Quarter Sale (payment of one-quarter of the sale price to the landlord) was a common device for impeding tenant alienation.

No matter how lenient in its terms, a leasehold was not ownership. Soon after the Revolution, charges of feudal oppression were made by aggrieved tenants against the entire system. Sporadic outbursts of violence occurred in 1791 and 1813. Resentment against the "aristocratic" landlords was fanned by gradual depletion of the soil and volatile wheat prices.

On January 26, 1839, Stephen Van Rensselaer III died, leaving an estimated 468,000 acres under leasehold and $400,000 in unpaid tenant debts. The will of "the Good Patroon" bequeathed Rensselaerwyck to his two sons and stipulated that the unpaid rents be collected. Bargaining between the Rensselaers and the tenants broke down and subsequent attempts by sheriffs to serve process on tenant debtors were resisted. Governor Seward was compelled to call out the state militia in December 1839 in order to restore civic order. Promising the tenants a fair hearing of grievances, Seward appointed a state commission to arrange a settlement, but the Rensselaers refused to relinquish their claim to past debts, and negotiations failed once more.

In April 1842 the Judiciary Committee of the New York State Assembly incensed the tenants by supporting the landlord's position. Declaring that all leaseholds were legal contracts, the committee denounced Seward's leniency, sustained the Rensselaer will, and denied the existence of tenant hardship. Widespread publication of these declarations caused the Anti-Rent struggle to pass beyond Rensselaerwyck into manors of adjoining counties.

Anti-Rent agitation, at its height between 1842 and 1847, followed a consistent pattern. Inflammatory lecturers with scant regard for fact addressed Anti-Rent gatherings in which resolutions were passed denying landlord titles and denouncing all leaseholds as feudal and antidemocratic. Tenants disguised as "Injins" in calico and warpaint gathered upon the sounding of tin horns that forewarned the approach of sheriff or lawyer. Attempts by landlords and legal officials to collect rent were forcibly defied. Papers, writs, and warrants were burned. In the Helderberg country, where resistance and hardship were greatest, sheriffs were tarred and feathered.

On August 7, 1845, Undersheriff Osman Steele of Delaware County was murdered while attempting to make an arrest. Governor Silas Wright declared Delaware County to be in a state of insurrection and again called out the militia. Judge Amasa Parker convicted sixty Delaware County tenants of manslaughter. With Governor Wright's support, a law was passed during the following winter making it a felony for a New York citizen to appear armed and disguised.

Anti-Rentism became a significant force in New York politics. On a local level, tenants organized into political committees that charged dues, financed the "Injins," paid all court costs, and supported candidates of both parties who were sympathetic to Anti-Rent. In January 1845 and February 1846, the Anti-Rent State Convention, composed of delegates from eleven counties, met to gather their powers for the forthcoming elections. The Democrats, split between the Hunker and Barnburner factions, became as solicitous of the Anti-Rent vote as the Whigs. Every candidate backed by the Anti-Rent convention in the election of 1846 was victorious. Even the governorship fell to John Young, who, by ousting Silas Wright, defeated the tenants' symbol of landlord oppression.

By 1845 the struggle began to assume national significance. Horace Greeley became a declared supporter of Anti-Rent, writing *Tribune* editorials that treated patroon landholdings as evidence of the national danger of land monopolies. George Henry Evans and the National Reformers attempted to gain control of the Anti-Rent Conventions and superimpose Fourieristic overtones upon an essentially local movement.

Tenant grievances had been effectively dramatized and their voting power fully exploited. In March 1846, a select committee appointed by the state assembly submitted the Tilden Report. Its recommendations included the following:

1. The landholders need not prove their titles in court.

2. Interest received through leases should be taxed.
3. Quarter sales, water and mineral reservations, frighten away potential immigrants and should be abolished.
4. Distress (seizure of a tenant's personal effects until payment of rent) should be abolished.
5. Leasehold tenures depress individual initiative and impede regional prosperity.
6. Upon the death of the landlord, the tenant shall have the right to convert a leasehold into a freehold at a stipulated price per acre.

The landlords, realizing that the decrees of 1842 had received a distinct setback, denounced the Tilden Report as a concession to political expediency.

When a convention to redraft the New York State Constitution met in 1846, the Anti-Rent movement had gained sufficient power to cause the enactment of the following provisions into law:

1. All New York lands are allodial; all existing contracts are valid.
2. Interest received through leases shall be taxed.
3. Quarter sales are invalid for all contracts written after 1846.
4. No future lease may demand rent or services for a period exceeding twelve years.

Although these changes in no way offered release from any obligations of existing leasehold contracts, the Tilden Report had in effect been legalized.

In 1850 quarter sales on all contracts were declared invalid. Two years later, a court decision stated that a lease in perpetuity was entitled to all the rights of an estate in fee. The landholding gentry, long unable to collect their rents, realized that time was against them. In August 1845 an agreement to sell had been made by seventeen landlords, including the Livingstons, Verplancks and De Peysters. Stephen Van Rensselaer IV soon followed suit, and in 1848 William Van Rensselaer consented to sell his lands. By 1850 the number of leaseholds on Livingston Manor was negligible. The slow compromise had worked in favor of the tenants. Thereafter, the institution of "aristocratic" leasehold underwent a lingering demise.

This historical outline has been compiled from two sources:

Ellis, D. M. *Landlords and Farmers in the Hudson-Mohawk Region 1790–1850*. Ithaca, N.Y.: Cornell University Press, 1946.

Christman, Henry. *Tin Horns and Calico*. New York: Henry Holt, 1945.

Thus the Littlepage trilogy, written in 1845 and 1846, appeared at the very height of the Anti-Rent turmoil. *The Redskins* was planned, finished, and published during the months following the release of the Tilden Report, but prior to the convention to redraft the state constitution. Cooper's fear that the Tilden Report would be enacted into law is evident throughout the work.

Works Cited

Adams, John, *The Political Writings of John Adams*. Edited by G. A. Peek, Jr. New York: Bobbs-Merrill, 1954.

Beard, James F. "Cooper and His Artistic Contemporaries," *New York History*, XXXV (1954), 480–495.

Bewley, Marius. *The Eccentric Design: Form in the Classic American Novel*. New York: Columbia University Press, 1963.

Brooks, Van Wyck. *The World of Washington Irving*. New York: E. P. Dutton, 1944.

Chase, Richard. *The American Novel and its Tradition*. New York: Doubleday, 1957.

Christman, Henry. *Tin Horns and Calico*. New York: Henry Holt, 1945.

Cooper, James Fenimore. *Cooper's Novels*, 32 vols., illustrated from drawings by F. O. C. Darley. New York: W. A. Townsend, 1861.

———. *The American Democrat*. Edited by George Dekker and Larry Johnston. Baltimore: Penguin Books, 1969.

———. *The Chronicles of Cooperstown*. Cooperstown, N.Y.: H. & E. Phinney, 1838.

———. *The Crater*. Edited by Thomas Philbrick. Cambridge, Mass.: Harvard University Press, 1962.

———. *Early Critical Essays: 1820–1822*. Edited by James F. Beard. Gainesville, Fla.: Scholars' Facsimiles and Reprints, 1959.

———. *Excursions in Italy*. Paris: Baudry's European Library, 1838.

———. *Gleanings in Europe: England.* Edited by R. E. Spiller. New York: Oxford University Press, 1930.

———. *Gleanings in Europe: France.* Edited by R. E. Spiller. New York: Oxford University Press, 1928.

———. *History of the Navy.* Cooperstown, N. Y.: H. & E. Phinney, 1847.

———. *Letter to General Lafayette.* New York: The Facsimile Text Society, 1931.

———. *A Letter to His Countrymen.* New York: John Wiley, 1834.

———. *The Letters and Journals of James Fenimore Cooper.* Edited by James F. Beard. 6 vols. Cambridge, Mass.: Harvard University Press, 1960–1968.

———. *Lives of Distinguished Naval Officers.* 2 vols. Philadelphia: Carey and Hart, 1846.

———. *New York.* New York: William Farquhar Payson, 1930.

———. *Notions of the Americans.* Edited by R. E. Spiller. 2 vols. New York: Frederick Ungar, 1963.

———. *The Pilot.* New York: Charles Wiley, 1823.

———. *The Pioneers.* New York: Charles Wiley, 1823.

———. *Sketches of Switzerland.* 2 parts. Philadelphia: Carey, Lea & Blanchard, 1836.

———. *The Spy.* New York: Wiley and Halstead, 1822.

———. *The Spy.* New York: Charles Wiley, 1824.

———. *The Spy.* Leipzig: Bernhardt Tauchnitz, 1842.

Cooper, Susan Fenimore. *The Cooper Gallery; or, Pages and Pictures from the Writings of James Fenimore Cooper, with Notes.* New York: James Miller, 1865.

———. "A Glance Backward." *Atlantic Monthly,* LIX (1887), 199–206.

Crèvecoeur, St. Jean de. *Letters from an American Farmer.* Garden City, N.Y.: Doubleday, 1961.

Dekker, George. *James Fenimore Cooper: the Novelist.* London: Routledge & Kegan Paul, 1967.

Ellis, D. M. "The Coopers and New York State Landholding Systems." *New York History,* XXXV (1954), 412–422.

————. *Landlords and Farmers in the Hudson-Mohawk Region*: 1790–1850. Ithaca, N. Y.: Cornell University Press, 1946.

Fiedler, Leslie A. *Love and Death in the American Novel*. New York: Criterion Books, 1960.

Fox, Dixon Ryan. *The Decline of Aristocracy in the Politics of New York*. New York: Harper & Row, 1965.

Frick, A. C. *History of the State of New York*. New York: Columbia University Press, 1934.

Fussell, Edwin. *Frontier: American Literature and the American West*. Princeton: Princeton University Press, 1965.

Grossman, James. *James Fenimore Cooper*. Stanford: Stanford University Press, 1967.

Hamilton, Jay and Madison. *The Federalist Papers*. Edited by R. P. Fairfield. New York: Doubleday, 1966.

Hicks, Granville. "Landlord Cooper and the Anti-Renters." *Antioch Review*, V (1945), 95–109.

House, Kay Seymour. *Cooper's Americans*. Columbus: Ohio State University Press, 1965.

Howard, Leon. "Introduction" to *The Pioneers*. New York: Holt Rinehart & Winston, 1959.

James, Henry. *Hawthorne*. New York: Macmillan, 1887.

Jefferson, Thomas. *The Life and Selected Writings*. Edited by Adrienne Koch and William Peden. New York: Random House, 1944.

Jones, H. M. "Prose and Pictures: James Fenimore Cooper." *Tulane Studies in English*, III (1952), 133–154.

Kaul, A. N. *The American Vision: Actual and Ideal Society in Nineteenth-Century Fiction*. New Haven: Yale University Press, 1963.

Kirk, Russell. "Cooper and the European Puzzle." *College English*, VII (1946), 198–207.

Koch, Adrienne. *The American Enlightenment*. New York: G. Braziller, 1965.

Lawrence, D. H. *Studies in Classic American Literature*. New York: The Viking Press, 1961.

Lewis, R. W. B. *The American Adam*. Chicago: University of Chicago Press, 1955.

Locke, John. *Locke on Politics, Religion and Education*. Edited with an Introduction by Maurice Cranston. New York: Macmillan, 1965.

Lounsbury, T. R. *James Fenimore Cooper*. Boston: Houghton Mifflin, 1883.

Lukács, George. *The Historical Novel*. New York: Humanities Press, 1965.

Marx, Leo. *The Machine in the Garden: Technology and the Pastoral Ideal in America*. New York: Oxford University Press, 1967.

McCloskey, John C. "Cooper's Political Views in *The Crater*." *Modern Philology*, LIII (1955), 113–116.

Melville, Herman. *Israel Potter*. New York: Hill and Wang, 1957.

Memorial of James Fenimore Cooper. New York: G. P. Putnam, 1852.

Mencken, H. L. *A Mencken Chrestomathy*. New York: Alfred A. Knopf, 1962.

Myers, Marvin. *The Jacksonian Persuasion*. Stanford: Stanford University Press, 1960.

Miller, Perry. *The Life of the Mind in America: From the Revolution to the Civil War*. New York: Harcourt Brace, Jovanovich, 1965.

Morison, S. E. *The Oxford History of the American People*. New York: Oxford University Press, 1965.

Outland, Ethel R. *The "Effingham" Libels on Cooper*. Madison: University of Wisconsin Studies in Language and Literature, 1929.

Palmer, R. R. *A History of the Modern World*. New York: Alfred A. Knopf, 1960.

Parkman, Francis. *The Conspiracy of Pontiac*. New York: Macmillan, 1962.

Pearce, Roy Harvey. "Civilization and Savagism: the World of The Leatherstocking Tales." *English Institute Essays*. New York: Columbia University Press, 1950.

————. "The Leatherstocking Tales Re-Examined." *SAQ*, XXXXVI (1947), 524–536.

————. *The Savages of America*. Baltimore: Johns Hopkins Press, 1953.

Philbrick, T. L. "Cooper's *The Pioneers*," *PMLA*, LXXIX (1964), 579–593.

————. *James Fenimore Cooper and the Development of American Sea Fiction*. Cambridge, Mass.: Harvard University Press, 1961.

Pickering, James H. "New York in the Revolution: Cooper's *Wyandotté*," *New York History*, XLIX (1968), 121–141.

Poe, Edgar Allan. "Cooper's *Wyandotté*," *The Works of Edgar Allan Poe*. Chicago: Stone & Kimball, 1895. VII, 3–18.

Porte, Joel. *The Romance in America*. Middletown, Conn.: Wesleyan University Press, 1969.

Ringe, Donald A. "Cooper's *The Crater* and the Moral Basis of Society." *Papers of the Michigan Academy of Science, Arts, and Letters*, XLIV (1959), 371–380.

————. "Cooper's Littlepage Novels: Change and Stability in American Society," *AL*, XXXII (1960), 280–290.

————. *James Fenimore Cooper*. New York: Twayne Publishers, 1962.

————. "James Fenimore Cooper and Thomas Cole: An Analogous Technique," *AL*, XXX (1958), 26–36.

Schlesinger, Arthur M. *The Age of Jackson*. Boston: Little, Brown, 1945.

Shulenberger, Arvid. *Cooper's Theory of Fiction*. Lawrence: University of Kansas Press, 1955.

Smith, Henry Nash. "Introduction" to *The Prairie*. New York: Holt Rinehart & Winston, 1950.

————. *Virgin Land*. New York: Vintage Books, 1957.

Spiller, Robert E. *Fenimore Cooper: Critic of His Times*. New York: Minton, Balch, 1931.

Van Deusen, G. G. *The Jacksonion Era*. New York: Harper & Row, 1963.

Wallace, Paul. "Cooper's Indians," *New York History*, XXXV
    (1954), 423–446.

Waples, Dorothy. *The Whig Myth of James Fenimore Cooper.*
    New Haven: Yale University Press, 1938.

Wasserstrom, William. "Cooper, Freud and the Origins of
    Culture," *The American Imago*, XVII (1960), 423–437.

Winters, Yvor. *Maule's Curse.* Norfolk, Conn.: New Direc-
    tions, 1938.

Zoellner, R. H. "Conceptual Ambivalence in Cooper's Leather-
    stocking." *AL*, XXXI (1960), 397–420.

Index of Subjects and Cooper's Ideas

Index of Cooper's Works

Index of Names